The Great Big Book of Personal Productivity

THE GREAT BIG BOOK OF PERSONAL PRODUCTIVITY

BY

RON FRY

Viva Books Private Limited
New Delhi • Mumbai • Chennai • Kolkata

First Indian Edition 2003

VIVA BOOKS PRIVATE LIMITED

- 4262/3 Ansari Road, Daryaganj, New Delhi 110 002
  E-mail: viva@vivagroupindia.net

- 215-216 New Apollo Estate, 2nd Floor, Mogra Lane,
  Andheri (E), Mumbai 400 069
  E-mail: vivabooks@mantraonline.com

- 7 Aziz Mulk, Seventh Street, Thousand Lights, Chennai 600 006
  E-mail: vivachennai@mantraonline.com

- 6-A, Rifle Range Road, Kolkata 700 019
  E-mail: vivakolkata@mantraonline.com

Published by arrangement with

Career Press
3 Tice Road
Franklin Lakes
N J 07417
USA

ISBN 81-7649-374-0

Rs. 295

Published by Vinod Vasishtha for Viva Books Private Limited, 4262/3 Ansari Road, Daryaganj, New Delhi 110 002 and printed at Print Perfect, Mayapuri, Delhi.

Contents

BOOK 2: IMPROVE YOUR READING

Book 3: Improve Your Memory

BOOK 4: IMPROVE YOUR WRITING

PREFACE

Ten years ago, I wrote and published a small book called ***How to Study***. I was surprised at the time that I couldn't find any book like it. Nothing about how to organize homework, reports, or projects. Nothing about how to do better on tests (except for those phone book-sized volumes with hints for all the alphabet tests). Nothing about improving reading (unless you just wanted to read very, very fast). Little on helping students learn memory techniques. Nothing on taking better notes.

You get the idea. There was seemingly one heck of a need out there!

History has proven that the need was *overwhelming*. ***How to Study*** has gone through four editions, which, combined, have sold more than one million copies.

As helpful as this single volume quickly became, many students, teachers and parents called or wrote me and asked for even more help. *More* examples. *More* practice. *More* quizzes. Pretty much more *everything*. Because I didn't want to create a 1,000-page book, I wrote a series of smaller volumes covering specific aspects of studying—***"Ace" Any Test, Get Organized, Improve Your Memory, Improve Your Reading, Improve Your Writing, Manage Your Time, Take Notes,*** and ***Use Your Computer***—many of which are now in second or third editions as well. My suggestion—and I still think it's valid—was to start with ***How to Study***, then purchase the books covering those topics in which special help was needed. All told, these eight additional books have sold another *two* million copies!

So much for the history lesson. Let me tell you about the book you're holding right now (and its companion volume, ***Ron Fry's Great Big Book of How to Study***). Although most people find the individual books a less expensive way to get the specific advice they need, those who feel they need help on *everything* have had to purchase *nine* different books, at a cost of more than $60. Now, I still think that's a good value, and I think being able to buy just two or three or four books is sensible. But some people want it all—all of the books in ***Ron Fry's How to Study Program*** in a single volume. A single *inexpensive* volume.

Okay, I compromised. *Two* volumes. Two *inexpensive* volumes—less than half the cost of the individual titles. ***Ron Fry's Big Book of Personal Productivity*** contains ***Get Organized, Improve Your Memory, Improve Your Reading,*** and ***Improve Your Writing***. And ***Ron Fry's Big Book of How to Study*** contains ***How to Study, Manage Your Time, Take Notes*** and ***Ace Any Test*** (with a smidgen of ***Use Your Computer*** thrown in).

One of the unavoidable problems with the individual books was duplication. ***Improve Your Reading***, for example, had to deal with retaining what you read, so it contained portions of ***Improve Your Memory***. And, of course, I needed to cover taking notes while you were reading, so some of ***Take Notes*** was incorporated. And because someone could conceivably just buy one of the books, each of them had to contain everything about that topic, even if each of those topics was also covered, in less detail, of course, in ***How to Study*** itself, which became almost a summary of all the other books.

Well, these two new volumes solve most of that problem. In ***Ron Fry's Big Book of How to Study***, you won't find the chapters in ***How to Study*** that covered time management, note-taking, or studying for tests, because ***Manage Your Time, Take Notes*** and ***"Ace" Any Test*** are included—in their entirety—in the same volume. And in ***Ron Fry's Big Book of Personal Productivity***, I edited each of the four books included-***Get Organized, Improve Your Memory, Improve Your Reading,*** and ***Improve Your Writing***—to remove all of the duplication between the volumes. (I'll admit, however, that there *is* some necessary duplication between the two volumes, primarily because ***Get Organized*** covers much of the same terrain already plowed by ***Manage Your Time*** and ***Take Notes***. But because some people will *still* only buy one of the two volumes, I felt it absolutely necessary to make each complete unto itself.)

I sincerely hope these new compilations will give parents, teachers, and students one more way to access this advice. Unlike some of the self-styled study gurus out there, I've never made some blanket, hyped-up guarantee like *Read This Book And Get Straight As In 30 Minutes Or Less*. And I'm not about to start now. *But* I will make you a promise: Read these two volumes cover-to-cover, take the quizzes, practice (just a little!) the techniques, and study just a little smarter (*not necessarily longer*)...*and* I guarantee you will see a difference in results. The more you apply these tips, tricks, and techniques, the more your grades will improve and, more important, the greater your ability to learn...anything...faster, better, easier.

Ron Fry
May, 1999

Book 1

Get Organized

INTRODUCTION

START AT THE BEGINNING

This year marks another major milestone in the near decade-long evolution of my ***How to Study Program***—the production of two compilation volumes: ***Ron Fry's Big Book of Personal Productivity*** (which you are holding in your hot little hands) and ***Ron Fry's Big Book of How to Study***. Together, they incorporate virtually all of the advice previously available in nine *separate* volumes, all of which are still available (and all of which will be updated and revised in the year 2000).

Why are these books the best-selling series of study guides ever published? Why are they still so *needed*, not only by students but by their parents who want so badly for them to do well?

Because virtually all of the conditions I've been writing and speaking about across the country since 1988 have remained...or gotten *worse:*

1. Despite modest recent improvements in test scores—in 1995, the average on the verbal portion of the SAT rose five points, math scores improved three points—U.S. students still score abysmally low compared to students in many other countries, especially on science and math tests.
2. Most parents, when polled, say improving our public schools is our nation's number-one priority. Those same parents do *not* think public schools are doing a very good job teaching their kids much of anything.
3. Business leaders continue to complain that far too many entry-level job candidates can barely read, write, add, or multiply. Many can't fill out job applications! As a result, businesses are spending billions to teach employees the basic skills they should have learned in school.

As a result, the need for my nine books will, unfortunately, continue, because they offer *exactly* the help most students need—and their parents demand.

So who are you?

A number of you are students, not just the high school students I always thought were my readers, but also college students (a rousing plug for their high school preparation), and *junior* high school students (which says something far more positive about their eventual success).

Many of you reading this are adults. Some of you are returning to school. And some of you are long out of school but have figured out that if you could learn *now* the study skills your teachers never taught you, you'd do better in your careers—especially if you knew how to meet pressing deadlines or remember the key points of a presentation.

All too many of you are parents with the same lament: "How do I get Jack (or Jill) to do better in school? If his life is as organized as his room, I fear for all of us!"

I want to briefly take the time to address every one of the audiences for this book and discuss some of the factors particular to each of you.

If you're a high school student

You should be particularly comfortable with both the language and format of this book—its relatively short sentences and paragraphs, occasionally humorous (I hope) headings and subheadings, a reasonable but certainly not outrageous vocabulary. I wrote it with you in mind!

If you're a junior high school student

Learning *now* how to organize your studying and your life is key to success now and in the future. You are trying to learn how to study at *precisely* the right time. Sixth, 7th, and 8th grades—before that sometimes cosmic leap to high school—are without a doubt the period in which these study skills should be mastered. If you're serious enough about studying to be reading this book, I doubt you'll have trouble with the concepts or the language.

If you're a "traditional" college student...

...having pretty much gone right from high school to college, learning how to organize your life and studies is not just a nice idea, it's the only thing that will enable you to survive. Trust me. You haven't even contemplated how busy life can be until you show up at old Klutzburg U., and get your first class schedule...and volunteer schedule...and athletics schedule...and work schedule.

If you're the parent of a student of any age

Your child's school is probably doing little if anything to teach him or her how to study. Which means he or she is not learning how to *learn*. And that means he or she is not learning how to *succeed*.

Should the schools be accomplishing that? Absolutely. After all, we spend $275 billion on elementary and secondary education in this country, *an average of $6,000 per student per year*. We ought to be getting more for that money than possible graduation, some football cheers, and a rotten entry-level job market.

What can parents do?

There are probably even more dedicated parents out there than dedicated students, because the first phone call at any of my radio or TV appearances comes from a sincere and worried parent asking, "What can I do to help my kid do better in school?" Okay, here they are, the rules for parents of students of any age:

1. **Set up a homework area.** Free of distraction, well lit, all necessary supplies handy.
2. **Set up a homework routine.** When and where it gets done. Same bat-time every day.
3. **Set homework priorities.** Actually, just make the point that homework *is* the priority—before a date, before TV, before going out to play, whatever.
4. **Turn off the TV.** Or at the very least, severely limit when and how much TV-watching is done. This may be the toughest one.

5. **Make reading a habit**—for them, certainly, but also for yourselves. Kids will inevitably do what you *do*, not what you *say* (even if you say *not* to do what you *do*).
6. **Talk to the teachers.** Find out what your kids are supposed to be learning. If you don't, you can't really supervise. You might even be teaching them things at odds with what the teacher's trying to do.
7. **Encourage and motivate,** but don't nag them to do their homework. It doesn't work.
8. **Supervise their work,** but don't fall into the trap of *doing* their homework.
9. **Praise them to succeed,** but don't overpraise them for mediocre work. Kids know when you're slinging it.
10. **Convince them of reality.** (This is for older students.) Okay, I'll admit it's almost as much of a stretch as turning off the TV, but learning and believing that the real world will not care about their grades, but measure them by what they know and what they can do, is a lesson that will save many tears (probably yours). It's probably never too early to (carefully) let your boy or girl genius get the message that life *is* not fair.
11. **If you can afford it, get your kid(s) a computer** and all the software they can handle. There really is no avoiding it: Your kids, whatever their age, absolutely must master technology (computers) in order to survive in and after school. A recent decade-long study has shown that kids who master computers learn faster and earn higher test scores.

The importance of your involvement

Your involvement in your child's education is absolutely essential to his or her eventual success. Surprisingly enough, the results of every study done in the last two decades about what affects a child's success in school clearly demonstrate that only one factor *overwhelmingly* affects it, every time: parental involvement. Not the size of the school, the money spent per pupil, the number of language labs, how many of the students go on to college, how many great teachers there are (or lousy ones). All factors, yes. *But none as significant as the effect you can have.*

So please, take the time to read this book (and its companion volume, ***Ron Fry's Big Book of How to Study***) yourself. Learn what your kids *should* be learning.

And you can help tremendously, *even if you were not a great student yourself, even if you never learned great study skills.* You can learn now with your child—not only will it help him or her in school, it will help *you* on the job, whatever your field.

If you're a nontraditional student

If you are going back to high school, college, or graduate school at age 25, 45, 65, or 85—you probably need the help offered in these volumes more than anyone! Why? Because the longer you've been out of school, the more likely you don't remember what you've forgotten. And you've probably forgotten what you're supposed to remember! As much as I emphasize that it's rarely too early to learn good study habits, I must also emphasize that it's never too *late*.

If you are returning to school and attempting to carry even a partial courseload while simultaneously raising a family, holding down a job, or both, there are some particular problems you face that you probably didn't the first time you were in school:

Time and money pressures. Let's face it, when all you had to worry about was going to school, it simply *had* to be easier than going to school, raising a family, and working for a living simultaneously. (And it was!) Mastering all of the techniques of time management is even more essential if you are to effectively juggle your many responsibilities to your career, family, clubs, friends, etc., with your commitment to school. Money management may well be another essential skill, whether figuring out how to pay for childcare (something you probably didn't have to worry about the last time you were in school) or how to manage all your responsibilities while cutting your hours at work to make time for school.

Self-imposed fears of inadequacy. You may well convince yourself that you're just "out of practice" with all this school stuff. You don't even remember what to do with a highlighter! Although some of this fear is valid, most is not. I suspect what many of you are really fearing is that you just aren't in that school "mentality" anymore, that you don't "think" the same way.

I think these last fears are groundless. You've been out there thinking and doing for quite a few years, perhaps very successfully, so it's really ridiculous to think school will be so different. It won't be. Relax.

Maybe you're worried because you didn't exactly light up the academic power plant the first time around. Well, neither did Edison or Einstein or a host of other relatively successful people. But then, you've changed rather significantly since those halcyon days of "boola boolaing," haven't you? Held a series of jobs, raised a family, saved money, taken on more and more responsibility? Concentrate on how much *more* qualified you are *now* than you were *then!*

Feeling you're "out of your element." This is a slightly different fear, the fear that you just don't fit in any more. After all, you're not 18 anymore. But then, neither are fully half the college students on campus today. That's right, fully 50 percent of all college students are older than 25. The reality is, you'll probably feel more in your element now than you did the first time around!

You'll see teachers differently. Probably a plus. It's doubtful you'll hold them in the same awe you did the first time around. At worst, you'll consider teachers your equals. At best, you'll consider them younger and not necessarily as successful or experienced as you are. In either event, you probably won't be quite as ready to treat your college professors as if they were gods.

There *are* differences in academic life. It's slower than the "real" world, and you may well be moving significantly faster than its normal pace. When you were 18, an afternoon without classes meant a game of Frisbee. Now it might mean catching up on a week's worth of errands, cooking (and freezing) a week's worth of dinners, and/or writing four reports due last week. Despite your own hectic schedule, do not expect campus life to accelerate in response. You will have to get used to people and systems with far less interest in speed.

Some random thoughts about learning

Learning shouldn't be painful and certainly doesn't have to be boring, though, far too often, it's both. However, it's not necessarily going to be wonderful and painless, either. Sometimes you actually have to work hard to figure something out or get a project done. That *is* reality.

It is also reality that everything is not readily apparent or easily understandable. That confusion reigns. Tell yourself that's okay and learn how to get past it. Heck, if you actually think you understand everything you've read the first time through, you're kidding yourself. Learning something slowly doesn't mean there's something wrong with you. It may be a subject that virtually everybody learns slowly.

A good student doesn't panic when something doesn't seem to be getting through the haze. He just takes his time, follows whatever steps apply, and remains confident that the light bulb will indeed inevitably go off.

Parents often ask me, "How can I motivate my teenager?" My initial response is usually to smile and say, "If I knew the answer to that question, I would have retired very wealthy quite some time ago." However, I think there *is* an answer, but it's not something *parents* can do, it's something you, the student, have to decide: Are you going to spend the school day interested and alert or bored and resentful?

It's really that simple. Why not develop the attitude that you have to go to school anyway, so rather than being bored or miserable while you're there, you might as well be active and learn as much as possible? The difference between a C and an A or B for many students is, I firmly believe, merely a matter of wanting to do better. As I constantly stress in interviews, inevitably you will leave school. And very quickly, you'll discover the premium is on what you know and what you can do. Grades won't count anymore, neither will tests. So you can learn it all now or regret it later.

How many times have you said to yourself, "I don't know why I'm even trying to learn this (calculus, algebra, geometry, physics, chemistry, history, whatever). I'll *never* use this again!"? I hate to burst bubbles, but unless you've got a patent on some great new fortune-telling device, you have *no clue* what you're going to need to know tomorrow or next week, let alone next year or next decade.

I've been amazed in my own life how things I did with no specific purpose in mind (except probably to earn money) turned out years later to be not just invaluable to my life or career, but essential. How was I to know when I took German as my language elective in high school that the most important international trade show in book publishing, my field, was in Frankfurt...Germany? Or that the basic skills I learned one year working for an accountant (while I was writing my first book) would become essential when I later started four companies? Or how important basic math skills would be in selling and negotiating over the years? (Okay, I'll admit it: I haven't used a differential equation in 20 years, but, hey, you never know!)

So learn it *all*. And don't be surprised if the subject you'd vote "least likely to ever be useful" winds up being the key to *your* fame and fortune.

There *are* other study guides

Although I immodestly maintain my ***How to Study Program*** to be the most helpful to the most people, there are certainly lots of other purported study books out there. Unfortunately, I don't think many of them deliver what they promise. In fact, I'm actually getting angry at the growing number of study guides out there claiming to be "the sure way to straight As" or something of the sort. These are also the books that dismiss reasonable alternative ways to study and learn with: "Well, that never worked for me," as if that is a valid reason to dismiss it, as if we should care that it didn't work for the author.

Inevitably, these other books promote the authors' "system," which usually means what *they* did to get through school. This "system," whether basic and traditional or wildly quirky, may or may not work for you. So what do you do if "their" way of taking notes makes no sense to you? Or you master their highfalutin "Super Student Study Symbols" and still get Cs?

I'm not getting into a Dennis Miller rant here, but there are very few "rights" and "wrongs" out there in the study world. There's certainly no single "right" way to attack a multiple choice test or absolute "right" way to take notes. So don't get fooled into thinking there *is*, especially if what you're doing seems to be working for you.

Don't change what "ain't broke" just because some self-proclaimed study guru claims what you're doing is all wet. Maybe *he's* all wet. After all, if his system works for you, all it *really* means is you have the same likes, dislikes, talents, or skills as the author.

Needless to say, don't read *my* books looking for the Truth—that single, inestimable system of "rules" that works for everyone. You won't find it, 'cause there's no such bird.

You will find a plethora of techniques, tips, tricks, gimmicks, and what-have-yous, some or all of which may work for you, some of which won't. Pick and choose, change and adapt, figure out what works for you. Because you are the one responsible for creating your study system.

Yes, I'll occasionally point out "my way" of doing something. I may even suggest that I think it offers some clear advantages to all the alternative ways of accomplishing the same thing. But that doesn't mean it's some carved-in-stone, deviate-from-the-sacred-Ron-Fry-study-path-under-penalty-of-a-writhing-death kind of rule.

I've used the phrase "Study smarter, not harder" as a sort of catch-phrase in promotion and publicity for the

How to Study Program for nearly a decade. So what does it mean to you? Does it mean I guarantee you'll spend less time studying? Or that the least amount of time is best? Or that studying isn't ever supposed to be difficult?

Hardly. It does mean that studying inefficiently is wasting time that could be spent doing other (okay, probably more *fun)* things and that getting your studying done as quickly and efficiently as possible is a realistic, worthy, and *attainable* goal. I'm no stranger to hard work, but I'm not a monastic dropout who thrives on self-flagellation. I try not to work harder than I have to!

That said, I can guarantee that the 1,000-plus pages of my ***How to Study Program*** contain the most wide-ranging, comprehensive, and complete system of studying ever published. I have attempted to create a system that is usable, that is useful, that is practical, that is learnable. One that *you* can use—whatever your age, whatever your level of achievement, whatever your IQ—to start doing better in school, in work, and in life *immediately*.

Ron Fry
May, 1999

CHAPTER 1

THE NEED FOR ORGANIZATION

Whether you're a high school student just starting to feel frazzled; a college student juggling five classes and a part-time job; or a parent working, attending classes, and raising a family; a simple, easy-to follow system of organization is crucial to your success. And despite your natural tendency to proclaim that you just don't have the *time* to spend scheduling, listing, and recording, it's also the best way to give yourself *more* time.

Taking time to make time

I'm sure many of you reading this are struggling with your increasing responsibilities and commitments. Some of you may be so overwhelmed you've just given up. Those of you who haven't probably figure it's your fault—if you just worked *harder*, spent more time on your papers and assignments, set up camp in the library—then everything would work out.

So you resign yourself to all-nighters, cramming for tests, and forgetting about time-consuming activities such as eating and sleeping. Trying to do everything—even when there's too much to do—without acquiring the skills to *control* your time, is an approach that will surely lead to burnout.

When does it all end?

With classes, homework, a part-time or full-time job, and all the opportunities for fun and recreation, life as a student can be very busy. But believe me, it doesn't suddenly get easier when you graduate.

Most adults will tell you that it only gets *busier.* There will always be a boss who expects you to work later; children who need to be fed, clothed, and taken to the doctor; hobbies and interests to pursue; community service to become involved in; courses to take, etc.

If you're an adult doing all of the latter, I sure don't have to tell you how important organization is, do I?

There may *not* be time for *every*thing

When I asked one busy student if she wished she had more time, she joked, "I'm *glad* there are only 24 hours in a day. Any more and I wouldn't have an excuse for not getting everything done!"

Let me give you the good news: There *is* a way that you can accomplish more in less time. And it doesn't even take more effort. You can plan ahead and make conscious choices about how your time will be spent, and how much time you will spend on each task. You can have more control over your time, rather than always running out of time as you keep trying to do everything.

Now the bad news: The first step to managing your time should be deciding just what is important...and what isn't. Difficult as it may be, sometimes it's necessary for us to recognize that we truly *can't* do it all; to slice from our busy schedules those activities that aren't as meaningful to us so that we can devote more energy to those that are.

You may be a *Star Trek* fan from way back. But is it really the best use of your time to run back to your room to catch the morning rerun each weekday?

You may love music so much, you want to be in the school orchestra, jazz band, choir, and play with your own garage band on weekends. But is it realistic to commit to all *four?*

Your job at the mall boutique may mean you get 20 percent off all the clothes you buy. But if you are working there four days a week, taking 15 hours of classes, and working at the food co-op on weekends, when do you expect to study?

If you're raising a family, working part-time, and trying to take a near-full class load, it's probably time to cure yourself of the Super Parent syndrome.

But there *is* enough time to plan

Yet, even after paring down our commitments, most of us are still challenged to get it all done. What with classes, study time, work obligations, extracurricular activities, and social life, it's not easy getting it all in—even without *Star Trek.*

Whether you're in high school, college, or graduate school, a "traditional" student, or one who's chosen to return to school after being out in the "real world" for a while, you'll find that the organizational plan I outline in this book is a manageable program that *will* work for you.

This program allows for flexibility. In fact, I encourage you to adapt any of my recommendations to your own unique needs. That means it will work for you whether you are living in a dorm, sharing accommodations with a roommate, or living with a spouse and children. That you *can* learn how to balance school, work, fun, and even family obligations.

The purpose of this book is to help you make *choices* about what is important to you, set *goals* for yourself, *organize* and *schedule* your time, and develop the *motivation* and *self-discipline* to follow your schedule and reach those goals, which will give you the time to learn all the other study skills I write about!

Wouldn't it be nice to actually have some *extra* time...instead of always running out of it?

To feel that you're exerting some control over your schedule, your schoolwork, your *life*...instead of caroming from appointment to appointment, class to class, assignment to assignment, like some crazed billiard ball?

It can happen.

I will not spend a lot of time trying to convince you that this is a "fun" idea—getting excited about calendars and to-do lists is a bit of a stretch. You will *not* wake up one morning and suddenly decide that organizing your life is just the most awesome thing you can think of.

But I suspect you *will* do it if I can convince you that effective organization will reward you in some very tangible ways.

Presuming all this is true (and I'll wager it is), unless you have some darn good reasons—a solid idea of some of the benefits effective organization *can* bring you—you will probably find it hard to consistently motivate yourself to do it. It has to become a habit, something you do without thinking, but also something you do *no matter what.*

More work, less time, more fun!

An organizational or time-management system that fits your needs can help you get more work done in less time. Whether your priority is more free time than you have now or improved grades, learning how to organize your life and your studies can help you reach your objective, because:

1. **It helps you put first things first.** Have you ever spent an evening doing a busy-work assignment for an *easy* class, only to find that you hadn't spent enough time studying for a crucial test in a more difficult one?

   Listing all of the tasks you are required to complete and *prioritizing* them ensures that the most important things will *always* get done—*even on days when you don't get* everything *done.*

2. **It helps you avoid time traps.** Time traps are the unplanned events that pop up, sometimes (it seems) every day. They're the fires you have to put out before you can turn to tasks like studying.

   You may fall into such time traps because they *seem* urgent...or because they seem *fun.* Or you may end up spending hours in them...without even realizing you're stuck.

   There's no way to avoid *every* time trap. But effective time management can help you avoid most of them. Time management is like a fire-*prevention* approach rather than a fire-*fighting* one: It allows you to go about your work systematically instead of moving from crisis to crisis or whim to whim.

3. **It helps you anticipate opportunities.** In addition to helping you balance study time with other time demands, effective time management can help make the time you *do* spend studying more productive. You'll be able to get more done in the same amount of time or (even better) do more work in less time. I'm sure you could find *some* way to spend those extra hours each week.

   Imagine that you and another student are working on the same term paper assignment. You plan out the steps to be completed well in advance and start on them early. The other student delays even thinking about the paper until a week before the assignment is due.

   If both of you were unable to find all the materials you needed in the local library, you, who started early, would have the opportunity to send away for them. The student who had only a week left would not have the same luxury, or the same good grade.

4. **It gives you freedom and control.** Contrary to many students' fears, time management is *liberating,* not restrictive. A certain control over *part* of your day allows you to be flexible with the *rest* of your day.

   In addition, you will be able to plan more freedom into your schedule. For example, you would know well in advance that you have a big test the day after a friend's party. Instead of having to call your friend the night of the party with a big sob story, you could make sure you allocate enough study time beforehand and go to the party without feeling guilty, without even *thinking* about the test.

5. **It helps you avoid time conflicts.** Have you ever lived the following horror story? You get out of class at 5:30, remember you have a big math assignment due, *then* realize you have no time to do it because you have a music rehearsal at 6 p.m. *Then* you remember that your softball game is scheduled for 7 p.m....just before that date you made months ago (which you completely forgot about until you came home and found a not-so-subtle message on your answering machine).

   Simply having all of your activities, responsibilities, and tasks written down in one place helps ensure that two or three things don't get scheduled for the same time. If time conflicts do arise, you will recognize them well in advance and be able to rearrange things accordingly.

6. **It helps you avoid feeling guilty.** When you know how much studying has to be done and you have the time scheduled to do it, you can relax—you *know* that the work will get done. It is much easier to forget about studying if you've already allotted the time for it. Without a plan to finish the work you are doing, you may feel like it's "hanging over your head"—even when you're not working on it. If you're going to spend time *thinking* about studying, you might as well just spend the time *studying!*

   Effective time management also helps keep your conscience off your back: When your studying is done, you can *really* enjoy your free time *without* feeling guilty because you're not studying.

7. **It helps you evaluate your progress.** If you know where you should be in class readings and assignments, you will never be surprised when deadlines loom. For example, if you've planned out the whole term and know you have to read an average of 75 pages a week to keep up in your business management class, and you only read *60* pages this week, you don't need a calculator to figure out that you are slightly behind. And it's easy enough to schedule a little more time to read next week so you can catch up to your schedule.

   On the other hand, if you only read when it doesn't cut into your leisure time (like when your assignment doesn't conflict with your favorite TV programs), you'll never know whether you're behind or ahead (but I'll bet you're behind!). Then one day you suddenly realize you have to be up to Chapter 7...by lunchtime.

8. **It helps you see the big picture.** Effective time management provides you with a bird's-eye view of the semester. Instead of being caught off guard when the busy times come, you will be able to plan ahead—*weeks* ahead—when you have big tests or assignments due in more than one class.

   Why not complete that German culture paper a few days early so it's not in the way when two other papers are due...or you're trying to get ready for a weekend ski trip? Conflicts can be worked out with fewer problems if you know about them in advance and do something to eliminate them.

9. **It helps you see the bigger picture.** Planning ahead and plotting your course early allows you to see how classes fit with your overall school career. For example, if you know you have to take chemistry, biology and pharmacology to be eligible for entrance into the nursing program, and the courses you will take later will build on those, you will at least be able to see why the classes are required for your major, even if you aren't particularly fond of one or two of them.

10. **It helps you learn how to study smarter, not harder.** Students sometimes think time management just means reallocating their time—spending the same time studying, the same time in class, the same time partying, just shifting around these time segments so everything is more "organized."

    This is only *partially* true—a key part of effective time management *is* learning how to prioritize tasks. But this simple view ignores one great benefit of taking control of your time: It may well be possible you will be *so* organized, *so* prioritized, *so in control of your time* that you can spend *less* time studying, get *better* grades and have *more* time for other things: extracurricular activities, hobbies, a movie, whatever.

It keeps getting better

Besides helping you to manage your time right now and reach your immediate study goals, learning how to organize your studying will *continue* to pay off.

Have you ever sat in a class and thought to yourself, "I'll *never* use this stuff once I get out of school"?

You won't say that about organizational skills. They will be useful throughout your life. Preparation is what school is all about—if you spend your time effectively now, you will be better prepared for the future.

And the better prepared you are, the more options you will have—effective learning and good grades *now* will increase your range of choices when you graduate. The company you work for or the graduate school you attend will be one *you* choose, not one whose choice was dictated by your poor past performance.

Learning how to manage your time now will develop habits and skills you can use outside of school. It may be difficult for you to develop the habits of effective time management, but don't think you're alone—time management presents just as much of a problem to many parents, professors, and nonstudents. How many people do you know who *never* worry about time?

If you learn effective time-management skills in school, the payoffs will come throughout your life. Whether you wind up running a household or a business, you will have learned skills you will use every day.

Time management is not a magic wand that can be waved to solve problems in school or after graduation. It is a craft that must be developed over time. There is no "time-management gene" that you either have or lack, like the ones that produce brown eyes or black hair.

These techniques are tools that can be used to help you reach your short-term and long-range goals successfully.

The important thing to remember is that you *can* be a successful time manager and a successful student *if* you are willing to make the effort to learn and apply the principles in this book.

If you hate the idea of being tied to a schedule, if you fear that it would drain all spontaneity and fun from your life, I know you'll be pleasantly surprised when you discover that just the *opposite* is true.

Most students are relieved and excited when they learn what a liberating tool time management can be.

Let's explode some myths that may be holding *you* back.

Do I have to *live* in the library?

Learning effective organizational skills will not turn you into a study-bound bookworm. How much time do you need to set aside for studying? Ask your career counselor, and he or she will probably echo the timeworn 2:1 ratio—spend two hours studying *out* of class for every hour you spend *in* class.

Hogwash. That ratio may be way out of line—either not enough time or too much. The amount of study time will vary from individual to individual, depending on your classes, abilities, needs, and goals.

Scheduling time to study doesn't mean that you have to go from three hours of studying a day to eight. In fact, laying out your study time in advance often means you can relax more when you're *not* studying because you won't be worrying about when you're going to get your schoolwork done—the time's been set aside.

How *long* you study is less important than how *effective* you are when you do sit down to study. The goal is not to spend *more* time studying, but to spend the same or less time, *getting more done in whatever time you spend.*

It's too complicated

Many fear that time management implies complexity. Actually, I recommend simplicity. The more complex your system, the harder it will be to use and, consequently, the less likely you *will* use it consistently. The more complex the system, the more likely it will collapse.

It's too inflexible

You can design your time-management system to fit your own needs. Some of the skills you will learn in this book will be more helpful to you in reaching your goals than others. You may already be using some of them. Others you will want to start using right now. Still others may not fit your needs at all.

Use the skills that are most likely to lead you to *your* study goals, meet *your* needs and fit with *your* personality.

Inflexibility is most people's biggest fear—"If I set it all out on a schedule, then I won't be able to be spontaneous and choose what to do with my time later."

Your time-management system can be as flexible as you want. In fact, the best systems act as guides, not some rigid set of "must do's" and "can't do's."

That's enough about the myths. Let's take a look at what is actually required to use your time-management skills effectively.

A good notebook and a sharp pencil

You have to be able to look at your plan when it's time to use it. It's nearly impossible to make detailed plans very far in advance without having a permanent record. Make it your rule: "If I plan it out, I will write it down."

And make sure that you have *one place to write and keep all your schedule information,* including class times, meetings, study times, project due dates, vacations, doctor appointments, social events, etc., so you always know exactly where to find them.

Your readiness to adapt and personalize

The time-management system that best suits you will be tailor-made to fit *your* needs and personality.

Consider this example: Although most parents turn the lights out and keep things quiet when their baby is trying to go to sleep, one baby I know, who spent two months in the hustle and bustle of a newborn intensive-care unit, couldn't sleep unless the lights were *on* and it was *noisy*.

Similarly, many students will study best in a quiet environment, but others may feel uncomfortable in a "stuffy" library and prefer studying in their living room.

Make your study schedule work for *you,* not your night-owl roommate who must plan every activity down to the minute. Alter it, modify it, make it stricter, make it more flexible. Whatever works for you.

You'll never be disorganized again!

We've all had the experience of missing an important appointment or commitment and saying, "I know I had that written down somewhere—I wonder *where*?"

It's easy to *think,* "I'll write it down so I won't forget," but a schedule that is not used regularly isn't a safety net at all. You must consistently write down your commitments. You must spend time filling out your schedule every week, every day.

Any efforts you make to manage your time will be futile if you do not have your schedule with you when you need it. For example, you are in art class without your schedule when your teacher tells you when your next project is due. You jot it down in your art notebook and promise yourself you'll add it to your schedule as soon as you get home.

You hurry to your next class, and your geology instructor schedules a study session for the following week. You scribble a reminder in your lab book.

Between classes, a friend stops to invite you to a party Thursday night. You promise you'll be there.

You arrive at work to find out your supervisor has scheduled your hours for the following week. She checks them with you, they seem fine, so you commit to them.

Had you been carrying your schedule with you, you would have been able to write down your art project and schedule the necessary amount of preparation time.

You would have realized that your study session for geology was the same night as your friend's party and you would have discovered that accepting the work schedule your supervisor presented left you with little time to work on your art project.

Take your schedule with you anywhere and everywhere you think you might need it.

When in doubt, take it along!

Keeping your schedule with you will reduce the number of times you have to say, "I'll just try to remember it for now," or "I'll write it down on this little piece of paper and transfer it to my planner later."

Always make a point of writing down tasks, assignments, phone numbers, and other bits of important information in your schedule *immediately*.

Use your new system consistently

In order to test its effectiveness, you must give any time-management system a chance to work—give it a trial run. No program can work unless it is utilized consistently. And consistency won't happen without effort.

It's just like learning to ride a bicycle. It's a pain at first; you may even fall down a few times. But once you're a two-wheel pro, you can travel much faster and farther than you could by foot.

The same goes for the techniques you will learn here—they may take practice and a little getting used to, but once you've lived a "reorganized" life for a couple of weeks, you'll probably find yourself in the habit of doing it. From then on, it will take relatively little effort to maintain.

That's when you'll really notice the payoff—when the task becomes second nature.

CHAPTER 2

ORGANIZE YOUR LIFE

In one of my all-time favorite Abbott & Costello routines, the hapless Costello stands in front of a huge roll-top desk. There are hundreds—no, *thousands*—of papers spilling out of it. Suddenly, Abbott, the supreme delegator, comes in and asks for "the Smerling contract, 1942." Costello pulls out a pair of enormous tongs, roots around in the cavernous desk, papers spilling everywhere, and pulls out a single sheet of paper. "Smerling contract, 1942," he announces.

Many of us are probably as disorganized as Costello's "filing system," though I suspect more than a few (okay, me included) would contend that we *really can* find things in the clutter we like to call a desk. Whether we're kidding ourselves or not, becoming more organized in our lives—whether we're students, homebodies, or career ladder-climbers—is key to succeeding at home, in school, and on the job.

Self-quiz: How's your planning IQ?

To learn something about your present orientation to planning, take this quiz adapted from Jonathan and Susan Clark's *Make the Most of Your Workday* (Career Press, 1994), circling the answer that describes your orientation: (3) agree (2) not sure (1) disagree.

I take regular time for planning every day.	3 2 1
I have a personally chosen calendar or organizational system.	3 2 1
I prioritize all my assignments... daily.	3 2 1
I usually complete a Daily Schedule (see pages 75 to 78).	3 2 1
I do not have difficulty making decisions.	3 2 1
I work daily on parts of projects due more than a week from now.	3 2 1
The gas tank in my car is presently at least half full.	3 2 1
I know exactly when my most productive time of day is.	3 2 1
I know my most important assignment for tomorrow.	3 2 1
I have a current Project Board (see pages 69 to 72).	3 2 1

How did you do?

25 or more	You have a plan, and are working on it.
15 to 24	Sometimes your day gets the better of you.
less than 15	How you are holding up under this crisis?

Why things don't get done

Are you frustrated at the end of the day? Is your to-do list nearly as long at the end of the day as it was in the beginning? Do you sometimes feel you've spent all day spinning your wheels? Nearly all productivity problems can be traced to one or more of the items on the following list:

- ☞ **No clear goals.** Without a specific sense of purpose, it's impossible to effectively manage and organize your priorities. If you don't have a clear idea of where you want to go, any road will take you there.
- ☞ **Lack of priorities.** The best to-do list ever written is useless if it hasn't been prioritized. Most people naturally work on the easy or fun things first. They may cross off a majority of their list, but miss the most important items!
- ☞ **No daily plan.** Beginning your day without a plan of action is a formula for spending all day doing the wrong things. It invites anyone and everyone to interrupt your activities. You will passively allow unwelcome intrusions, because you'll have no way to defend yourself.
- ☞ **Procrastination.** It always seems like a good idea to "Scarlett O'Hara" your schedule. After all, tomorrow is another day. But it catches up with you!

- ☞ **Personal disorganization.** No matter how organized your priorities or how effective your daily plan, you may be losing irretrievable time searching for things that are lost in the messes on your desk, in your files, closets and even your car.
- ☞ **Perfectionism.** Are you unable to complete and release an assignment (paper, lab report, presentation, whatever) until it is done perfectly? Can you still see ways for something to be done better? Even if you can't see anything, does it nag you that there must be something you overlooked?
- ☞ **Interruptions.** Your day can be going according to schedule...until a friend drops in or a game of "Killer Frisbee" commences. Many of these occurrences can be eliminated; those that can't must be controlled.

If some or all of these apply to you, it's time to change some habits. If you're resolved to do so, I have some great news: Not only can bad habits be broken, but they can be replaced by good habits relatively easily. In fact, it's much easier to replace a habit than to break it. Just replace the "slob habit" with the good organizational habits in this book. Here's your battle plan:

- ☞ Begin today. The best time to start working on your resolve to be better organized is today. Don't procrastinate. Your motivation and resolve will not be stronger in a month than they are now. Start now and set a goal to acquire this new habit in the next 30 days!

☞ Spread the word. Don't keep your resolve a secret. Commit yourself to positive change by telling your friends and family what you've decided to do and by challenging them to keep you to your commitment.

☞ Practice, practice, practice. Practice is the oil that lubricates any habit's engine. The more you do something, the more ingrained it becomes.

The goal pyramid

One way to visualize all your goals—and their relation to each other—is to construct what I call a *goal pyramid.* Here's how to do it:

1. Centered at the top of a piece of paper, write down what you ultimately hope to gain from your education. This is your long-range goal and the pinnacle of your pyramid.
2. Below your long-range goal(s), list mid-range goals—milestones or steps that will lead you to your eventual target.
3. Below the mid-range goals, list as many short-range goals as you can—smaller steps that can be completed in relatively short periods of time.

Change your goal pyramid as you progress through school. You may eventually decide on a different career. Or your mid-range goals may change as you decide on a different path leading to the long-range goal. The short-range goals will undoubtedly change, even daily.

The process of creating your own goal pyramid allows you to see *how* all those little daily and weekly steps you take can lead to your mid-range and long-term goals, and will thereby motivate you to work on your daily and weekly tasks with more energy and enthusiasm.

Make goal-setting a part of your life

The development of good study skills is the highway to your goals, whatever they are. No matter how hard you have to work or how much adversity you have to overcome along the way, the journey will indeed be worth it.

How do you make setting goals a part of your life? Here are some hints I think will help:

1. **Be realistic when you set goals.** Don't aim too high or too low, and don't be particularly concerned when (not if) you have to make adjustments along the way.
2. **Be realistic about your expectations.** An improved understanding of a subject you have little aptitude for is preferable to getting hopelessly bogged down if total mastery of the subject is just not in the cards.
3. **Don't give up too easily.** You can be overly realistic—too ready to give up just because something is a trifle harder than you'd like. Don't aim too high and feel miserable when you don't come close, or aim too low and never achieve your potential—find the path that's right for you.
4. **Concentrate on areas that offer the best chance for improvement.** Unexpected successes can do wonders for your confidence and might make it possible for you to achieve more than you thought you could even in other areas.
5. **Monitor your achievements and keep resetting your goals.** Daily, weekly, monthly, yearly, ask yourself how you've done and where you'd like to go now.

How perfect are you?

What is a perfectionist, and are you one? And if you are, why is it a problem?

Perfectionists care perhaps *too* much, finding it impossible to be satisfied with anything less than "perfect" work (as they define it), presuming that such an ideal can actually be attained.

It is possible, of course, to score a "perfect" 100 on a test or to get an A+ on a paper the teacher calls "Perfect!" in the margin. But in reality, doing anything "perfectly" is an impossible task.

What does all this have to do with you? Nothing, unless you find yourself spending two hours polishing an already A+ paper, or half an hour searching for that one "perfect" word, or an hour rewriting great notes to make them "absolutely perfect." In other words, while striving for perfection may well be a noble trait, it can very easily, perhaps inevitably, become a major problem. It can become an uncontrollable and unstoppable urge that seriously inhibits your enjoyment of your work and your life.

If you really would prefer spending another couple of hours polishing that A+ paper to taking in a movie, reading a book, or getting some *other* assignment done, be my guest. Is the last 10 percent or so really worth it? In some cases it is, but not usually.

3 more rules to help you get organized

As you begin to make goal-setting and organization a part of your daily life, following are three concepts that will make a huge difference in your success.

Small changes, over time, make a big difference

A simple, tiny change in your behavior may have virtually negligible results, but make *hundreds* of small changes, and the effects can be earth-shattering!

Make this rule become an automatic part of your thought process and your actions. It will help you understand the often small difference between success and failure, productivity and frustration, happiness and agony. It's so simple, it's deceptive. Maybe just a little more training. Maybe a slightly better method of planning. Maybe just one tiny habit overcome. Maybe all of these and more. Each one alone is almost inconsequential, but when added up, the advantage is incredible!

The 80-20 Rule (Pareto Principle)

Another rule that you can apply to make a difference in how well you organize and manage your priorities is the 80-20 Rule, also known as the Pareto Principle.

Victor Pareto was an Italian economist and sociologist at the turn of the 20th century who studied the ownership of land in Italy. Pareto discovered that more than 80 percent of all the land was owned by less than 20 percent of the people. As he studied other things that people owned (including money), he found the same principle held true: 20 percent or less of the people always ended up with 80 percent or more of whatever he measured.

The most astonishing revelation about the 80-20 Rule is its opposite side: If 20 percent of activities are producing 80 percent of the results, then the other 80 percent of activities are, in total, only giving 20 percent of the results.

Remember: To apply the 80-20 Rule to managing your priorities, remind yourself that 20 percent of the activities on your list are going to produce 80 percent of the results and payoff. Your question must constantly be, "Which activities are the 20-percenters?"

Take advantage of "in-between" time

You can be even more productive by identifying the little windows of opportunity that pass through your life each day. They don't arrive with much fanfare, so if you're not alert to them, they will sneak right past you. What must you do with this "in-between" time? Recognize it as soon as it occurs *and* utilize it immediately by taking a premeditated action. If you don't have a plan, you will waste this time!

Here are some suggestions:

☞ Make phone calls.

☞ Read something.

☞ Mail letters.

☞ Pick up groceries (or make your grocery list).

☞ Clean up your desk and return things to their proper places.

☞ Review your Daily Schedule and reprioritize, if necessary.

☞ Go through your mail.

☞ Write a quick note or letter home.

☞ Proofread some or all of one of your papers.

☞ Think! (About an upcoming assignment, a paper you're writing, and so forth.)

☞ Relax!

Chapter 3

Organize Your Studying

You *can* study smarter. You *can* put in less time and get better results. But learning how *is* hard, because learning of *any* kind takes discipline. And learning self-discipline is, to many of us, the most difficult task of all.

If you're currently doing little or nothing in the way of schoolwork, then you *are* going to have to put in more time and effort. How much more? Or even more generally, how long should you study, period? Until you get the results you want to achieve.

The smarter you are and the more easily you learn and adapt the techniques in this book, the more likely you'll be spending less time on your homework than before. But the further you need to go—from Ds to As rather than from Bs to As—the more you need to learn and the longer you need to give yourself to learn it.

Don't get discouraged. You will see results surprisingly quickly.

Get ready for a lifelong journey

Learning how to study is really a long-term process. Once you undertake the journey, you will be surprised at the number of landmarks, pathways, side streets, and road signs you'll find. Even after you've transformed yourself into a better student than you ever hoped to be, you'll inevitably find one more signpost that offers new information, one more pathway that leads you in an interesting new direction.

Consider learning how to study a *lifelong process* and be ready to modify anything you're doing as you learn other methods.

This is especially important right from the start when you consider your overall study strategies. How long you study per night, how long you work on a particular subject, and how often you schedule breaks are going to vary considerably depending on how well you were doing before you read this book, how far you have to go, how interested you are in getting there, how involved you are in other activities, the time of day, your general health, and so forth. Are you getting the idea?

It gets more complicated: What's your study sequence? Hardest assignments first? Easiest? Longest? Shortest? Are you comfortable switching back and forth from one to another, or do you prefer to focus on a single assignment from start to finish?

This gets even more difficult when you consider that the tasks themselves may have a great effect on your schedule. Fifteen-minute study increments might work well for you most of the time (though I suspect a half-hour is an ideal unit for most of you, an hour only for those of you who can work that long without a break and who have assignments that traditionally take that long to complete).

On the other hand, you may have no problem at all working on a long project in fits and starts, 15 or 20 minutes at a time, without needing to retrace your steps each time you pick it up again.

What's the lesson in all of this? There is no ideal, no answer, and certainly no "right" answer to many of the questions I've posed. It's a message you'll read in these pages over and over again: Figure out what works for you and keep on doing it. If it later stops working or doesn't seem to be working as well, change it.

None of the organizational techniques discussed at length in this book is carved in stone. You not only should feel free to adapt and shape and bend them to your own needs, you *must* do so.

Creating your study environment

On page 54, I have included a checklist for you to rate your study environment. It includes not just *where* you study—at home, in the library, at a friend's—but when and *how* you study, too. Once you've identified what works for you, avoid those situations in which you *know* you don't perform best. If you don't know the answer to one or more of the questions, take the time to experiment.

Study groups: What are friends for?

I was 35 years old and a devoted watcher of the television show *The Paper Chase* before I was introduced to the concept of a study group. This series was to be about a law school that seemed to be on this side of hell. Sharing the load with other students wasn't just a good idea, it was virtually mandatory. My high school wasn't hell, not even a mild purgatory, but I still think a study group would have been beneficial. If I had thought of the idea I would have probably started one.

My ideal study environment

How I receive information best:

1. ❑ Orally ❑ Visually

In the classroom, I should:

2. ❑ Concentrate on taking notes ❑ Concentrate on listening
3. ❑ Sit in front ❑ Sit in back ❑ Sit near window or door

Where I study best:

4. ❑ At home ❑ In the library ❑ Somewhere else: ______________

When I study best:

5. ❑ Every night; little on weekends ❑ Mainly on weekends ❑ Spread out over seven days
6. ❑ In the morning ❑ Evening ❑ Afternoon
7. ❑ Before dinner ❑ After dinner

How I study best:

8. ❑ Alone ❑ With a friend ❑ In a group
9. ❑ Under time pressure ❑ Before I know I have to
10. ❑ With music ❑ In front of TV ❑ In a quiet room
11. ❑ Organizing an entire night's studying before I start
    ❑ Tackling and completing one subject at a time

I need to take a break:

12. ❑ Every 30 minutes or so ❑ Every hour
    ❑ Every 2 hours ❑ Every ____ hours

The idea is simple: Find a small group of like-minded students and share notes, question each other, prepare for tests together. Obviously, to be effective, the students you pick to be in your group should share all, or at least most, of your classes.

Even if you find only one or two other students willing to work with you, such cooperation will be invaluable, especially in preparing for major exams.

Tips for forming your own study group

☞ I suggest four students minimum, probably six maximum. You want to ensure everyone gets a chance to participate while maximizing the collective knowledge and wisdom of the group.

☞ Although group members need not be best friends, they shouldn't be overtly hostile to one another, either. Seek diversity of experience, demand common dedication.

☞ Try to select students who are at least as smart, committed, and serious as you. That will encourage you to keep up and challenge you a bit. Avoid a group in which you're the "star"—at least until you flicker out during the first exam.

☞ Avoid inviting members who are inherently unequal—boyfriend/girlfriend combinations, in which one may be inhibited by their *amore*'s presence; situations where one student works for another; situations where underclassmen and upperclassmen may stifle one another, etc.

☞ Decide early on if you're forming a study group or a social group. If the latter, don't pretend it's the former. If the former, don't just invite your friends and sit around discussing your teachers.

☞ There are a number of ways to organize. My suggestion is to assign each class to one student. That student must master that assigned class, doing, in addition to the usual assignments, any extra reading (recommended by the professor or not) necessary to achieve that goal, taking outstanding notes, outlining the course (if the group so desires), being available for questions, and preparing various practice quizzes, midterms and finals as needed, to help test the other students' mastery.

Needless to say, all of the other students attend all classes, take their own notes, and do their own reading and homework assignments. But the student assigned that class attempts to learn as much as the professor, to actually be the "substitute professor" of that class in the study group. (So if you have five classes, a five-person study group is ideal.)

☞ Make meeting times and assignments formal and rigorous. Consider establishing rigid rules of conduct. Better to shake out the frivolous students early. You don't want anyone who is working as little as possible but hoping to take advantage of *your* hard work.

☞ Consider appointing a chair (rotating weekly, if you wish) in charge of keeping everyone on schedule and settling disputes before they disrupt the study group.

☞ However you organize, clearly decide—early—the exact requirements and assignments of each student. Again, you never want the feeling to emerge that one or two of you are trying to "ride the coattails" of the others.

Where should *you* study?

1. **At the library.** There may be numerous choices, from the large reading room, to quieter, sometimes deserted specialty rooms, to your own, solitary study cubicle. My favorite "home away from home" at Princeton was a little room that seemingly only four or five of us knew about—with four wonderfully comfortable chairs, subdued lighting, phonographs with earplugs, and a selection of some 500 classical records. For someone like me, who requires music to study, it was a custom-made study haven!

2. **At home.** Remember that this is the place where distractions are most likely to occur. No one tends to telephone you at the library, and little brothers (or your own kids) will not find you easily in the "stacks." It is, of course, usually the most convenient place to make your study headquarters. It may not, however, be the most effective.

3. **At a friend's, neighbor's, or relative's.** This may not be an option at all for most of you, even on an occasional basis, but you still may want to set up one or two alternative study sites. Despite many experts' opinion that you must study in the same place every night (with which I don't agree, by the way), I have a friend who simply craves some variety to help motivate him. He has four different places in which he likes to study and simply rotates them from night to night. Do whatever you find works best for you.

4. **In an empty classroom.** Certainly an option at many colleges and perhaps some private high schools, it is an interesting idea mainly because so few students have ever thought of it! While not a likely option at a public high school, it never hurts to ask if you can't make some arrangements. Since many athletic teams practice until 6 p.m. or later, even on the high school level, there may be a part of the school open—and usable with permission—even if the rest is locked up tight.
5. **At your job.** Whether you're a student working part-time or a full-time worker going to school part-time, you may be able to make arrangements to use an empty office, even during regular office hours, or perhaps after everyone has left (depending on how much your boss trusts you). If you're in junior high or high school and a parent, friend or relative works nearby, you may be able to work from just after school until closing time at that person's workplace.

When should you study

As much as possible, create a routine time of day for your studying. Some experts contend that doing the same *thing* at the same *time* every day is the most effective way to organize any ongoing task. Some students find it easier to set aside specific blocks of time during the day, each day, in which they plan on studying.

No matter who you are, the time of day you'll study is determined by the following factors

1. **Study when you're at your best.** What is your peak performance period—the time of day you do your best work? This period varies from person to person. You may be dead to the world until noon but able to study well into the night, or up and alert at the crack of dawn but distracted and tired if you try to burn the midnight oil.
2. **Consider your sleep habits.** Habit is a very powerful influence. If you always set your alarm for 7 a.m., you may find that you wake up then even when you forget to set it. If you have grown accustomed to going to sleep around 11 p.m., you will undoubtedly become quite tired if you try to stay up studying until 2 a.m., and probably accomplish very little in those three extra hours.
3. **Study when you can.** Although you want to sit down to study when you are mentally most alert, external factors also play a role in deciding when you study. Being at your best is a great goal, but is not always possible: Study whenever circumstances allow.
4. **Consider the complexity of the assignment when you allocate time.** The tasks themselves may have a great effect on your schedule. Don't schedule one hour for an 80-page reading assignment when you know you read half a page per minute...on a good day.

Evaluate your study area

Whatever location you choose as your study base, how you set up your study area can affect your ability to stay focused and, if you aren't careful, seriously inhibit quality study time. Sit down at your desk or study area right now and evaluate your own study environment:

1. Do you have one or two special places reserved just for studying? Or do you study wherever seems convenient or available at the time?
2. Is your study area a pleasant place? Would you offer it to a friend as a good place to study? Or do you dread it because it's so depressing?
3. How's the lighting? Is it too dim or too bright? Is the whole desk well lit? Or only portions of it?
4. Are all the materials you need handy?
5. What else do you do here? Eat? Sleep? Write letters? Read for pleasure? If you try to study at the same place you sit to listen to your music or chat on the telephone, you may find yourself doing one when you think you are doing the other!
6. Is your study area in a high-traffic or low-traffic area? How often are you interrupted by people passing through?
7. Can you close the door to the room to avoid disturbances and outside noise?
8. When do you spend the most time here? What time of day do you study? Is it when you are at your best? Or do you inevitably study when you're tired and less productive?
9. Are your files, folders and other class materials organized and near the work area? Do you have some filing system in place for them?

Staying focused on your studies

If you find yourself doodling and dawdling more than reading and remembering, try these solutions:

1. **Create a comfortable work environment.** The size, style, and placement of your desk, chair, and lighting may all affect whether or not you're distracted from the work at hand. Take the time to design the area that's perfect for you.
2. **Turn up the lights.** Experiment with the placement and intensity of lighting in your study area until you find what works for you, both in terms of comfort and as a means of staying awake and focused.
3. **Set some rules.** Let family, relatives, and especially friends know how important your studying is and that specific hours are inviolate.
4. **Take the breaks you need.** Don't just follow well-intentioned but bogus advice about how long you should study before taking a break. Break when *you* need to.

Fighting tiredness and boredom

You've chosen the best study spot and no one could fault you on its setup. You're still using pencils to prop up your eyelids? Help is on the way:

Take a nap. What a concept! When you're too tired to study, take a short nap to revive yourself. Maximize that nap's effect by keeping it short—20 minutes is ideal, 40 minutes absolute maximum. After that, you go into another phase of sleep and you may wake even more tired than before.

Have a drink. A little caffeine won't harm you—a cup of coffee or tea, a glass of soda. Just be careful not to mainline it—caffeine's "wake-up" properties seem to reverse when you reach a certain level, making you far more tired than you were!

Turn down the heat. You needn't build an igloo out back, but too warm a room will inevitably leave you dreaming of sugarplums...while your paper remains unwritten on your desk.

Shake a leg. Go for a walk, high step around the kitchen, do a few jumping jacks—even mild physical exertion will give you an immediate lift.

Change your study schedule. Presuming you have some choice here, find a way to study when *you* are normally more awake and/or most efficient.

Studying with small kids

So many more of you are going to school while raising a family, I want to give you some ideas that will help you cope with the Charge of the Preschool Light Brigade:

Plan activities to keep the kids occupied. The busier you are in school and/or at work, the more time your kids will want to spend with you when you *are* home. If you spend some time with them, it may be easier for them to play alone, especially if you've created projects *they* can work on while *you*'re working on your homework.

Make the kids part of your study routine. Kids love routine, so why not include them in yours? If 4 p.m. to 6 p.m. is always "Mommy's Study Time," they will soon get used to it, especially if you make spending other time with them a priority and if you take the time to give them something to do during those hours.

Use the television as a baby sitter. While many of you will have a problem with this—it's one that I and my daughter deal with weekly, if not daily—it may be the lesser of two evils. And you can certainly rent (or tape) enough quality shows so you don't have to worry about the little darlings watching street gangs bash skulls (or bashing skulls themselves on some video game system).

Plan your study accordingly. Unless you are right up there in the Perfect Parent Pantheon, all these things will not keep your kids from interrupting every now and then. While you can minimize such intrusions, it's virtually impossible to eliminate them entirely. So don't try—plan your schedule *assuming* them. For one, that means taking more frequent breaks to spend five minutes with your kids. They'll be more likely to give you the 15 or 20 minutes at a time *you* need if they get periodic attention themselves.

Find help. Spouses can occasionally take the kids out for dinner and a movie (and trust me, the kids will encourage you to study *more* if you institute this!), relatives can baby-sit (at their homes) on a rotating basis, or playmates can be invited over (allowing you to send your darling to their house the next day). You may be able to trade baby-sitting chores with other parents at school and professional day care may be available at your child's school or in someone's home for a couple of hours a day.

Finally, use the Pre-Test Organizer on pages 64 and 65 to figure out your plan of action for the next test.

You *can* be successful without killing yourself!

Pre-Test Organizer

Class:________________ **Teacher:**______________________
Test date:____________ **Time:** From__________ to__________
Place:____
Special instructions to myself (take calculator, dictionary, etc.):__________________________________

Materials I need to study for this test (check all needed):

- ❑ Book
- ❑ Workbook
- ❑ Class notes
- ❑ Handouts
- ❑ Tapes/videos
- ❑ Old tests
- ❑ Other ______________

Format of the test will be (write the number of T/F, essays, etc., and total points for each section):

____

____

____

____

____

Study group meetings (times, places):

1. ____
2. ____
3. ____
4. ____
5. ____

Material to be covered:

Indicate topics, sources and amount of review (light or heavy) required. Check box when review is completed.

Topic	Sources	Review
________	________	☐____
________	________	☐____
________	________	☐____
________	________	☐____
________	________	☐____
________	________	☐____
________	________	☐____

After the test:

Grade I expected________Grade I received________

What did I do that helped me?________________________

____

____

____

____

What else should I have done?________________________

____

____

____

____

____

____

Chapter 4

Organize Your Months, Weeks, and Days

Now you're ready to plan!

We'll begin by developing a time-management plan for an entire term...before it begins, of course. This term plan will allow you to keep your sights on the "big picture." You'll see the forest, even when you're in the midst of the trees…and a majority of them are oversized redwoods.

By being able to take in your entire term—every major assignment, every test, every paper, every appointment—you will be less likely to get caught up spending more time on a lower-priority class, just because it requires regularly scheduled reports, while falling behind in a more important one, which only requires reading.

And when you can actually *see* you have a test in accounting the same week your zoology project is due, you can plan ahead and finish the project early. If you decide (for whatever reason) not to do so, at least you won't be caught by surprise when crunch time comes.

Start planning early

For your long-term planning to be effective, however, you must start early. Students who fail to plan *before* the school term begins often find themselves wasting time filling in their schedules one event at a time during the term. They may also find themselves feeling disorganized throughout the term. Starting early, on the other hand, increases your ability to follow a systematic plan of attack.

All college students—and some high school students—are able to pick and choose courses according to their own schedules, likes, dislikes, goals, and so forth. The headiness of such freedom should be tempered with the commonsense approach you're trying to develop through reading this book. Here are a few hints to help you along:

1. Whenever possible, consider each professor's reputation as you decide whether to select a particular course (especially if it is an overview or introductory course that is offered in two or three sessions). Word soon gets around as to which professors' lectures are stimulating and rewarding—an environment in which learning is a joy, even if it isn't a subject you like!
2. Attempt to select classes so that your schedule is balanced on a weekly and even a daily basis, though this will not always be possible or advisable. (Don't change your major just to fit your schedule!) Try to leave an open hour or half-hour between classes—it's ideal for review, post-class note-taking, quick trips to the library, and so forth.

3. Try to alternate challenging classes with those that come more easily to you. Studying is a process of positive reinforcement. You'll need encouragement along the way.
4. Avoid late-evening or early-morning classes, especially if such scheduling provides you with large gaps of "down time."
5. Set a personal study pace and follow it. Place yourself on a study diet, the key rule of which is: *Don't overeat.*

Identify the starting line

You can't race off to your ultimate goal until you figure out where *your* starting line is. So the first step necessary to overhaul your current routine is to *identify* that routine in detail. My suggestion is to chart, in 15-minute increments, how you spend every minute of every day *right now.* While a day or two might be sufficient for some of you, I recommend you chart your activities for an entire week, including the weekend.

This is especially important if, like many people, you have huge pockets of time that seem to disappear, but in reality are devoted to things like "resting" after you wake up, putting on makeup or shaving, reading the paper, waiting for transportation or driving to and from school or work. Could you use an extra hour or two a day, either for studying or for fun? Make better use of such "dead" time and you'll find all the time you need.

For example, learn how to do multiple tasks at the same time. Listen to a book on tape while you're working around the house; practice vocabulary or math drills while you're driving; have your kids, parents or roommates quiz you for an upcoming test while you are doing the dishes, vacuuming or dusting; and always carry your calendar, notebook(s), pens and a textbook with you—you can get a phenomenal amount of reading or studying done while in line at the bank, library or supermarket or while commuting by bus or train.

Strategy tip: Identify those items on your daily calendar, whatever their priority, that can be completed in 15 minutes or less. These are the ideal tasks to tackle at the launderette, while waiting for a librarian to locate a book you need or while standing in line anywhere.

Collect what you need

As you begin your planning session, make sure you have all the information and materials you need to make a quality plan. Gather your class syllabuses; work schedule; dates of important family events, vacations or trips; other personal commitments (doctor appointments, birthday parties, and so forth.); and a calendar of any extracurricular events in which you plan to participate.

Keeping track of your day-to-day activities—classes, appointments, regular daily homework assignments and daily or weekly quizzes—will be dealt with later in this chapter. For now, I want to talk about the projects—term papers, theses, studying for midterm and final exams, etc.—that require completion over a long period of time—weeks, maybe even months.

Creating your Project Board

There are two excellent tools you can use for your long-term planning. The first is a Project Board, which you can put on any blank wall or right above your desk. (See pages 70 and 71 for a sample Project Board.)

Sample Projects Board

MONTH/WEEK		PROJECT: STUDENT CORPORATION
1st MONTH	Week 1	Initial group meeting: Discuss overall assignment and possible products or services—bring list of three each to meeting (1 hour)
	Week 2	Finalize product or service; finalize organization of group and longterm responsibilities of each subgroup. (3)
	Week 3	Subgroup planning and short-term assignments (2)
	Week 4	Work on individual assignment from subgroup (?)
2nd MONTH	Week 1	Work on individual assignment from subgroup (?)
	Week 2	Work on individual assignment from subgroup (?)
	Week 3	Integrate individual assignment with rest of subgroup (?)
	Week 4	Meet with entire group to integrate plans (?)
3rd MONTH	Week 1	Finalize all-group plan; draft initial report (?)
	Week 2	Type and proof final report (?)
	Week 3	
	Week 4	
	DUE DATE	3RD MONTH/end of Week 2

PROJECT: DANTE TERM PAPER	REVIEW/EXAM SCHEDULE
Finalize topic (1 hour)	Review prior month's History notes (3)
Initial library research (2) General outline (1)	Review prior month's English notes (2)
Detailed library research (3)	Review prior month's Science notes (4)
Detailed library research (3)	Review prior month's Math notes (4)
Detailed library research (3)	Review 1st MONTH History notes (3)
Detailed outline (1)	Review 1st MONTH English notes (2)
First draft (4), Additional research (2)	Review 1st MONTH Science notes (4)
	Review 1st MONTH Math notes (4)
Second draft, spellcheck, proof (10)	2nd MONTH History notes (3)
Independent proof (1)	2nd MONTH English notes (2)
	2nd MONTH Science notes (4)
Type final draft and proof (4)	2nd MONTH Math notes (4)
end of 3RD MONTH	end of 3RD MONTH

It's not necessary for you to construct your own Project Board, though it is certainly the least expensive alternative. There are ready-made charts for professionals available in a variety of formats for your convenience, including magnetic and erasable. (Once again you're learning something that you can use throughout your entire life: Professionals call their Project Boards "flow charts.") Your local art supply, stationery or bookstore may have a selection of such items.

How does the Project Board work? It is just a variation on a typical calendar. You can set it up vertically, with the months running down the left-hand side and the projects across the top. Or you can certainly switch it around and have the dates across the top and the projects running vertically (in fact, that's the way a lot of the ready-made ones are sold). It all depends on the available space you have on your wall.

Using your Project Board

In the case of each project, there is a key preparatory step before you can use the chart: You have to break down each general assignment into its component parts, the specific tasks involved in any large project.

Also include on your Project Board time for studying for all your final exams. Cramming for tests doesn't work very well in the short term and doesn't work at all over the long term, so take my advice and make it a habit to review your class notes on each subject on a *weekly or monthly* basis.

As a result of this plan, you'll allocate little time to last-minute cramming or even studying for a specific final the week before it is given (just a couple of hours to go over any details you're still a little unsure of or spend on areas you think will be on the test).

While others are burning the midnight oil in the library the night before each exam, you're getting a good night's sleep and will enter the tests refreshed, relaxed, and confident. Seems like a better plan to me.

As a byproduct of this study schedule, you will find that salient facts and ideas will remain with you long after anybody is testing you on them.

Now that you have your Project Board, what do you do with it? Keep adding any and all other important projects throughout the term and continue to revise it according to actual time spent, as opposed to time allocated. Getting into this habit will make you more aware of how much time to allocate to future projects. The more you do this, the more accurate your estimates will be.

Using a Term-Planning Calendar

The Term-Planning Calendar, an example of which is shown on page 79, can be used in concert with or in place of the Project Board.

To use it with the Project Board, start by transferring all the information from the Project Board to your Term Planning Calendar. Then *add* your weekly class schedule, work schedule, family celebrations, vacations and trips, club meetings, and extracurricular activities. *Everything.* The idea is to make sure your Calendar has *all* your scheduling information, while your Project Board contains just the briefest summary that you can ingest in a glance.

Leave your Project Board on your wall at home; carry your Term-Planning Calendar with you. Whenever new projects, appointments, meetings, etc. are scheduled, add them immediately to your Calendar. Then transfer the steps involving major projects to your Project Board.

To use it in place of the Project Board, just don't make a Project Board. Put all the information—including the steps of all your projects and the approximate time you expect each to take—right on the Calendar.

It's up to you which way to go. Personally, I prefer using *both,* for one simple reason: I like being able to look at the wall and see the entire term *at a glance.* I find it much easier to see how everything "fits together" *this* way than trying to "glance" at a dozen different weekly calendars or even three monthly ones.

The fat lady isn't singing yet

It's time to become even more organized. The Project Board and Term-Planning Calendar have given you a good start by helping you schedule the entire term. Now it's time to learn about the tools that will help you organize your days and weeks.

Step 1: Make your "to-do" list

First, identify everything you need to do this week. Look at your Project Board and/or Term-Planning Calendar to determine what tasks need to be completed this week for all of your major school projects. Add any additional tasks that must be done—from sending a birthday present to your sister to attending your monthly volunteer meeting to completing homework that may have just been assigned.

Once you have created your list, you can move on to the next step, putting your tasks in order of importance.

Step 2: Prioritize your tasks

When you sit down to study without a plan, you just dive into the first project that comes to mind. The problem with this approach has been discussed earlier: There is no guarantee that the first thing that comes to mind will be the most important. The point of the weekly Priority Task Sheet is to help you arrange your tasks *in order of importance.* That way, even if you find yourself without enough time for *everything,* you can at least finish the most important assignments.

First, ask yourself this question, "If I only got a few things done this week, what would I want them to be?" Mark these high-priority tasks with an "H." After you have identified the "urgent" items, consider those tasks that are least important—items that could wait until the following week to be done, if necessary. These are low-priority items, at least for this week—mark them with an "L."

All the other items fit somewhere between the critical tasks and the low-priority ones. Mark them with an "M," for middle priority.

Strategy tip: If you push aside the same low-priority item day after day, week after week, at some point you should just stop and decide whether it's something you need to do at all!

A completed Priority Task Sheet is on page 80. A blank form you can photocopy is on page 82.

Step 3: Fill in your Daily Schedule

Before you start adding papers, projects, homework, study time, etc., to your calendar, fill in the "givens"—the time you need to sleep, eat, work, and attend class. Even if your current routine consists of meals on the run and sleep whenever you find it, build the assumption *right into your schedule* that you are going to get eight hours of sleep and three decent meals a day. You may surprise yourself and find that there is still enough time to do everything you need. (Though all of us probably know someone who sleeps three hours a night, eats nothing but junk and still finds a way to get straight As, most experts would contend that regular, healthy eating and a decent sleep schedule are key attributes to any successful study system.)

Now you're ready to transfer the items on your Priority Task Sheet to your Daily Schedule forms. (See page 81 for a sample completed Daily Schedule, page 83 for a blank form you can photocopy.)

Put in the "H" items first, followed by the "M" items. Then, fit in as many of the "L" items that you still have room for. By following this procedure, you'll make sure you devote the amount of time needed for your most important priorities. You can schedule your most productive study time for your most important tasks, and plug in your lower priorities as they fit.

Other considerations

Besides the importance of the task and the available time you have to complete it, other factors will determine how you fit your Daily Schedules together. Some factors will be beyond your control—work schedules, appointments with professors, counselors, or doctors. But there are plenty of factors you *do* control and should consider as you put together your Daily Schedules each week.

Schedule enough time for each task—time to "warm up" and get the task accomplished, particularly when working on long-term projects, but not so much time that you "burn out." Every individual is different, but most students study best for blocks of one and a half to three hours, depending on the subject.

Don't overdo it. Plan your study time in blocks, breaking up work time with short leisure activities. (It's helpful to add these to your schedule as well.) For example, you've set aside three hours on Wednesday afternoon for that research assignment. Schedule a 15-minute walk to the ice cream shop somewhere in the middle of that study block. You'll find that these breaks help you think more clearly and creatively when you get back to studying.

Even if you tend to like longer blocks of study time, be careful about scheduling study "marathons"—a six- or eight-hour stretch rather than a series of two-hour sessions. The longer the period you schedule, the more likely you'll have to fight the demons of procrastination. Convincing yourself that you're really studying your heart out, you'll also find it easier to justify time-wasting distractions, scheduling longer breaks, and, before long, quitting before you should.

Use your Daily Schedule *daily*

Each night (or in the morning before the day begins) look at your schedule for the upcoming day. How much free time is there? Are there "surprise" tasks that are *not* on your schedule but need to be? Are there conflicts you were unaware of at the beginning of the week?

If you plan well at the beginning of the week, this shouldn't happen often, but it invariably does. Just as often, you'll discover a class is canceled or a meeting postponed, which leaves you with a schedule change. By checking your Daily Schedule *daily*—either the night before or the first thing in the morning—you'll be able to respond to these changes.

How do you know whether to enter an assignment on your Daily Schedule or put it on the Project Board first?

If it's a simple task *and* if it will definitely be accomplished within a week—read pages 201-274 of your history text, study for quiz, meet to discuss cheerleading tryouts—put it on the appropriate Daily Schedule Sheet(s).

If, however, it's a task that is complicated—requiring further breakdown into specific steps—and/or one that will require more than a week to complete, it should be "flow charted" on your Project Board. *Then* the individual steps should be added to your Daily Schedules. (I like to plan everything out the night before. It's a fantastic feeling to wake up and start the day completely organized.)

The most important 15 minutes of the day

Set aside 15 minutes every day to go over your daily and weekly priorities. Although many businesspeople like to make this the first 15 minutes of their day, I recommend making it the *last* 15 minutes of *your* day. Why? Three great reasons:

1. **Your ideas will be fresher.** It's easier to analyze at the end of the day what you have accomplished...and what you haven't.
2. **It's a great way to end the day.** Even if your "study day" ends at 11 p.m., you will feel fully prepared for the next day, and ready to relax, anxiety-free.
3. **You'll get off to a great start the next morning.** If you use the morning to plan, it's easy to turn a 15-minute planning session into an hour of aimless "thinking." While others are fumbling for a cup of coffee, you're off and running!

Term Planning Calendar

Fill In due dates for assignments and papers, dates of tests, and important non-academic activities and events

Month	Mon	Tue	Wed	Thu	Fri	Sat	Sun

Priority Rating	Scheduled?	**Priority Tasks This Week** *Week of* 3/28 *through* 4/3
		Sociology Paper
H		– Library Search
M		– Outline
L		– Rough Draft
		Math Assignments
H		– Ch. 4
M		– Ch. 5
M		– Study for test

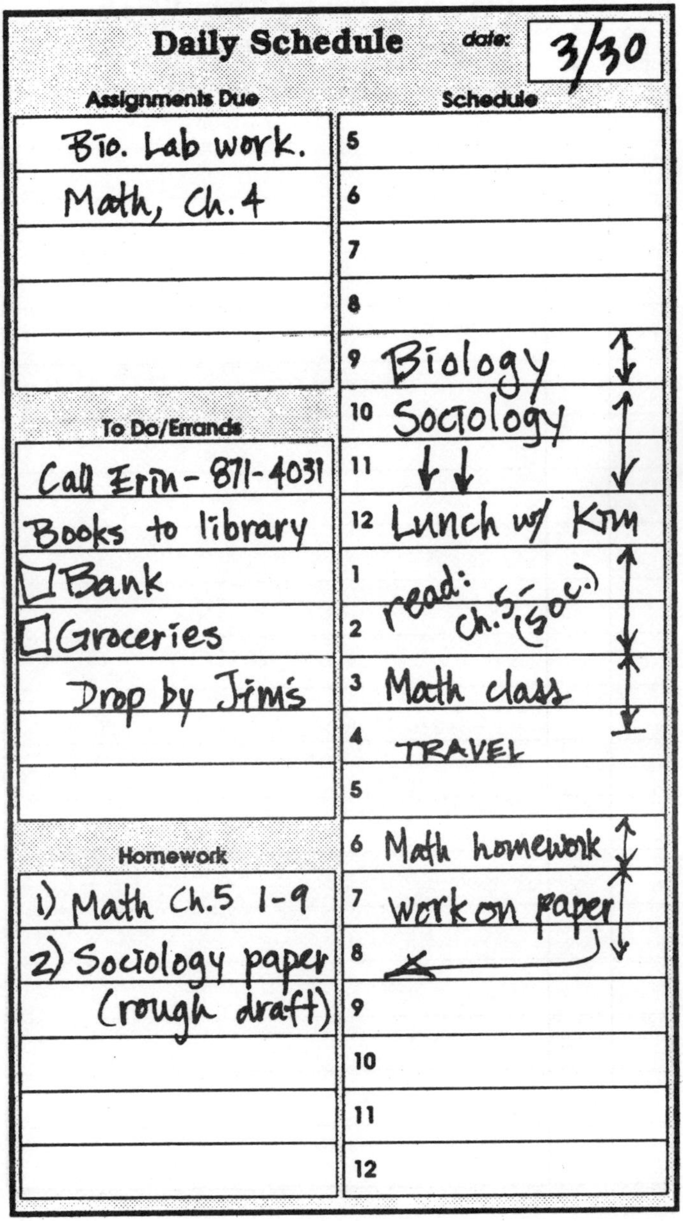

Daily Schedule date: 3/30

Assignments Due	Schedule	
Bio. Lab work.	5	
Math, Ch. 4	6	
	7	
	8	
	9	Biology
To Do/Errands	10	Sociology
Call Erin - 871-4031	11	↓↓
Books to library	12	Lunch w/ Kim
☐ Bank	1	read: Ch. 5 (soc.)
☐ Groceries	2	
Drop by Jim's	3	Math class
	4	TRAVEL
	5	
Homework	6	Math homework
1) Math Ch. 5 1-9	7	work on paper
2) Sociology paper	8	
(rough draft)	9	
	10	
	11	
	12	

Priority Rating	Scheduled?	**Priority Tasks This Week** *Week of* *through*

Daily Schedule

date:

Assignments Due

To Do/Errands

Homework

Schedule

5	
6	
7	
8	
9	
10	
11	
12	
1	
2	
3	
4	
5	
6	
7	
8	
9	
10	
11	
12	

CHAPTER 5

DEALING WITH LIFE'S DAILY TRAUMAS

Your organizational plan should be simple. Why commit to another complicated project that wastes your time and saps your already depleted mental energies? Unfortunately, no matter how basic your time management system, ease-of-use doesn't guarantee that you won't be plagued with occasional time-crunch problems.

As you try to implement these skills, you're bound to have some glitches. Learn some problem-solving skills so these study roadblocks don't stop your progress completely.

If you run into a "wall" on your path to organizational success, the best solution is to find creative ways to get *around* it, rather than trying to crash your way *through* it.

Time flies when you're having fun...

...and sometimes even when you're *not*. No matter how hard you try to stick to your schedule, you find that your assignments always take a lot longer than you had planned. You schedule an hour to do your economics homework, and it takes you twice that long. You plan an afternoon at the library for research, and it's closing time before you're ready to leave. It seems like you spend all your time studying—and you're *still* not getting it done.

Solutions: It's time for an attitude check. Are you being too much of a perfectionist? Is it taking you so long to read because you're trying to memorize every word? Make sure your expectations for yourself are realistic. And don't exaggerate the importance of lower-priority assignments.

Consider altering your behavior—with a little help from an alarm clock. If you've planned an hour for your reading assignment, set the clock to go off when you should have completed it. Then, *stop reading* and go on to the next assignment. If you're not done, reassure yourself that you can go back to it later. You'll probably become conditioned to complete your assignments more quickly, and you won't run the risk of leaving your other, perhaps more important, work unfinished.

"I'm allergic to my desk"

There's nothing wrong with your study area. It's in a quiet corner of the house with few distractions. All your materials are nearby, and the area is well-lit and well-ventilated. But...every time you sit down to study, you find yourself coming up with *any* excuse to leave. Unable to focus on any assignment, your mind would be wandering out the window if there were one in front of you.

Solution: It can happen. You set up the ideal study area, follow your time management system, and stick to your schedule religiously. Your intentions are good, but, for some reason, it just doesn't work. Bad vibes, maybe.

What can you do?

Change your environment!

Just as you can condition yourself to study, you can also condition yourself *not* to study in a particular location. Stick to your schedule, but try another area—another floor in the library, or even a place that may not seem to be as conducive to quiet study. Maybe you're one of those people who needs a little music or activity in the background to concentrate.

If changing your environment doesn't help, consider altering your study behavior. Are you trying to study at a time of day when you have far too much pent-up energy? Maybe switching your study time earlier or later would help. Try taking a brisk walk or exercising before you begin studying.

Think about other behavior: Have you had several cups of coffee (or cans of soda) prior to your study period? Caffeine overdose—or too much sugar *and* caffeine—could make it very difficult to concentrate.

A conspiracy to keep you from studying

Friends and family call when you're studying because they know that's the best time to reach you at home. Or you're interrupted by phone calls for family members or roommates. Worse yet are the calls from people taking surveys, asking for donations, or trying to sell you something.

Solutions: A ringing phone is virtually impossible to ignore. Even if you're determined not to pick it up, it still demands your attention and interrupts your concentration. An answering machine will eliminate your getting roped into lengthy conversations, but your train of thought will still be derailed.

There are a few environment-altering solutions: Turn off the ringer or unplug the phone and let your answering machine take calls while you're studying. Or remove yourself from within hearing distance—go to the library.

A little help from your "friends"

Your roommate, whose study hours differ from yours, always seems to want to spend "quality bonding time" in the middle of your heavy-duty reading assignments.

Solutions: It's not rude to refuse to talk to someone while you're studying. But it often feels like that, and I'd rather feel guilty about not studying than be rude to a friend. A favorite tip from human-relations specialists is to respond in a positive but diverting way—for example, "It sounds like this is important to you. I really want to hear more. Can we talk in an hour when I'm done with this, so I can concentrate more on your problem?" (Granted, your roommate would consider you crazy—or worse—if you actually talked like this. Put it in your own words—it's the attitude that's important.)

Another solution might be to put up a "Do Not Disturb" sign, indicating the time you will be available to talk. The visual signal helps remind others that you're busy *before* they unintentionally interrupt you with small talk.

You can't count on anyone

You painstakingly plan your schedule each week, religiously keeping track of each appointment, assignment, and commitment you have. Unfortunately, others don't seem to have the same sense of responsibility you do. Your friends cancel social engagements, you arrive on time for a meeting and no one else in the group shows up, even your teacher postpones the pre-test study session.

Solution: Yes, its time for another attitude adjustment. Welcome to the real world!

First of all, there's really nothing you can do when someone else cancels or postpones a scheduled appointment. But if you remember, in the very first chapter of ***Get Organized***, I said that fanaticism is not an element of a good time management program.

Occasional—and sometimes more than occasional—cancellations, postponements or schedule shuffles should *not* ruin your plan.

Try looking at such last-minute changes as *opportunities.* Your doctor canceled your appointment? That means a free hour to get ahead in calculus, read your history, work out at the gym...or just do nothing!

Old habits die hard

As you begin to implement your own organizational system for success, you may need to rid yourself of some old habits:

1. **Don't make your schedule overly vague.** When you're scheduling your time, be specific about which tasks you plan to do, and when you plan to do them.
2. **Don't delay your planning.** It's easy to convince yourself that you will plan the details of a particular task when the time comes. But that way it's much too easy to forget your homework when your friends invite you to go to the park or out for a snack.
3. **Write *everything* down.** Not having to remember all these items will free up space in your brain for the things you need to concentrate on or *do* have to remember. As a general

rule, write down the so-called little things and you'll avoid data overload and clutter.

4. **Learn to manage distractions.** Don't respond to the urgent and forget the important. It's easy to become distracted when the phone rings, your baby brother chooses to trash your room or you realize your favorite TV show is coming on. But don't just drop your books and run off. Take a few seconds to make sure you have reached a logical stopping point.

5. **Don't "shotgun" plan.** Even if you haven't been following a systematic time-management approach, you may have had some way of keeping important dates and events in mind. Some students use what might be called the "shotgun" approach—writing down assignments, dates, and times on whatever is available. They wind up with so many slips of paper in so many places, their planning attempts are virtually worthless.

   Record all upcoming events and tasks on your Project Board and/or Term-Planning Calendar. And always have your calendar with you so you can refer to it when you are planning a specific week or day or need to add an appointment or assignment to it.

6. **Don't "over-schedule."** As you begin to follow a time-management program, you may find yourself trying to schedule too *much* of your time. Once you get the "effectiveness bug" and become aware of how much you can accomplish, it might be tempting to squeeze more and more into your life.

7. **Be honest with yourself** when determining those things that require more effort, that come easier to you. Chances are, you can't complete the outline for your term paper, study three chapters of biology, and do your French assignment in the two hours you have between class and work. Schedule enough time to get each assignment done. Whenever possible, schedule pleasurable activities after study time, not before so they act as incentives, not distractions.
8. **Remember that time is relative.** Car trips take longer if you have to schedule frequent stops for gas, food, necessities, etc. The trip is longer still if you start out during rush hour. Likewise, libraries are more crowded at certain times of the day or year, which will affect how fast you can get books you need, etc. So take the time of day into account.
9. **Be prepared.** As assignments are entered on your calendar, make sure you also enter items needed for their completion—texts, other books you have to buy, borrow, or get from the library, special materials, and the like. There's nothing worse than sitting down to do that assignment you've put off until the last minute, realizing that though *you're* finally ready to get to work, but that your supplies *aren't*. And at 10 p.m., you don't have a lot of options!
10. **Be realistic.** Plan according to *your* schedule, *your* goals, and *your* aptitudes, not some ephemeral "standard." Allocate the time you expect a project to take *you*, not the time it might take someone else, or how long your teacher tells you it should take.

11. **Be flexible, monitor, and adjust.** No calendar is an island. Any new assignment will affect whatever you've already scheduled. If you have a reasonably light schedule when a new assignment suddenly appears, it can just be plugged right into your calendar and finished as scheduled. But if you've already planned virtually every hour for the next two weeks, *any* addition may force you to change a whole day's plan. Be flexible and be ready. It'll happen.
12. **Look for more time savings.** If you find that you are consistently allotting more time than necessary to a specific chore—you allocate one hour to review your English notes every Sunday but always finish in 30 minutes or less—adjust your future schedule accordingly.
13. **Accomplish one task before going on to the next one**—don't skip around.
14. **Do your least favorite chores** (study assignments, projects, whatever) first—you'll feel better having gotten them out of the way!
15. **Try anything that works.** You may decide that color coding your calendar—red for assignments that must be accomplished that week, blue for steps in longer-term projects (which give you more flexibility), yellow for personal time and appointments, green for classes, etc.—makes it easier for you to tell at a glance what you need to do and when you need to do it.
16. **Adapt these tools to your own use.** Try anything you think may work—use it if it does, discard it if it doesn't.

There are thinkers and there are doers.

And there are those who think a lot about doing.

Organizing your life requires you to actually *use* the Project Board, Term-Planning Calendar, Priority Task Sheets, and Daily Schedules we've discussed, not just waste more time "planning" instead of studying!

Planning is an ongoing learning process. Dive in and plan for your upcoming school term. Or if you're in the middle of a term now, plan the remainder of it right now. As you use your plan in the upcoming weeks and months, you will come up with new ideas for improving your time-management system in the future and tailoring it to your own needs.

CHAPTER 6

GET ORGANIZED FOR CLASS

The pitfalls of poor note-taking skills

Most students take too many notes or too few.

Many of you will develop severe cases of carpal-tunnel syndrome in crazed efforts to reproduce every single word your teachers utter.

Others take notes so sparse that when reviewed weeks—or merely hours—later, they'll make so little sense that they might as well have been etched in Sanskrit.

If you feel compelled to take down your teacher's every pearly word, or recopy your entire text, you certainly won't have much of a social life—where would you ever find the time? Maybe you're so horrified at the prospect of *reliving* those hours of lectures and chapters of text that you simply *never* review your notes. And if you skip note-taking altogether...well, I don't need to tell you what kind of grades you should expect.

Note-taking should be the ultimate exercise in good-old American pragmatism. Take notes only on the material that helps you develop a thorough understanding of your subject...and get good grades. And you should do it in a way that is, first and foremost, useful and understandable to *you*. A method that's easy to use would be a real plus.

Most students have a difficult time developing a good note-taking technique and recognizing the information that always shows up on tests—an understanding of which is essential for good grades.

Failing to learn good note-taking methods, they resort to what *I* think are useless substitutes, such as tape recorders and photocopying machines.

Know your teacher

First and foremost, you must know and understand the kind of teacher you've got and his or her likes, dislikes, preferences, style, and what he or she expects you to get out of the class. Depending on your analysis of your teacher's habits, goals, and tendencies, preparation may vary quite a bit, whatever the class format.

Take something as simple as asking questions during class (which I encourage you to do whenever you don't understand a key point). Some teachers are very confident fielding questions at any time during a lesson; others prefer questions to be held until the end of the day's lesson; still others discourage questions (or any interaction for that matter) entirely. Learn when and how your teacher likes to field questions, and ask them accordingly.

No matter how ready a class is to enter into a freewheeling discussion, some teachers fear losing control and veering away from their very specific lesson plan. Such teachers may well encourage discussion but always try to steer it into a predetermined path (their lesson plan). Other teachers thrive on chaos, in which case you can never be sure what's going to happen.

Approaching a class with the former teacher should lead you to participate as much as possible in the class discussion, but warn you to stay within whatever boundaries he or she has obviously set.

Getting ready for a class taught by the latter kind of teacher requires much more than just reading the text—there will be a lot of emphasis on your understanding key concepts, interpretation, analysis and your ability to apply those lessons to cases never mentioned in your text at all!

In general, here's how you should plan to prepare for any class before you walk through the door and take your seat:

Complete all assignments

Regardless of a particular teacher's style or the classroom format he or she is using, virtually every course you take will have a formal text (or two or three or more) assigned to it. Though the way the text explains or covers particular topics may differ substantially from your teacher's approach to the same material, your text is still the basis of the course and a key ingredient in your studying. You *must* read it, plus any other assigned books, *before* you get to class.

You may sometimes feel you can get away without reading assigned books beforehand, especially in a lecture format where you *know* the chance of being called on is slim to none. But fear of being questioned on the material is certainly not the only reason I stress reading the material that's been assigned. You will be lost if the professor decides—for the first time ever!—to spend the entire period asking *the students* questions. I've seen it happen. And it was *not* a pleasant experience for the unprepared.

You'll also find it harder to take clear and concise notes because you won't know what's in the text (in which case you'll be frantically taking notes on material you could have underlined in your books the night before) or be able to evaluate the relative importance of the teacher's remarks.

Remember: Completing your reading assignment includes not just reading the *main* text but any *other* books or articles previously assigned, plus handouts that may have been passed out. It also means completing any non-reading assignments—turning in a lab report, preparing a list of topics, or being ready to present your oral report.

Review your notes

Both from your reading and from the previous class. Your teacher is probably going to start this lecture or discussion from the point he or she left off last time. And you probably won't remember where that point was from week to week...unless you check your notes.

Have questions ready

Go over your questions before class. That way, you'll be able to check off the ones the lecturer or teacher answers along the way and only ask those left unanswered.

Prepare required materials

Including your notebook, text, pens or pencils, and other such basics, plus particular class requirements like a calculator, drawing paper, or other books.

Learn "selective" listening

Taking concise, clear notes is first and foremost the practice of discrimination—developing your ability to separate the essential from the superfluous, key concepts, key facts, key ideas from all the rest. In turn, this requires the ability to listen to what your teacher is saying and copying down only what *you* need to understand the concept. For some, that could mean a single sentence. For others, a detailed example will be the key.

Just remember: The quality of your notes usually has little to do with their *length*—three key lines that reveal the core concepts of a whole lecture are far more valuable than paragraphs of less important data.

So why do some people keep trying to take verbatim notes, convinced that the more pages they cover with scribbles the better students they're being? It's probably a sign of insecurity—they haven't read the material and/or don't have a clue about what's being discussed, but at least they'll have complete notes!

Even if you find yourself wandering helplessly in the lecturer's wake, so unsure of what she's saying that you can't begin to separate the important, noteworthy material from the nonessential verbiage, use the techniques discussed in this book to organize and condense your notes anyway.

If you really find yourself so lost that you are just wasting your time, consider adding a review session to your schedule (to read or reread the appropriate texts) and, if the lecture or class is available again at another time, attend again. Yes it *is*, strictly speaking, a waste of your precious study time, but *not* if it's the only way to learn and understand important material.

Take notes on what you don't know

You *know* the first line of the Gettysburg Address. You *know* the chemical formula for water. You *know* what date Pearl Harbor was bombed. So why waste time and space writing them down?

Frequently, your teachers will present material you already know in order to set the stage for further discussion or to introduce material that is more difficult. Don't be so conditioned to automatically copy down dates, vocabulary, terms, formulas and names that you mindlessly take notes on information you already know. You'll just be wasting your time—both in class and later, when you review your overly detailed notes.

This is why some experts recommend that you bring your notes or outline of your textbook reading to class and *add your class notes to it.* I think it's an effective way to organize all your notes for that class, even if it effectively kills the idea of highlighting or underlining your text.

Observe your instructor's style

All instructors (perhaps I should say all *effective* instructors) develop a plan of attack for each class. They decide what points they will make, how much time they will spend reviewing assignments and previous lessons, what texts they will refer to, what anecdotes they will bring into the lecture to provide comic relief or human interest and how much time they'll allow for questions.

Building a note-taking strategy around each instructor's typical plan of attack for lectures is another key to academic success.

Throughout junior high school and much of high school, I had to struggle to get good grades. I took copious notes, studied them every night, and pored over them before every quiz and exam.

I was rewarded for my efforts with straight As, but resented the hours I had to put in, while my less ambitious buddies found more intriguing ways to spend their time.

But some of the brighter kids had leisure time, too. When I asked them how they did it, they shrugged their shoulders and said they didn't know.

These students had an innate talent that they couldn't explain, a sixth sense about what to study, what were the most important things a teacher said and what instructors were most likely to ask about on tests.

In fact, when I was in a study group with some of these students, they would say, "Don't worry, she'll never ask about that." And sure enough, she never did.

What's more, these students had forgotten many of the details I was sweating. They hadn't even bothered to write any of them down, let alone try to remember them.

What these students innately knew was that items discussed during any lesson could be grouped into several categories, which varied in importance:

- ☞ Information not contained in the class texts and other assigned readings.
- ☞ Explanations of obscure material covered in the texts and readings but with which students might have difficulty.
- ☞ Demonstrations or examples that provided greater understanding of the subject matter.
- ☞ Background information that put the course material in context.

As you are listening to an instructor, decide which of these categories best fits the information being presented to you. This will help you determine how detailed your notes on the material should be. (This will become especially easy as some time passes and you get to know the instructor.)

Read, read, read

Most good instructors will follow a text they've selected for the course. Likewise, unless they've written the textbook themselves (which you will find surprisingly common in college), most teachers will supplement it with additional information. Good teachers will look for shortcomings in textbooks and spend varying amounts of class time filling in these gaps.

As a result, it makes sense to stay one step ahead of your instructors. Read ahead in your textbook so that, as an instructor is speaking, you know what part of the lesson you should write down and what parts of it are *already* written down in your textbook. Conversely, you'll immediately recognize the supplemental material on which you might need to take more detailed notes.

Will you be asked about this supplemental material on your exams?

Of course, if you ask your teacher that question, he'll probably say something like, "You are expected to know everything that's mentioned in this class." That's why it's best to pay attention (and not ask stupid questions you already know the answers to!).

You will quickly learn to tell from a teacher's body language what he considers important and what he considers tangential.

In addition, your experience with the teacher's exams and spot quizzes will give you a great deal of insight into what he or she considers most important.

Sit near the front of the room

Minimize distractions by sitting as close to the instructor as you can.

The farther you sit from the teacher, the more difficult it is to listen. Sitting toward the back of the room means more heads bobbing around in front of you, more students staring out the window—encouraging you to do the same.

Sitting up front has several benefits. You will make a terrific first impression on the instructor—you might very well be the only student sitting in the front row. He'll see immediately that you have come to class to listen and learn, not just take up space.

You'll be able to hear the instructor's voice, and the instructor will be able to hear *you* when you ask and answer questions.

Finally, being able to see the teacher clearly will help ensure that your eyes don't wander around the room and out the windows, taking your brain with them.

So, if you have the option of picking your desk in class, sit right down in front.

Avoid distracting classmates

The gum cracker. The doodler. The practical joker. The whisperer. Even the perfume sprayer. Your classmates may be wonderful friends, entertaining lunch companions, and ultimate weekend party animals, but their quirks, idiosyncrasies and personal hygiene habits can prove distracting when you sit next to them in class.

Knuckle-cracking, giggling, note-passing, and whispering are just some of the evils that can divert your attention in the middle of your math professor's discourse on quadratic equations. Avoid them.

Listen for verbal clues

Identifying noteworthy material means finding a way to separate the wheat—that which you *should* write down—from the chaff—that which you should *ignore*. How do you do that? By *listening* for verbal clues and *watching* for the nonverbal ones.

Certainly not all teachers will give you the clues you're seeking. But many will invariably signal important material in the way they present it—pausing (waiting for all the pens to rise), repeating the same point (perhaps even one already made and repeated in your textbook), slowing down their normally supersonic lecture speed, speaking more loudly (or more softly), even by simply stating, "I think the following is important."

There are also numerous words and phrases that should *signal* noteworthy material (and, at the same time, give you the clues you need to logically organize your notes): "first of all," "most importantly," "therefore," "as a result," "to summarize," "on the other hand," "on the contrary," "the following (number of) reasons (causes, effects, decisions, facts, etc.)."

Such words and phrases give you the clues to not just write down the material that follows, but also to put it in context—to make a list ("first," "the following reasons"); to establish a cause-and-effect relationship ("therefore," "as a result"); to establish opposites or alternatives ("on the other hand," "on the contrary"); to signify a conclusion ("to summarize," "therefore"); or to offer an explanation or definition.

Look for nonverbal clues

If the teacher begins looking out the window, or his eyes glaze over, he's sending you a clear signal: "Put your pen down. This isn't going to be on the test. (So don't take notes!)"

On the other hand, if she turns to write something on the blackboard, makes eye contact with several students and/or gestures dramatically, she's sending a clear signal about the importance of the point she's making.

Learn how to be a detective—don't overlook the clues.

Ask questions often

Being an active listener means asking *yourself* if you understand everything that has been discussed. If the answer is no, you must ask the instructor questions at an appropriate time or write down the questions you need answered later in order to understand the subject fully.

To tape or not to tape

I am opposed to using a tape recorder in class as a substitute for an active brain for the following reasons:

- ☞ **It's time-consuming.** Not only will you have to waste time sitting in class, you'll have to waste more time listening to that class *again*!
- ☞ **It's virtually useless for review.** Fast-forwarding and rewinding cassettes to find the salient points of a lecture is torture. During the hectic days before an exam, do you really want to waste time listening to a whole lecture when you could just reread your notes?
- ☞ **It offers no backup.** Only the most diligent students record *and* take notes. What happens if your tape recorder malfunctions? How useful will blank or distorted tapes be when it's review time?

☞ **It costs money.** Compare the price of blank paper and pen to that of recorder, batteries, and tapes. The cost of batteries *alone* should convince you that you're better off with a pen and paper.

☞ **You miss the "live" clues** discussed earlier. When all you have is a tape, you don't see that flash in your teacher's eyes, passionate arm-flailing, stern set of the jaw, any and all of which scream, "Pay attention. This will be on your test!"

Create your own shorthand

You don't have to be a master of shorthand to streamline your note-taking. Here are five ways:

1. **Eliminate vowels.** As a sign that was ubiquitous in the New York City subways used to proclaim, "If u cn rd ths, u cn gt a gd jb." (If you can read this, you can get a good job.) And, we might add, "u cn b a btr stdnt."
2. **Use word beginnings** ("rep" for representative, "con" for congressperson) and other easy-to-remember abbreviations.
3. **Stop putting periods** after abbreviations.
4. **Create your own symbols** and abbreviations based on your needs and comfort level.

   There are two specific symbols you may want to create—they'll be needed again and again:

   Ⓦ That's my symbol for "*What?*" as in "What the heck does that mean?" "What did she say?" or "What happened? I'm completely lost!" It denotes something that's been missed—leave space in your notes to fill in the missing pieces of the puzzle after class.

Ⓜ That's my symbol for "My idea" or "My thought." I want to clearly separate my own thoughts during a lecture from the professor's—include too many of your own ideas (without noting that they *are* yours) and your notes begin to lose some serious value!

5. **Use standard symbols** in place of words. The following list may help you. You may also recognize some of these from math and logic:

≈	Approximately
w/	With
w/o	Without
wh/	Which
→	Resulting in
←	As a result of/consequence of
+	And or also
*	Most importantly
cf	Compare; in comparison; in relation to
ff	Following
<	Less than
>	More than
=	The same as
↑	Increasing
↓	Decreasing
esp	Especially
Δ	Change
⊂	It follows that
∴	Therefore
∵	Because

Feel free to use your own code for these two instances; you certainly don't have to use mine.

Although I recommend using all the "common" symbols and abbreviations listed previously *all* the time, in *every* class, in order to maintain consistency, you may want to create specific symbols or abbreviations for each class. In chemistry, for example, "TD" may stand for thermodynamics, "K" for the Kinetic Theory of Gases (don't mix it up with the "K" for Kelvin). In history, "GW" is the Father of our Country, "ABE" is Mr. Honesty, "FR" could be the French Revolution (or "freedom rider"), "IR" the Industrial Revolution.

How do you keep everything straight? Create a list on the first page of that class's notebook or binder section for the abbreviations and symbols you intend to use regularly through the semester.

Expanding on your "shorthand"

Continue to abbreviate *more* as additional terms become readily recognizable—in that way, the speed and effectiveness of your note-taking will increase as the school year grinds on.

Many students are prone to write *big* when they are writing fast and to use only a portion of the width of their paper. I guess they figure that turning over pages quickly means they are taking great notes. All it really means is that they are taking notes that will be difficult to read or use when it's review time.

Force yourself to write small and take advantage of the entire width of your note paper. The less unnecessary movement, the better.

What to do *after* class

As soon as possible after your class, review your notes, fill in the "blanks," mark down questions you need to research in your text or ask during the next class, and remember to mark any new assignments on your weekly calendar.

I tend to discourage recopying your notes as a general practice, since I believe it's more important to work on taking good notes the first time around and not wasting the time it takes to recopy. *But* if you tend to write fast and illegibly, it might also be a good time to rewrite your notes so they're readable, taking the opportunity to summarize as you go. The better your notes, the better your chance of capturing and recalling the pertinent material.

It is not easy for most high school students to do so, but in college, where you have a greater say in scheduling your classes, I recommend "one period on, one off"—an open period, even a half hour, after each class to review that class's notes and prepare for the next one.

If you find yourself unable to take full advantage of such in-between time, schedule as *little* time between classes as you can.

Are you among the missing?

Even if you diligently apply all of the tips in this chapter, it will all be moot if you regularly miss class. So don't! It's especially important to attend all classes near semester's end. Teachers sometimes use the last week to review the entire semester (what a great way to minimize your *own* review time!) and/or clarify specific topics they feel might still be fuzzy and/or answer questions. Students invariably ask about the final exam during this period, and some teachers virtually outline what's going to be on the test!

If you *must* miss a class, find that verbatim note-taker who hasn't followed my advice and borrow *his* or *her* notes. That way, *you* get to decide what's important enough to copy down. (Some professors might even lend you *their* notes. It's worth asking!)

CHAPTER 7

ORGANIZE YOUR READING AND WRITING

Taking *effective* notes from your texts should:

☞ *Help you recognize* the most important points of a text.

☞ *Make it easier* for you to understand those important points.

☞ Enhance your memory of the text.

☞ Provide a *highly efficient* way to study for your exams.

Go for the gold, ignore the pyrite

Step one in effective note-taking from texts is to write down the *principle* points the author is trying to make. These main ideas should be placed either in the left-hand margin of your note paper, or as headings. *Do not write complete sentences.*

Then, write down the most important details or examples the author uses to support each of these arguments. These details should be noted under their appropriate main idea. I suggest indenting them and writing each idea on a new line, one under the other. Again, *do not use complete sentences.* Include only enough details so that your notes are not "Greek to you" when you review them.

I'm sure it's abundantly clear to all of you that not many best-selling authors moonlight writing textbooks. Most of the tomes given to you in classes—even the ones for *literature* classes—are poorly written, badly organized cures for insomnia. Dull is the kindest word to describe all but a few of them.

That said, it's also clear that no matter how dull the prose, your job is to mine the important details from your textbooks in order to get good grades. Lest you have to wade through that lifeless mass of words more than once, why not take great notes the *first* time through?

You can borrow many of the strategies you implement for taking notes in class for your attack on your reading assignments. Just as you use your active brain to listen carefully to what your teacher talks about, you can use that same piece of equipment to *read* actively:

☞ Read, then write.

☞ Make sure you understand the big picture.

☞ Take notes on what you don't know.

These same principles we discussed in conjunction with taking notes in class apply to taking notes on your reading materials. But there are some additional strategies you should consider.

Change the way you read

When we read books for pleasure, we tend to read, naturally, from beginning to the end. (Though some of us may be guilty of taking a peek at the last chapter of a suspenseful mystery novel.) Yet this linear approach, beginning at point A and moving in a direct manner to point B, is not necessarily the most effective way to read texts for information.

If you find yourself plowing diligently through your texts without having the faintest clue as to what you've read, it's time to change the way you read. The best students don't wade through each chapter of their textbooks from beginning to end. Instead, they read in an almost circular fashion. Here's how:

Look for clues

If we're curled up with the latest Stephen King thriller, we fully expect some clues along the way that will hint at the gory horror to come. And we count on Agatha Christie to subtly sprinkle keys to her mysteries' solutions long before they are resolved in the drawing room.

But most of you probably never tried to solve the mysteries of your own textbooks by using the telltale signs and signals almost all of them contain. That's right, *textbooks are riddled with clues* that will reveal to the perceptive student all the noteworthy material that must be captured. Here's where to find them:

Chapter heads and subheads. Bold-faced headings and subheadings announce the detail about the main topic. And, in some textbooks, paragraph headings or bold-faced lead-ins announce that the author is about to provide finer details. So start each reading assignment by going through the chapter, beginning to end, *reading only the bold-faced heads and subheads.*

Knowing what the author is driving at in a textbook will help you look for the important building blocks for his or her conclusions while you're reading. While it may not be as much fun to read a mystery novel this way, when it comes to textbook reading and note-taking, it will make you a much more *active* reader, and, consequently, make it much less likely that you will doze off while being beaten senseless by the usual ponderous prose.

Pictures, graphs, and charts. Most textbooks, particularly those in the sciences, will have charts, graphs, numerical tables, maps and other illustrations. All too many students see these as mere fillers—padding to glance at, then forget.

If you're giving these charts and graphs short shrift, you're really shortchanging *yourself.* You don't have to re-draw the tables in your notes, but observe how they supplement the text and what points they emphasize, and make note of these. This will help you put them into your own words, which will help you remember them later. And it will ensure that you don't have to continually refer to your textbooks when brushing up for an exam.

Highlighted terms, vocabulary, and other facts. In some textbooks, you'll discover that key terms and other such information are highlighted within the body text. (And I *don't* mean by a previous student; consider such yellow-swathed passages with caution—their value is directly proportional to that student's final grade, which you don't know.) Whether boldface, italic or boxed, this is usually an indication that the material is noteworthy.

Questions. Some textbook publishers use a format in which key points are emphasized by questions, either within the body of the text or at the end of the chapter. If you read these questions *before* reading the chapter, you'll have a better idea of what material you need to pay closer attention to.

These standard organizational tools should make your reading job simpler. The next time you have to read a history, geography or similar text, try skimming the assigned pages first. Read the heads, the subheads, and the callouts. Read the first sentence of each paragraph. Then go back and start reading the details.

To summarize the skimming process:

1. Read and be sure you understand the title or heading. Try rephrasing it as a question for further clarification of what you will read.
2. Examine all the subheadings, illustrations, and graphics—these will help you identify the significant matter within the text.
3. Read *thoroughly* the introductory paragraphs, the summary, and any questions at chapter's end.
4. Read the first sentence of every paragraph—this generally includes the main idea.
5. Evaluate what you have gained from this process: Can you answer the questions at the end of the chapter? Can you intelligently participate in a class discussion of the material?
6. Write a brief summary that capsulizes what you have learned from your skimming.
7. Based on this evaluation, decide whether a more thorough reading is required.

Now for the fine print

Now that you have gotten a good overview of the contents by reading the heads and subheads, reviewing the summary, picking up on the highlighted words and information and considering the review questions that may be included, you're finally ready to read the chapter.

If a more thorough reading is then required, turn back to the beginning. *Read one section (chapter, etc.) at a time.* And do not go on to the next until you've completed the following exercise:

1. Write definitions of any key terms you feel are essential to understanding the topic.
2. Write questions and answers you feel clarify the topic.
3. Write any questions for which you *don't* have answers—then make sure you find them through rereading, further research, or asking another student or your teacher.
4. Even if you still have unanswered questions, move on to the next section and complete numbers one to three for that section (and so on, until your reading assignment is complete).

See if this method doesn't help you get a better handle on any assignment right from the start.

Because you did a preliminary review first, you'll find that your reading will go much faster.

*But...*don't assume that now you can speed through your reading assignment. Don't rush through your textbook, or you'll just have to read it again.

Sure, we've all heard about the boy and girl wonders who can whip through their physics texts at 1,000 or even 2,000 words per minute *and* retain everything, but most of us never will read that fast. That's fine—it's better to read something slowly and *remember* it than rush it into oblivion. Many great students—even those in law school or taking umpteen courses on the 19th-century novel—never achieve reading speeds even close to 1,000 words per minute. Some of them have to read passages they don't understand again and again to get the point. *There's nothing wrong with that.*

The most intelligent way to read is with comprehension, not speed, as your primary goal.

Many students underline in their textbooks or use magic markers to "highlight" them. This is a sure sign of masochism, as it guarantees only one thing: They will have to read a great deal of the deadly book again when they review for their exams.

Others write notes in the margin. This is a little bit better as a strategy for getting higher grades, but marginalia usually make the most sense only in context, so this messy method also forces the student to reread a great deal of text.

What's *the* most effective way to read and remember your textbooks?

The importance of outlining

Outlining a textbook, article, or other secondary source is a bit like what the Japanese call reverse engineering—a way of developing a diagram for something so that you can see exactly how it's been put together. Seeing how published authors build their arguments and marshal their research will help you when it comes time to write your own papers.

Seeing that logic of construction will also help you a great deal in remembering the book—by putting the author's points down in *your* words, you will be building a way to retrieve the key points of the book more easily from your memory.

What's more, outlining will force you to distinguish the most important points from those of secondary importance, helping you build a true understanding of the topic.

Do like the Romans do

Standard outlines use Roman numerals (I, II, III), capital letters, Arabic numerals (1, 2, 3, 4), and lower-case letters and indentations to show relationship and importance of topics in the text. While you certainly don't have to use the Roman-numeral system, your outline should be organized in the following manner:

Title
Author

I. First important topic in the text
- A. First subtopic
  - 1. First subtopic of A
    - a. First subtopic of 1
    - b. Second subtopic of 1
  - 2. Second subtopic of A

II. The second important topic in the text

Get the idea? In a book, the Roman numerals would usually refer to chapters; the capital letters to subheadings; and the Arabic numbers and lower-case letters to blocks of paragraphs. In an article or single chapter, the Roman numbers would correspond to subheadings, capital letters to blocks of paragraphs, Arabic numerals to paragraphs and small letters to key sentences.

The discipline of creating outlines will help you zero in on the most important points an author is making and capture them, process them and, thereby, retain them.

Sometimes an author will put the major point of a paragraph in the first sentence. But just as often the main idea of a paragraph or section will follow some of these telltale words: "therefore," "because," "thus," "since," "as a result."

When we see these words we should identify the material they introduce as the major points in our outline. The material immediately preceding and following almost always will be in support of these major points. The outline is an extraordinary tool for organizing your thoughts and your time.

Create a timeline

I always found it frustrating to read textbooks in social studies. I'd go through chapters on France and the Far East, and have a fairly good understanding of those areas, but no idea where certain events stood in a global context. As more and more colleges add multicultural curricula, you may find it even more difficult to "connect" events in 17th-century France or 19th-century Africa with what was happening in the rest of the world (let alone the U.S.).

An excellent tool for overcoming that difficulty is a timeline that you can update periodically. It will help you visualize the chronology and remember the relationship of key world events.

A simple, abridged timeline of Charles Dickens's literary life would look like the following timeline. (I suggest you create a horizontal timeline, but the layout of this book makes it difficult to reproduce that way difficult, so here's a vertical version).

1812 Birth
1836 First book published (*Sketches by Boz*)
1837 Pickwick Papers
1838 Oliver Twist
1850 *David Copperfield*
1853 *Bleak House*
1857 *Little Dorrit*
1861 *Great Expectations*
1870 Death

This makes it easy to see that he was born as the United States was entering the War of 1812 and died soon after the end of the Civil War. If you added other literary figures from the same period, you would not soon forget that Dickens, Dostoyevsky, Tolstoy, Kierkegaard, Ibsen, Noah Webster, Emerson, Longfellow, Melville and Hawthorne, among many others, were literary contemporaries. Adding nonliterary events to your timeline would enable you to make connections between what was being written and what was going on in the United States, Britain, Europe, Africa, and so forth.

Draw a concept tree

Another terrific device for limiting the amount of verbiage in your notes and making them more memorable is the concept tree. Like a timeline, the concept tree is a visual representation of the relationship among several key facts. For instance, one might depict the categories and examples of musical instruments this way:

Musical Instruments

- **Brass**
  - Bugle
  - Cornet
  - French horn
  - Saxophone
  - Trombone
  - Trumpet
  - Tuba
- **Percussion**
  - Bongo
  - Cymbal
  - Drum
  - Piano
  - Tambourine
  - Triangle
  - Xylophone
- **String**
  - Banjo
  - Bass
  - Cello
  - Guitar
  - Harp
  - Viola
  - Violin
- **Wind**
  - Bagpipes
  - Bassoon
  - Clarinet
  - Flute
  - Harmonica
  - Oboe
  - Recorder

Now we can give credence to the old saying, "A picture is worth a thousand words," since timelines and concept trees will be much more helpful than mere words in remembering material, particularly conceptual material. Developing them will ensure that your interest in the text will not flag too much.

Add a vocabulary list

Many questions on exams require students to define the terminology in a particular discipline. Your physics professor will want to know what vectors are, your calculus teacher will want to know about differential equations, your history professor will want you to be well-versed on the Cold War, and your English literature professor will require you to know about the Romantic Poets.

As you read your textbook, be sure to write down all new terms that seem important and their definitions. I used to draw a box around terms and definitions in my notes, because I knew these were among the items most likely to be asked about, and the box would always draw my attention to them when I was reviewing.

Wait, you're not done yet

After you've finished taking notes on a chapter, go through them and identify the most important points, either with an asterisk or a highlighter. You'll probably end up marking about 40 to 50 percent of your entries. When you're reviewing for a test, you should read *all* of your notes, but your asterisks will indicate which points you considered the most important while the chapter was very fresh in your mind.

To summarize, when it comes to taking notes from your texts or other reading material, you should:

☞ Take a cursory look through the chapter before you begin reading. Look for subheads, highlighted terms and summaries at the end of the chapter to give you a sense of the content.

☞ Read each section thoroughly. Although your review of the chapter "clues" will help you understand the material, you should read for comprehension rather than speed.

☞ Take notes immediately after you've finished reading, using mapping, the outline, timeline, concept tree and vocabulary list methods of organization, as necessary.

☞ Mark with an asterisk or highlight the key points as you review your notes.

Notes on library materials

Sometime during your high school or college years, you will undoubtedly be called upon to do some extensive research, either for a term paper or some other major project. Such a task will indeed be a major undertaking. Note-taking will be only one aspect of the process, albeit an important one.

(Although I will give you a terrific system for taking notes for a term paper or report in this chapter, I urge you to also read ***Improve Your Writing***, which thoroughly covers *all* the important steps, from selecting a topic and developing an outline to researching and taking notes to writing, rewriting and proofreading your final paper.)

As you will discover, writing a term paper will require you to take notes from a number of sources, most of them available at the library. But the more periodicals, reference books and even microfiche you uncover as terrific sources of information for your project, the more likely you'll be told that you can't take these materials out of the library. You'll have to take your notes *at the library,* not at your leisure in the comfort of your room.

So you'll definitely want a note-taking system that is quick, thorough, efficient and precludes the necessity of having to return to the source *again*. What's the answer?

No, it's not photocopying.

Why photocopying is redundant

You've found a resource that's perfect for your term paper. Your first impulse might be to find the library photocopying machine and pump some quarters into it.

Is photocopying a help or a hindrance?

I used to employ a system of photocopying when preparing for my term papers. I would go to the library with nothing except a roll of dimes (photocopying was a lot cheaper in those days), and comb the card catalog, the stacks, and the periodicals index for possible sources, using the library-supplied pencils to write the information down on call slips. I'd stack the volumes and periodicals around me at one of the tables and comb through them for hours, looking for juicy quotes and fun factoids.

I'd mark the books with those handy call slips. Then, I'd haul all of the useful sources over to the photocopier and begin Xeroxing away my hard-earned money.

I'd wind up going home with a pile of photocopies that I had to *reread*, which I'd do armed with pens of as many different colors as I could find. I'd underline all of the related passages with the same color, pick up another pen, and go sifting through the photocopies again. This method certainly helped me produce some darned good papers, but it also ensured that I spent too much time rereading information, organizing and reorganizing the research before I ever began actually writing.

You *can* be superorganized

I'm not going to go into detail about the right way to do all this right now—I've included the entire text from ***Improve Your Writing*** later in this volume. But I can tell you that there is a dynamite note-taking system in that book, one that will revolutionize the way you prepare any paper, any report, or, for that matter, any speech.

This simple note-card system is, in fact, one that many professional writers—including this one—swear by long after they leave the world of term papers and class reports behind.

Book 2

Improve Your Reading

Chapter 1

Reading: The Mother of All Study Skills

I think you'll find this is a book unlike any you've read before. And if you take the time to read it, I promise it will make everything else you have to read—whatever your student status, whatever your job, whatever your age—a lot easier to get through.

Why? Because I'm going to show you how to plow through *all* your reading assignments—whatever the subjects—better and faster...*and* how to remember *more* of what you read.

This book is *not* a gimmicky speed-reading method. It's not a spelling and grammar guide. Nor is it a lecture on the joys of reading. It's a *practical* guide, geared to *you*—a student of any age who isn't necessarily a poor reader, but who wants to get more from reading and do better in school and in life.

Personally, I love to read—the classics, spy thrillers, sports magazines, the newspaper, the back of the cereal box. When bored, tired, relaxing, or eating, I'll read just about anything handy, just to be able to read *some*thing.

But believe me, just because I love to read didn't mean it was easy for me to face some of those deadly textbook reading assignments. As a student, you inevitably will be required, as I was, to spend hours wading through ponderous, fact-filled, convoluted textbooks for subjects that are required but, at best, will never be favorites.

You may love reading for pleasure, but have trouble reading textbook assignments for certain subjects. You may get the reading done, but forget what you've read nearly as quickly as you read it. Or you just may hate the thought of sitting still to read *anything*. What*ever* kind of student you are—and whatever your reading skill—I've written this book to help you surmount your reading challenge, *whatever it may be.*

And that includes, for those of you long out of school, reading those nap-inducing business tomes, trade magazine articles, and other work-related stuff that's rarely reader-friendly.

You'll learn what you *should* read—and what you don't *have* to. You'll discover how to cut down on the time you spend reading, how to identify the main idea in your reading, as well as the important details, and how to remember more of what you read.

I'll show you different ways to read various types of books, from dry science texts to cumbersome classics.

Who knows? I might even convince you reading is fun!

When you're a *good* reader, the world is your oyster—you qualify for better schools, better jobs, better pay. Poor readers qualify for poor jobs and less fulfilling lives.

Ready to begin? Get motivated!

Any attempt to improve your reading must begin with motivation. Reading is not a genetic trait that is written in your DNA—there's no gene that makes you a good or bad reader like the ones that decide your hair or eye color. For the most part, reading is an *acquired* skill. A skill *you* can secure, grow and sharpen. You just have to *want* to.

Within this book, I will address a number of very practical techniques that are sure to increase your reading comprehension. But they are just *techniques.*

You'll invariably find them utterly useless if you are not motivated to read in the first place.

As the Nike commercial lambastes all of us weekend warriors—"Just Do It!" This attitude—not technique—is where the quest for improved reading begins. You must make reading a habit.

Good reader vs. poor reader

Look at the following comparison of a good reader and a poor reader as if you were some corporate hot shot who could hire just one of the individuals:

Good reader: You read for purpose. You've clearly defined your reason for reading—a question you want answered, facts you must remember, ideas you need to grasp, current events that affect you, or just the pleasure of following a well-written story.

Poor reader: Yes, you read, but often have no real reason for doing so. You aimlessly struggle through assigned reading, with little effort to grasp the "message."

Good reader: You read and assimilate thought. You hear and digest the concepts and ideas communicated.

Poor reader: You get lost in the muddle of words, struggling to make sense of what the author is trying to say. You are often bored because you force yourself to read every word to "get the message"...which you don't.

Good reader: You read critically and ask questions to evaluate whether the author's arguments are reasonable or off-the-wall. You recognize biases and don't just "believe" everything you read.

Poor reader: You swallow everything you read—hook, line, and sinker. You suffer from the delusion that everything in print is true, and are easily swayed from what you formerly believed to be true by any argument that sounds good.

Good reader: You read a variety of books, magazines, and newspapers—not limiting your reading to a *Far Side* humor book. You enjoy all types of reading—fiction, poetry, biography, current events.

Poor reader: You're a one-track reader—you read the sports pages, comics, or Gothic novels. Current events? You catch updates about your world from occasional TV news "sound bites."

Good reader: You enjoy reading and embrace it as an essential tool in your desire to better yourself.

Poor reader: You hate to read, deeming it a chore to be endured only when you have to. Reading is "boring."

Take a minute and ask yourself, who would *you* hire? Yes, you might hire Mr. Poor Reader...in some low-paying job. But would you ever put someone with such low-level skills in a responsible position?

At this point, I won't ask you to evaluate your own level of reading skills. Characterizing yourself as a "good" or "poor" reader was not the point of this exercise. What is important is to realize that Ms. Good Reader didn't spring full-blown from Zeus's cranium reading Shakespearean sonnets and quoting Winston Churchill. She learned to read the same way you and I did—with "See Spot run."

In time and through making reading a habit, Ms. Good Reader acquired and honed a skill that will open a world of opportunity to her.

Mr. Poor Reader, at some point, decided that being a good reader was not worth the effort and made *poor* reading his habit.

The good news is that being a poor reader is not a life sentence—you *can* improve your reading. The challenge is to find the motivation!

How fast can you understand?

When we read too fast or too slowly, we understand nothing.

—Pascal

Are you worried that you read too slowly? You probably shouldn't be—less-rapid readers are not necessarily less able. What counts is what you comprehend and remember. And like anything else, practice will probably increase your speed levels. If you must have a ranking, read the 500-word selection on pages 130 and 131 from start to finish, noting the elapsed time on your watch. Score yourself as follows:

Less than 30 seconds	very fast
31-45 seconds	fast
46-60 seconds	high average
61-89 seconds	average
90-119 seconds	slow
120 seconds or more	very slow

If you're like most members of the third estate, you wonder if there are any real differences between politicians who say they're liberal Democrats and those who say they're conservative Republicans. Aren't they all just a bunch of slick-talking, vote-seeking, pocket-lining, power-hungry egomaniacs bent on getting elected? Maybe some are, but they also tend to have basic philosophical differences guiding their slick-talking, vote-seeking, pocket-lining, power-hungry pursuit of office.

Let's look at some fundamental political, social, and economic differences between these groups.

Conservatives tend to champion free enterprise, or limited governmental control of the economy. They make the argument that people should be rewarded for their hard work and shouldn't expect government handouts through the welfare system. They are also heavily into national defense, law enforcement, and promotion of the fundamental values of family, God, and country. (Makes you want to break out into several verses of the "Star Spangled Banner," doesn't it?)

Liberals take a more paternalistic view of government. It is the last and only hope for many members of society who have suffered at the unscrupulous or uncaring hands of others. They contend that business would run amuck, exploiting workers and consumers in every market exchange, if not for government oversight. They also tend to be more concerned that everyone in society has equal access to a fair share of the economic pie, regardless of race, creed, sex, religion, shoe size, bank account, eye color, or planet of birth. Their hearts bleed for all.

These differences often place conservatives and liberals, Republicans and Democrats, on different sides of issues such as school prayer, welfare reform, environmental quality, worker safety, abortion, the death penalty, business regulation, sex education, and, well, just about every other newsworthy topic over the past 10 gadzillion years.

Of course, some of you might claim to be registered Democrats, yet say you support school prayer and welfare reform, or contend you're a Republican but you sure as heck want clean air and water and are willing to fight for them. Does this make you schizophrenic or hypocritical? Not necessarily. In fact, there are few *truly* liberal Democrats or *absolutely* conservative Republicans who support, without questions, the "straight" party line. Many members of the third estate have a combination of liberal and conservative views...just like you.

Now answer the following questions *without referring back to the text:*

1. According to the author, which of the following do traditional Republicans *not* favor?

A. School prayer
B. Sex education
C. Welfare reform
D. Banning abortion

2. Republicans favor:

A. Limited governmental control of the economy

B. Free enterprise

C. Both

D. Neither

3. Democrats favor:

A. Less stringent environmental laws

B. Lower taxes

C. Both

D. Neither

4. The author is probably:

A. A Democrat

B. A Republican

C. An independent

D. A smart aleck

A good reader should be reading fast or very fast and have gotten at least four of the five questions correct.

You should only worry—and plan to do something about it—if you fall into the slow or very slow range and/or missed two or more questions. Otherwise, you are probably reading as fast as you need to and retaining most of what you read.

Again, the relationship between speed and comprehension is paramount: Read *too* fast and you may comprehend *less*; reading more slowly does not necessarily mean you're not grasping the material.

What *decreases* reading speed/comprehension

1. Reading aloud or moving your lips when you read.
2. Reading mechanically—using your finger to follow words, moving your head as you read.
3. Applying the wrong *kind* of reading to the material.
4. Lacking sufficient vocabulary.

There are several things you can do to improve these reading mechanics.

To increase your reading speed:

1. Focus your attention and concentration.
2. Eliminate outside distractions.
3. Read in an environment that is uncluttered and comfortable.
4. Don't get hung up on single words or sentences, but *do* look up (in the dictionary) key words that you must understand in order to grasp an entire concept.
5. Try to grasp overall concepts rather than attempting to understand every detail.
6. If you find yourself moving your lips when you read (vocalization), practice reading with a pen or some other (nontoxic, nonsugary) object in your mouth. If it falls out while you're reading, you know you have to keep working!

To increase comprehension:

1. Try to make the act of learning sequential—comprehension is built by adding new knowledge to existing knowledge.

2. Review and rethink at designated points in your reading. Test yourself to see if the importance of the material is getting through.
3. If things don't add up, discard your conclusions. Go back, reread, and try to find an alternate conclusion.
4. Summarize what you've read, rephrasing it in your notes, in your own words.

Most importantly, read at the speed that's comfortable for you. Though I *can* read extremely fast, I *choose* to read novels much more slowly so I can appreciate the author's word play. Likewise, any material that I find particularly difficult to grasp slows me right down. I read newspapers, popular magazines, and the like very fast, seeking to grasp the information but not worrying about every detail.

Should you take some sort of speed-reading course, especially if your current speed level is low?

Reading for speed has some merit—many people who are slow readers read as little as possible, simply because they find it so tedious and boring. But just reading faster is not the answer to becoming a good reader.

I can't see that such a course could particularly *hurt* you in any way. I can also, however, recommend that you simply keep practicing reading, which will increase your speed naturally.

Don't remember less...faster

Retention is primarily a product of what you understand. It has little to do with how *fast* you read, how great an outline you can construct, or how many fluorescent colors you can buy to mark your textbooks. Reading a text, grasping the message, and remembering it are the fundamentals that make for high-level retention. Reading at a 1,000-word-per-minute clip does not necessarily mean that you have a clue as to what a text really says.

As you work toward improving your reading, realize that speed is secondary to comprehension. If you can read an assignment faster than anyone in class, but can't give a one-sentence synopsis of what you just read, you lose. If you really get the author's message—even if it takes you an hour or two longer than some of your friends—your time will pay off in huge dividends in class and later in life.

That's why this book concentrates on how to increase what you retain from your reading assignments. Whether you're reading a convoluted textbook that bores even the professor to tears or a magazine article, newspaper feature, or novel, you follow a certain process to absorb what you've read, which consists of:

1. Grasping the main idea.
2. Gathering the facts.
3. Figuring out the sequence of events.
4. Drawing conclusions.

When you spend an hour reading an assignment, then can't recall what you've just read, it's usually because a link in this chain has been broken. You've skipped one of these crucial steps in your reading process, leaving your understanding of the material filled with gaps.

To increase your retention rate, you need to master *each level* in this chain of comprehension. Not everything you will read will require that you comprehend on all four levels. Following a set of cooking directions, for example, simply requires that you discern the sequence for adding all ingredients. Other reading will demand that you are able to compile facts, identify a thesis, and give some critical thought as to its validity.

Ms. Good Reader is not only able to perform at each level of comprehension, but also has developed an instinct: She recognizes that certain things she reads can be read *just* to gather facts or *just* to grasp the main idea. She then is able to read quickly to accomplish this goal and move on to her next assignment—or to that Steven King novel she's been dying to read.

This book will help you develop a sense of what is involved in *each* step of the reading process.

The first chapters will address these different steps and provide exercises designed to help you master each stage in the process of retaining what you read.

In the final chapters, we will look at how to read literature, how to read a math or science textbook, and how to outline so that you can easily review a text.

By the time you finish this short book, you should find that by following the procedures I've suggested, you have significantly improved your reading comprehension.

Finding other textbooks

Few textbooks are written by what most of us would even remotely call professional writers. Although the authors and editors might well be experts, even legends, in a particular subject, writing in jargon-free, easy-to-grasp-prose is probably not their strong suit. You will occasionally be assigned a textbook that is so obtuse you aren't even sure whether to read it front to back, upside down, or inside out.

If you find a particular chapter, section, or entire textbook as tough to read as getting your baby brother to do you a favor, get to the library or the bookstore and find *another* book covering the *same* subject area that you *can* understand. (You might even consider asking your teacher or professor for recommendations. He or she will probably make your job of finding a *readable* text a lot easier. You may even score some brownie points for your seeming initiative—as long as you don't wonder aloud what caused him or her to select that torturous text in the first place!

"Ron," I hear you grumbling, "what happened to the 'study smarter, not harder' bit? This can't *possibly* be a time saver. Heck, I'll bet the books don't even cover the subject in the same way, let alone follow the same sequence! I'll be stuck slogging through *two* books."

All true, possibly. But if you just don't get it, maybe it's because the *author* just doesn't know how to *explain* it. *Maybe it's not your fault!* Too many students have sweated, moaned, dropped classes, even changed majors because they thought they were dumb, when it's possible it's the darned textbook that's dense, not you. So instead of continuing to slog though the mire, find an expert who can actually write—they're out there—and learn what you need to. After finally understanding the subject by reading this other text, you'll find much of the original textbook much easier to use...presuming you need it at all.

Answers to quiz: B, C, D, D.

CHAPTER 2

READING WITH PURPOSE

Even if you consider yourself "not much of a reader," you read *something* each and every day: a magazine article, instructions for hooking up the VCR, telephone messages tacked on the refrigerator, notes from your latest heartthrob.

Regardless of *what* you are reading, you have a purpose that dictates *how* you are going to read it—and you read different items in different ways. You wouldn't read the VCR instructions as you would a novel, any more than you'd read the magazine article in the same way as a grocery list. Without a purpose, you'd find yourself reading aimlessly and very inefficiently.

Unfortunately, many of the students I've talked to have not yet realized the importance of having a purpose for reading. Their lack of reading purpose can be summed up by the proverb: "If you aim at nothing, you will hit the bulls-eye every time."

Before you can understand what you're reading—and *remember* it—you must know *why* you're reading it in the first place.

Defining your purpose for reading

What is your purpose in reading? If the best answer you can come up with is, "Because my teacher said so," we need to come up with some better reasons. Reading a chapter just so you can say, "I finished my assignment," is relatively futile. You may as well put the book under a pillow and hope to absorb it by osmosis.

Unless you identify some purpose to read, you will find yourself flipping the pages of your textbooks while seldom retaining anything more than the chapter titles.

According to reading experts, there are six fundamental purposes for reading:

1. To grasp a certain message.
2. To find important details.
3. To answer a specific question.
4. To evaluate what you are reading.
5. To apply what you are reading.
6. To be entertained.

Because reading with purpose is the first step toward improved comprehension, let me suggest some simple techniques you can use to identify a purpose for *your* textbook reading.

Find the clues in every book

There is a group of special sections found in nearly all textbooks and technical materials (in fact, in almost all books except novels) that contain a wealth of information and can help you glean more from your reading. Becoming familiar with this data will enrich your reading experience and often make it easier. Here's what to look for:

The first page after the title page is usually the *table of contents*—a chapter-by-chapter list of the book's contents. Some are surprisingly detailed, listing every major point or topic covered in each chapter.

The first prose section (after the title page, table of contents, and, perhaps, *acknowledgments page,* in which the author thanks other authors, his editor, researcher, friends, relatives, teachers, etc., most of which you can ignore), is the *preface,* usually a description of what information you will find in the book. Authors may also use the preface to point out unique aspects of their books.

The *introduction* may be in place of or in addition to the preface and may be written by the author or some "name" the author has recruited to lend additional prestige to his or her work. Most introductions are an even more detailed overview of the book—chapter-by-chapter summaries are often included to give the reader a feel for the material to be covered.

Footnotes may be found throughout the text (a slightly elevated number following a sentence, quotation, etc., for example, "jim-dandy"[24]) and either explained at the bottom of the page on which they appear or in a special section at the back of the text. Footnotes may be used to cite sources of direct quotes or ideas and/or to further explain a point, add information, etc., outside of the text. You may make it a habit to ferret out sources cited for further reading.

If a text tends to use an alarmingly high number of terms with which you may not be familiar, the considerate author will include a *glossary*—essentially an abridged dictionary that defines all such terms.

The *bibliography*, usually at the end of the book, may include the source material the author used to research the textbook, a list of "recommended reading," or both. It is usually organized alphabetically by subject, making it easy for you to go to your library and find more information on a specific topic.

Appendices containing supplementary data or examples relating to subject matter covered in the text may also appear in the back of the book.

The last thing in a book is usually the *index*, an alphabetical listing that references, by page number, every mention of a particular name, subject, topic, etc., in the text.

Making it a habit to utilize all of these tools in your textbook can only make your studying easier.

Look for the clues in each chapter

Every textbook offers some clues that will help you define a purpose for reading. Begin with a very quick overview of the assignment, looking for questions that you'd like answered. Consider the following elements of your reading assignment *before* you begin your reading.

Much like the headlines of a newspaper clue you into what the story is about, these elements will give insight into what the section or chapter is trying to communicate.

Chapter heads and subheads

Chapter titles and bold-faced subheads announce the detail of the main topic. And in some textbooks, paragraph headings or bold-face "lead-ins" announce that the author is about to provide finer details.

So start each reading assignment by going through the chapter, beginning to end, *reading only the bold-faced heads and subheads.*

For example, suppose you encountered the heading, "The Demise of the American Indian," in your history text. You might use it to form the following questions:

A. *What* caused the demise of the American Indian?

B. *Who* caused it?

C. *When* did it occur?

D. *Why* did it occur?

As you read the chapter, you'll find yourself seeking answers to these questions. You now have a purpose!

Often you may find headings that contain words or terms you don't recognize. Seeking to define these terms or explain a concept should then define your purpose.

This process of headline-reading takes only a few minutes, but it lays the groundwork for a more intelligent and efficient reading of the chapter. You'll have some idea where the author is headed, which will give you a greater sense of what the most important details are and clarify where you should be concentrating your studying.

End-of-chapter summaries

If you read a mystery from start to finish, the way the author hopes you will, you're likely to get thrown off the scent by "red herrings" and other common detective novel devices. However, if you read the last page first, knowing the outcome will help you detect how the author constructed the novel and built an open-and-shut case for his or her master sleuth. You'd perceive a wealth of details about the eventually unmasked murderer that might have gone *unnoticed* had he been just another of the leading suspects.

Similarly, knowing what the author is driving at in a *textbook* will help you look for the important building blocks for his conclusions while you're reading.

It may not be fun to read a mystery novel this way, but when it comes to textbook reading, it will help you define your purpose for reading. And further, it will transform you into a much more *active* reader, making it less likely you'll doze off while being beaten senseless by the usual ponderous prose.

Pictures, graphs, and charts

Most textbooks, particularly those in the sciences, will have charts, graphs, numerical tables, maps, and other illustrations. All too many students see these as fillers—padding to glance at quickly, and, just as quickly, forget.

If you're giving these charts and graphs short shrift, you're really shortchanging *yourself.* Be sure to observe how they supplement the text, what points they emphasize, and make note of these.

Highlighted terms, vocabulary, and other facts

In some textbooks, you will discover that key terms and information are highlighted within the body text. (I don't mean highlighted by a previous student—treat such yellow-streaked passages with caution!) To find the definitions of these terms or the application of facts may then be your purpose for reading.

Questions

Some textbook publishers use a format in which key points are emphasized by questions, either within the body or at the end of the chapter. If you read these questions *before* reading the chapter, you'll have a better idea of the material on which to concentrate.

Prereading your assignment

If you begin your reading assignment by seeking out these heads, subheads, and other purpose-finding elements of the chapter, you'll have completed your prereading step. What is prereading? It is simply beginning your assigned reading by reviewing these clues and defining your purpose (or purposes) for reading.

I advise that you *always* preread every assignment! Why? Have you ever spent the better part of an evening plowing through an assignment only to finish with little or no understanding of what you just read? If the answer is yes, then you probably failed to preread it.

Reading faster without speed reading

While the heads, subheads, first sentences, and other author-provided hints we've talked about will help you get a quick read on what a chapter's about, some of the *words* in that chapter will help you concentrate on the important points and ignore the unimportant. Knowing when to speed up, slow down, ignore, or really concentrate will help you read both faster *and* more effectively.

When you see words like "likewise," "in addition," "moreover," "furthermore," and the like, you should know nothing new is being introduced. If you already know what's going on, speed up or skip what's coming entirely.

On the other hand, when you see words like "on the other hand," "nevertheless," "however," "rather," "but," and their ilk, slow down—you're getting information that adds a new perspective or contradicts what you've just read.

Lastly, watch out for "payoff" words such as, "to summarize," "in conclusion," "therefore," "consequently," "thus"—especially if you only have time to "hit the high points" of a chapter or you're reviewing for a test. Here's where the real meat is, where everything that went before is happily tied up in a nice bow and ribbon, a present that enables you to avoid having to unwrap the entire chapter.

Purpose defines reading method

Typically, your purpose for reading dictates how you read. There are basically three types of reading we all do:

1. **Quick reference reading** focuses on seeking specific information that addresses a particular question or concern we might have.
2. **Critical reading** involves discerning ideas and concepts that require a thorough analysis.
3. **Aesthetic or pleasure reading** is what we do for sheer entertainment or to appreciate an author's style and ability.

As you define your purpose for reading, you'll determine which method of reading is necessary to accomplish this purpose. The table on page 146 identifies some examples of types of reading, why you might read them, and the method you should use.

If you are a good reader, or desire to be one: You will always fit your reading *method* to your reading *purpose;* you have trained or are training yourself in a variety of reading skills; you have no problem switching your method to accommodate your purpose; and you are unsatisfied reading only one type of material.

Type	Purpose	Method
Newspaper advertisement	To locate best price for car	*Quick reference*
Magazine	To stay aware of current events	*Quick reference*
Self-help book	To learn to get along better with your family	*Critical*
Biology text	To prepare for an exam	*Critical*
New issue of *Rolling Stone*	To take your mind off biology!	*Pleasure*

A poor reader, on the other hand, reads everything the same way—doggedly plowing through the biology assignment, the newspaper, and the Stephen King novel...word by painful word. Reading with purpose is both foreign and foreboding to such a person, which makes it difficult for him or her to adapt a method of reading.

Become an active reader

Reading with purpose is as vital to your comprehension and retention as oxygen is to life. It is the cornerstone of *active* reading, reading that involves thinking—that process of engaging your mind and emotions in what the author is trying to communicate. Too many readers seek to absorb information passively as their eyes move across the page. The active reader *involves* him- or herself in receiving a message—a fact, an idea, an opinion—that is readily retained because he or she had a *purpose.*

Following is a passage adapted from *Make the Most of Your Workday* by Jonathan and Susan Clark (Career Press, 1994). *Preread* the passage in order to determine a *purpose* for reading. Be sure to use the note page following to jot down questions that may have been raised through your preread, and the purpose.

Are You Really Trying to Do Too Much?

We all need checks and balances to manage life's resources and responsibilities, and that's what this chapter is all about. You may be overloaded with responsibilities and demands. You may feel incapable of effectively organizing and managing all of your projects. You may be hoping for a mixture of ideas and solutions that, blended together, can restore a feeling of control.

It's possible that all your concerns about your time boil down to one simple fact: You may simply be trying to do too much!

The best organized schedule, the most well-planned "Daily Action Plan," the most effectively applied list of 10 steps or 12 ideas, cannot change your situation if you are trying to accomplish more than you have time to do.

How can you determine if self-overload conditions already exist? What can you do to change those conditions? Generally speaking, if you feel overloaded, you *are* overloaded. If you *don't* feel that you're presently overloaded, you may fear that you're heading that way...fast. Your question then is, "How can I keep this from happening?"

Whether you've already reached the breaking point or see the point approaching fast, to avoid certain demise you must take a long, hard look at all of your commitments and activities. You must be honest and realistic.

The very first step is to ask yourself: "If I were not already doing this, would I choose to get involved?"

A case study

Jim North, a personnel director for a small manufacturing firm, began attending monthly meetings of a local organization of personnel directors.

Although Jim enjoyed the association with other professionals in his field, he found it difficult to attend the breakfasts every month. He frequently got his most productive work done early in the day, and sometimes the meetings seemed to have only marginal professional benefits, since a number of the members seemed mainly interested in the meeting as a social occasion.

Jim was surprised when Gerry Duckworth, a member he knew only casually, called one day and asked if he would consider running for vice president of the organization for the coming year. When Jim asked what the position involved, Gerry said, "Oh, you really don't have to do anything. We just need someone to hold that office."

As it turned out, Jim's was the only name placed in nomination, and he was elected to the office.

A few days later, Kathy Cornell, the president, called Jim and told him there was a lunch meeting scheduled later that week for all the officers of the organization.

When Jim went to the officers' meeting, he discovered that the vice president had numerous responsibilities, including planning the programs for the breakfasts each month and heading up the annual new members campaign. Kathy excitedly told the group that she had just learned her company was sending her across the country for three months to oversee the opening of a new office. This meant Jim would function as president for that time!

Jim obviously realized this new job was a lot bigger than he had been told it was. If he had known it entailed so much responsibility, he probably would have declined the nomination. He began to envision the additional hours and energy required (which he really didn't have) to serve an organization of questionable value to him, and felt overwhelmed. He also found himself feeling resentful that the importance of the job had been misrepresented to him.

What was Jim's biggest mistake? If you were Jim, what would you do now?

What actually happened

Jim quickly reassessed his own priorities and determined that this new responsibility didn't fit into them. He analyzed what impact giving up that much additional time and energy would have on the activities to which he had already committed. He wondered how much more he could do in those areas if he were to direct the same time and energy to his priorities.

At the end of the meeting, he asked Kathy to stay for a few minutes. Then he told her: "Kathy, if I had realized the scope of this job, I never would have agreed to serve. I'm sorry I didn't ask more questions when Gerry called, and I realize this will put the association in a temporary bind, but I'm going to have to resign from the office."

Kathy reluctantly accepted Jim's resignation. She appointed another vice president before the next meeting and made the announcement in the chapter's newsletter.

For a few months, Jim felt a little uncomfortable at the meetings. A few people teased him about "chickening out" of the job, but the teasing eventually stopped. When the election of officers came around the next year, Jim reflected gratefully on his decision, realizing he had been wise to put his efforts into his priorities.

What it all meant to Jim

Jim could have decided to make the best of his position and plan great programs and spearhead an enthusiastic member campaign. Maybe he would have even gotten more out of the meetings and his opportunities to network with the other members of the chapter.

But sometimes people simply spread themselves too thin—trying to do too much and please too many people. When you identify your priorities by asking, "What's important to me?" it's often far more satisfying and rewarding to redirect additional time and effort to previous commitments than to add even more activities to an already jammed calendar.

And what it means to you

Put yourself in this story. Change the situation to one you're facing. Wouldn't you really rather be out from under this responsibility than trying to juggle it and fit it in with other, more important matters? Won't you feel good when that commitment is no longer on your list?

Remember, for any project that you're already involved in or are thinking about taking on, ask yourself this question: "Can I make a strong personal commitment to invest my time and abilities in this purpose, project, or pursuit?" If the answer is, "I can't make a full commitment," then it's best not to start it or, if already involved, to find a way out.

Your notes

What clues can you find that help you define a purpose for reading this passage?

What purpose or purposes did you determine for reading this passage?

What method, based on your purpose, would you use to read this passage?

CHAPTER 3

FINDING THE MAIN IDEA

In all good writing, there is a controlling thesis or message that connects all of the specific details and facts. This concept or idea is usually expressed as a generalization that summarizes the entire text.

Good comprehension results when you are able to grasp this main message, even if you sometimes forget some of the details. When you understand the intent, you have a context in which to evaluate the reasoning, the attitude, and whether the evidence cited really is supportive of the conclusions drawn.

An obsession for facts can obscure the "big picture," giving you an understanding of the trees but no concept of the forest. How many of you have spent hours studying for an important exam, collecting dates, names, terms, and formulas, but failed to ferret out the main idea, the underlying concept that is composed of these facts?

In longer, more involved readings, many messages are combined to form a chain of thought, which, in turn, may or may not be communicating one thesis or idea.

Your ability to capture this chain of thought determines your level of comprehension—and what you retain.

Dissecting your reading assignment

To succeed in identifying the main idea in any reading assignment, you must learn to use these helpful tools:

1. The topic sentence of a paragraph.
2. Summary sentences.
3. Supporting sentences.
4. Transitional statements.

As you learn to dissect your reading assignment paragraph by paragraph, identifying its many parts and their functions, you'll grasp the main idea much more quickly—and remember it much longer.

Recognizing a topic sentence

Every paragraph has a *topic sentence*—the sentence that summarizes what the paragraph is about. Even if a paragraph does not have such a clearly stated sentence, it can be implied or inferred from what is written.

Generally, the topic sentence is the first or last sentence of a paragraph—the one statement that announces, "Here's what this paragraph is all about!"

When the topic sentence is obscured or hidden, you may need to utilize two simple exercises to uncover it:

1. Pretend you're a headline writer for your local newspaper—write a headline for the paragraph you just read.

2. Write a five-word summary describing what the paragraph is about.

Exercise: Identifying a topic sentence

Write a headline or five-word summary for each of the following paragraphs:

It's very exciting to venture through display homes or visit open houses and dream of moving in. Just remember to treat home buying or selling very seriously and take time for a reality check now and then. This is a decision you'll live with for many years. "Home"-work is the key. Knowing the numbers ahead of time and setting your limits will definitely pay off.

More than ever, we are looking for meaning, fulfillment, and personal growth in our lives. And we're demanding those qualities in our jobs and business as well. An organization that understands this tends to have a happier and more productive workforce. If an organization has a clearly articulated statement of philosophy and values, there can be a meshing of corporate and personal goals known as *alignment*.

Like it or not, government is with us and will be for a long time to come. One can't even imagine a society that would not involve some sort of government. In that numerous needs-satisfying goods are produced only by the government, we have no choice but to keep it around. And because we have it, we have to pay taxes. The question then is whether our tax dollars are spent wisely. No. They aren't and they never will be, because government is incredibly inefficient and incompetent. The problem is, if the government doesn't perform duties badly, they probably won't be performed at all.

As you can see from these three paragraphs, the topic sentence is not always clearly stated. This is especially true in a number of the convoluted textbooks all of us have read. When trying to discern the main idea of such writing, you may need a more in-depth analysis.

You can begin your analysis by turning, once again, to our helpful questions. Is the passage written to address one of these questions?

1. **Who?** The paragraph focuses on a particular person or group of people. The topic sentence tells you *who* this is.
2. **When?** The paragraph is primarily concerned with *time.* The topic sentence may even begin with the word "when."
3. **Where?** The paragraph is oriented around a particular place or location. The topic sentence states *where* you are reading about.
4. **Why?** A paragraph that states reasons for some belief or happening usually addresses this question. The topic sentence answers *why* something is true or *why* an event happened.
5. **How?** A paragraph that identifies the way something works or the means by which something is done. The topic sentence explains the *how* of what is described.

You will notice that I didn't include the question "What?" in this list. This is not an oversight. "What?" addresses such a broad range of possibilities that asking this question will not necessarily lead you to the topic sentence.

The best test to determine whether you have identified the topic sentence is to rephrase it as a question. If the paragraph answers the question that you've framed, you have found the topic sentence.

Summary, support, or transitional?

Another technique that will lead you to the topic sentence is to identify what purpose *other* sentences in the paragraph serve—kind of a process of elimination.

Generally, sentences can be characterized as *summary, support,* or *transitional.*

Summary sentences state a general idea or concept. As a rule, a topic sentence is a summary sentence—a concise yet inclusive statement that expresses the general intent of the paragraph. (By definition, the topic sentence is never a support sentence.)

Support sentences provide the specific details and facts that give credibility to the author's points of view. They give examples, explain arguments, offer evidence, or attempt to prove something as true or false. They are not meant to state generally what the author wants to communicate; they are intended to be specific, not conceptual, in nature.

Transitional sentences move the author from one point to another. They may be viewed as bridges connecting the paragraphs in a text, suggesting the relationship between what you just finished reading and what you are about to read. Good readers are attuned to the signals such sentences provide—they are buzzers that scream, "This is what you are going to find out next!"

Transitional sentences may also alert you to what you should have just learned. Unlike support sentences, transitional sentences provide invaluable and direct clues to identifying the topic sentence.

Some examples of transitional signals

Any sentence that continues a progression of thought or succession of concepts is a transitional sentence. Such a sentence may begin with a word such as "first," "next," "finally," or "then" and indicate the before/after connection between changes, improvements, or alterations.

Transitional sentences that begin in this way should raise these questions in your mind:

1. Do I know what the previous examples were?
2. What additional example am I about to learn?
3. What was the situation prior to the change?

Other transition statements suggest a change in argument or thought or an exception to a rule. These will generally be introduced by words such as "but," "although," "though," "rather," "however," or similar conjunctions that suggest an opposing thought.

Such words ought to raise these questions:

1. What is the gist of the argument I just read?
2. What will the argument I am about to read state?
3. To what rule is the author offering an exception?

In your effort to improve your reading, developing the ability to recognize the contrast between general, inclusive words and statements (summary sentences) and specific, detail-oriented sentences (transitional or support sentences) is paramount.

Taking notes

The final step toward grasping and retaining the main idea of any paragraph is taking notes. There are several traditional methods students employ—outlining, highlighting, mapping, and drawing concept trees.

An exhaustive review of all these methods is not within the scope of this particular book, but for a complete discussion of note-taking techniques, be sure to read ***Take Notes***, another of the nine books in my ***How to Study Program***.

Whichever method you employ to retain the main idea, focus on the topic sentences, not on the specific details.

If you are a highlighter—you enjoy coloring textbooks with fluorescent markers—you will want to assign one color that you will always use to highlight topic sentences. Avoid what too many students do—highlighting virtually every paragraph. This practice will just extend your review time considerably—you'll find yourself rereading instead of reviewing.

If you utilize outlining or mapping (diagramming what you read rather than spending time worrying about Roman numerals and whether to use lower case letters or upper case letters on certain lines) you will find that your time will best be spent writing five-word summaries of the topic sentences.

If you find yourself getting bogged down in details and specifics, you are wasting valuable time. Again, writers are using these details to communicate their concepts—they are not necessarily to be remembered.

Read the following passage from *Economic Literacy* by Orley M. Amos, Jr. (Career Press, 1994), seeking out the topic sentences. Then summarize the main idea or ideas in five-word phrases.

An Altogether Look at Unions

Unions are organizations of workers—in the same industry, working for the same company, or in the same occupation—that negotiate with their employers about things such as wages, fringe benefits, working conditions, hiring and firing procedures, and other job-related items. The formal negotiation, where the union and the company seek to work out a contractual agreement on these various issues is termed *collective bargaining*.

In recent years, most of these collective bargaining agreements have been pretty straightforward. Unions demand a few things, companies return with their "best" offers, then they haggle back and forth until they reach a compromise. If this sounds a lot like buying a car or house, it is. It's the same sort of one-on-one negotiation that takes place in many markets.

Although the sorts of things that unions and management do to each other might appear childish, they have a serious and violent history. Their confrontations are as fundamental as the differences between the second and third estates. We can find the seeds of their conflicts growing out of our economy's transition from the simple fabrication methods of blacksmiths, carpenters, and other medieval craftsmen to the large factories that marked the onset of the Industrial Revolution.

In the early years of the Industrial Revolution, with hundreds or even thousands of workers in a single factory, the balance of market control was tipped to the side of the second estate. The handful of employers were pretty much able to dictate wages and working conditions.

Workers had about the same status as felled trees, molten steel or railroad cars filled with slaughterhouse-bound cattle. Wages were extremely low and working conditions were, at best, downright deadly. That's when unions came on the scene.

Battles between the new unions and the fat-cat employers often turned bloody. Companies didn't hesitate to use force—armed security guards and government soldiers—on the rabble-rousers. The unions fought back with an assortment of their own guerrilla tactics. Most of the violence ended with laws and court cases in the 1930s that forged a set of collective bargaining rules.

Let's try again with this brief excerpt from, "A National Care Agenda," by Suzanne Gordon, which appeared in the January 1991 edition of *The Atlantic Monthly*:

The United States is experiencing an extreme crisis in caring. As a society we cannot seem to muster the political will to care for the most precious things we produce: other human beings.

The United Sates has slipped to 25th place in the world in its infant-mortality rate. Twenty percent of America's children are destitute. More then 37 million people have no health insurance; 20 million to 30 million more are underinsured. Today, as patients are discharged earlier and earlier from the nation's hospitals, family members are increasingly asked to provide for their complex medical and emotional needs.

It is estimated that 1.8 million women care for children and elders simultaneously, and 33 percent of women do so in addition to holding down jobs.

> Yet not only do these caregivers, who relieve our health-care system of a tremendous financial burden, receive little help; they are often penalized for providing such care, through the loss of wages or of the job itself.

The author is throwing around a lot of statistics to impress upon her readers that the United States must give some consideration to people who provide infants and older people with home health care. Should we remember the statistics about infant mortality, inadequate health insurance, the burdens on working women? Should these statistics appear in our notes?

If we read linearly, starting at the beginning and plodding along to the last word, we probably would be tempted to write down the numbers and what they mean in our notes. But if we were to look ahead in the article (and glance at the subheads), we'd find that the author is actually making a case for investments in home care by the federal government and talking about where the money should come from.

Therefore, the statistics are not especially important, but the enormity of the problem to which they give credence *is*.

I didn't always keep my summaries to five words, but I distilled the main ideas to the fewest words I could.

Nor did I always write one summary statement per paragraph—just what was needed to capture the main idea or ideas from each paragraph.

CHAPTER 4

GATHERING THE FACTS

Now, what I want is Facts. Teach these boys and girls nothing but Facts. Facts alone are wanted in life. Plant nothing else, and root out everything else. You can only form the minds of reasoning animals upon Facts: Nothing else will ever be of any service to them. This is the principle on which I bring up my own children, and this is the principle on which I bring up these children. Stick to Facts, sir!

—Charles Dickens, *Hard Times*

Seeking out the facts, as Dickens's character would have us do, is also an effective way to confront your classroom reading assignments.

Although such a straightforward approach is not the complete formula for scholastic success, you'll find that the vast majority of your assigned reading requires a thorough recall of the facts.

In the previous chapter, we discussed the "forest"—the main idea. In this chapter, we will concentrate on "the trees"—how to read to gather facts, the specific details that support and develop the author's main point.

Facts: building blocks for ideas

Facts are the building blocks that give credibility to concepts and ideas. Your ability to gather and assimilate these facts will dramatically enhance your success at remembering what the author wanted to communicate.

If, however, you spend so much time studying the trees that you lose sight of the forest, your reading effectiveness will be limited. You must learn to discern what facts are salient to your understanding, and which ones to leave for the next *Trivial Pursuit* update.

If you are trying to identify your purpose for reading this chapter, it's threefold:

1. To develop the skill of scanning a text for facts as quickly as possible.
2. To distinguish between an important detail and a trivial one.
3. To learn how to *skim* text—reading and absorbing its essence, even when you're not looking for anything in particular.

Deciphering the message

The author of any kind of writing should have something to say, a message to communicate.

Unfortunately, such messages are often lost in the glut of verbiage many authors use to "dress up" their basic point. It's your job to rake through the mess and get to the heart of the text.

You need to approach each reading assignment with the mindset of Sherlock Holmes (or Agatha Christie, if you prefer): There is a mystery to be solved, and you are the master detective. The goal is to figure out what the text is trying to communicate—regardless of how deeply it is buried in the quagmire of convoluted language.

What is the message?

The first step in any good investigation is to collect all of the clues. What are the facts? By spending a few minutes of your time discerning these concrete facts, you will be far better equipped to digest what it is the author is trying to communicate.

But how do you extract the facts when they appear to be hidden in an impenetrable forest of words? You may need a little help—from "who-what-when-where-why-and-how." It seems that the facts readily sally forth when these six trusty questions are called upon the scene.

Exercise: Read the following excerpt, keeping these six words in mind. After you have finished reading it, answer the questions that follow. Be careful—you may have to slow way down!

> As Boris Yeltsin seeks to overcome an approval rating that hasn't reached double digits in months and confound countrymen who have declared he has no chance in the June elections, the Communists, sensing a chance for victory in a popular election, have suddenly become courteous and willing to compromise. Because they already dominate the newly-elected Parliament, their aim seems to be to keep the other political parties fighting among

themselves, giving them little reason or excuse for establishing an anti-Communist coalition.

Gennadi Seleznyov, Speaker of the Parliament's lower house, or Duma, and a former editor of *Pravda*, looks more like a German banker than an old-style Communist Party apparatchik. That and his poise were two of the reasons he won out over former Central Committee member Valentin Kuptsov in the bid to become spokesperson for the "new and improved" Russian Communists, though the fight was prolonged and nasty.

And the new Speaker has his share of enemies, among them the ultra-nationalist Vladimir Zhirnovsky, who backed the candidate of the nationalist Our Home is Russia centrist party, Ivan Rybkin, in a bid to deny the powerful position to Seleznyov. While repeatedly calling for Yeltsin's resignation, Zhirnovsky has nevertheless supported the perhaps lame duck President on many fronts, including the invasion of Chechnya, the only party in Parliament to do so.

Luckily for Seleznyov, Grigory A. Yavlinsky, the liberal economist who leads Yablonko, the most reformist party in opposition to Yeltsin, refused to go along with Our Home is Russia and, by extension, Zhirnovsky. By withholding his votes, he assured Seleznyov's victory. While he maintained that he held out because he was anti-Communist, it was rumored that he had cut a deal for a couple of much-sought-after committee posts as the price of his votes.

All of this bitter infighting suggests that Seleznyov's gamble might just pay off—it is unlikely that an anti-Communist front will emerge in time for the elections. In addition, the results of the last election must leave him sanguine. Although his party won 149 votes, more than any other (Mr. Zhirinovsky's party was in second place, with 51), in reality the Communists are only a few votes shy of the 226 needed for an outright majority. It turns out that many of the 225 "independent" candidates who ran successfully were not as independent as they had declared—nearly one-third of them can be counted on to support Seleznyov's programs.

Such control, unfortunately, tends to indicate that the new Duma will be far less flamboyant and much duller than the old, though undoubtedly more disciplined. Unlike the Speaker, many of the new Communist deputies *are* old-time apparatchiks who are quite accustomed to towing the party line and far less anxious to indulge in free speech.

1. The liberal economist who leads Yablonko is:
A. Vladimir Zhirnovsky
B. Boris Yeltsin
C. Grigory A. Yavlinsky
D. Ivan Rybkin
E. Valentin Kuptsov

2. Which of these ideas is *not* suggested in the passage?
A. Vladimir Zhirnovsky is an ultra-nationalist.
B. The Parliament's lower house is also known as the Duma.
C. Ivan Rybkin was the candidate of the Our Home is Russia centrist party.
D. Boris Yeltsin has had a high approval rating throughout the past few months.
E. Yablonko is the most reformist party in opposition to Yeltsin.

3. How many votes are needed for an outright majority?
A. 225
B. 226
C. 51
D. 149
E. None of the above

4. The main purpose of this passage is to explain:
A. The history of Communism.
B. The lifestyle of Ivan Rybkin.
C. The odds of the June election are in favor of the Communist party.
D. The fight for the Speakership.
E. The old and new Duma.

5. Using the context of the passage, how would "apparatchiks" be best described?
A. Radical
B. Bold
C. Pioneering
D. Inexperienced
E. Traditional

In the preceding exercise, you should have quickly read through the text and been able to answer all five questions. If it took you more than three minutes to do so, you spent too much time. You were reading *only* to answer our six questions—"who?", "what?", "when?", "where?", "why?" and "how?" Your purpose was to get to the facts, nothing more.

Scanning, skimming, reading, remembering

Most everyone I know confuses *skim* and *scan*. Let me set the record straight. *To skim is to read quickly and superficially. To scan is to read carefully but for a specific item.* So when you *skim* a reading selection, you are reading it in its entirety, though you're only hitting the "highlights."

When you *scan* a selection, you are reading it in detail but only until you find what you're looking for. Scanning is the technique we all employ when using the phone book—unless, of course, you're in the habit of reading every name in the book to find the one you're looking for. When you scan, your eyes do not look at every word, read every sentence, or think about every paragraph. Instead, they rapidly move across the page to find just what you are looking for and then read that carefully.

Scanning is the *fastest* reading rate of all—although you are reading in detail, you are *not* seeking to comprehend or remember anything that you see until you find the bit of information you're looking for.

When I was in college, I would begin any assignment by reading the first sentence of every paragraph and trying to answer the questions at the chapter's end. If this did not give me a pretty good idea of the content and important details of that chapter, then—and only then—would I read it more thoroughly.

I'm sure this method of skimming for the facts saved me countless hours of time (and boredom).

Ask first, then look

When skimming for detail, you will often have a particular question, date, or fact to find. You should approach the text much like the dictionary—knowing the word, you just skim the pages to find its definition. If you must answer a specific question or read about a historic figure, you simply find a source—book, magazine, or encyclopedia—and quickly skim the text for the answer or person.

You probably are assigned a lot of reading that can be accomplished by skimming for facts. By establishing the questions you want answered *before* you begin to read, you can quickly browse through the material, extracting only the information you need.

Let's say you're reading a U.S. history text with the goal of identifying the key players in the Watergate Affair. You can breeze through the section that paints a picture of the day's political scene. You can whiz through the description of the Watergate Towers. And you can briefly skim the highlights of other questionable and clandestine political activity in the American past. You *know* what—or who—you're looking for. And there they are—Chuck Colson, John Dean, Mitchell, Liddy—the whole gang. Now you can start to *read.*

By identifying the questions you wanted to answer (*a.k.a.* your purpose) in advance, you would be able to skim the chapter and answer your questions in a lot less time than it would have taken to painstakingly read every word.

As a general rule, if you are reading textbook material word for word, you probably are wasting quite a bit of your study time. Good readers are able to discern what they should read in this manner and what they can afford to skim. When trying to simply gather details and facts, skimming a text is a simple and very important shortcut.

Alternatively, our ability to skim a chapter—even something you need to read more critically—will enable you to develop a general sense of what the chapter is about and how thoroughly it needs to be read.

Exercise: Answer the following questions by scanning the paragraph that follows.

1. How many days are in an astronomical year?
2. Calendar years have how many days? Hours? Minutes? Seconds?
3. To regain the fraction of a day lost each calendar year, what is done?

> Why do we have leap years? They occur to make up the day lost by the fact that our calendar year and the astronomical year do not coincide exactly. An astronomical year has 2,424 days. In calendar years, this is 365 days, five hours, 45 minutes, and 12 seconds. The extra fraction of a day is made up by what we call leap years—when we add an extra day to February. This is done to keep our calendar year in step with the seasons, which are based on the astronomical year.

If this were part of your assigned reading, you would be finished when you had answered the questions. "But I didn't read it," you protest. Can you write a one-sentence summary of the paragraph? If you *can*, and you answered the questions correctly, then you know all you need to.

Skimming, or prereading, is a valuable step even if you aren't seeking specific facts. When skimming for a general overview, there's a very simple procedure to follow:

1. If there is a title or heading, *rephrase it as a question.* This will be your purpose for reading.
2. Examine all the *subheadings, illustrations, and graphics,* as these will help you identify the significant matter within the text.

3. Read thoroughly the *introductory paragraphs,* the summary, and any questions at the chapter's end.
4. Read the *first sentence* of every paragraph. As we discussed in Chapter 3, this is generally where the main idea of a text is found.
5. *Evaluate* what you have gained from this process: Can you answer the questions at the end of the chapter? Could you intelligently participate in a class discussion of the material?
6. *Write* a brief summary that encapsulates what you have learned from your skimming.
7. Based on this evaluation, *decide* whether a more thorough reading is required.

Exercise: Let's see how well you can skim for an overview, rather than for specific facts. Read the following two passages, then follow the seven steps outlined above for each:

Passage #1:

Five major scandals tainted the administration of President Ulysses S. Grant. Although the hero of Vicksburg was the first president to encounter charges of substantial wrongdoing during his administration, it was never proved that he was directly involved in any criminal acts nor that he profited from any of the acts of others.

The first incident occurred in 1869, the first year of his presidency. Known as Black Friday, it involved speculators James Fisk and Jay Gould and their attempt to corner the gold market. By involving Grant's brother-in-law, they hoped to prevent the government from "dumping" its gold onto the market, which would make it impossible for their scheme to succeed. Grant was not directly involved in Fisk's and Gould's machinations, but he certainly gave the appearance of complicity, allowing himself to be entertained lavishly and publicly on Fisk's yacht. However, when the pair's aggressive purchases of gold sent its price skyrocketing in a matter of days, Grant acted swiftly, ordering the Treasury Department to sell off $4 million in gold reserves. While this ended Fisk's and Gould's attempt, this step brought ruin to a number of individuals and businesses that were "riding the wave" of gold fever and resulted in a national economic shock not matched until the 1929 stock market crash.

The second major scandal involved the embezzlement of massive amounts of money by the Credit Mobilier holding company, which was involved with the construction of the Union Pacific railway. To avoid being discovered, the conspirators heavily bribed members of Congress and officials of the Republican Party, of which Grant was the nominal head. Although this scandal erupted during a heated reelection campaign against newspaper publisher Horace Greeley, Grant was evidently completely uninvolved and was reelected handily.

Two other scandals involved taxes and the officials appointed to collect them. One tax collector, John Sanborn, managed to keep nearly half of the delinquent taxes he collected, a total that exceeded $200,000. But that paled in comparison to the fraud discovered by Treasury Secretary Benjamin H. Bristow among liquor distillers and the officials charged with collecting taxes from them. Although Grant called for swift action against all the conspirators, his fervor flagged when his trusted personal secretary, Orville Babcock, was implicated in the scheme. Although Grant slowed the investigation, 110 conspirators were eventually found guilty.

In the final year of Grant's second term, evidence mounted that Secretary of War W.W. Belknap had been taking bribes from corrupt white traders at Indian trading posts. Since Grant had made much of his earlier attempts to institute a fair and nonabusive set of policies toward the Indians, the scandal was a personal embarrassment, though, again, Grant was in no way directly involved. Faced with certain impeachment, Belknap resigned.

Passage #2:

Self-fulfilling Prophesies and Other Scientific Marvels*

A combination of proper analytic skills and common sense is required for an executive to be effective. Call it the place where art and science meet. When you have the overly scientific, you find yourself in Dr. Frankenstein's laboratory, which I did one day at a large consumer products company in California.

The organization was looking at a decline in business caused by a combination of more aggressive competition and their own failure to launch some new products that their plan had heavily relied on. So the employees were going to bear the brunt of management's failure in these two areas. A senior management meeting was held to decide how best to downsize and to create several levels of contingency to react to various levels of revenue losses (and various degrees of shareholder ire). You see, it's simple to earn the big bucks: The management team was putting a hierarchy of firings in place to deal with a bad year, a horrible year, and a disastrous year. Imagine what would've happened if this talent and time had been devoted to trying to *improve* the year.

A particularly officious young woman from staffing and planning was invited to the meeting to provide some of the details of implementing the phased reductions. As the session progressed, I became mesmerized by her high-tech language for what was, to me, a high-touch problem. When asked at what point the second level of discharges would begin, for example, she replied:

"Attrits from the prime round should have been in the outplace mode, offsite, if they were of grades 8 or higher. Other attrits would simply be gone. If profit levels for the second quarter fall below 85 percent of plan as determined by this group, I will initiate secondary attrits. Human resources will inform and escort on the same day, which we advise be a Friday, if possible. Tertiary attrits will occur if profit falls below 75 percent of plan. Tertiary attrits will receive no outplace assistance, unless they are supergrade."

What this all meant, I deciphered, was that the people being let go were being referred to as "attrits" (short for *attrition*). This helped dehumanize the situation significantly. We could have been discussing reducing inventory or equipment leases.

> This was a case of all head, all science. It was a pragmatic approach using computerlike precision to remove people as though they were merely expense items on a balance sheet. The result was disastrous for morale and did not address the underlying cause of the company's marketplace problems.
>
> *Excerpted from *Our Emperors Have No Clothes* by Alan Weiss (Career Press, 1995)

Although it may not be evident at first, you'll soon see how *skimming* can save you a lot of reading time. Even if a more in-depth reading is necessary, you will find that by having gone through this process, you will have developed the kind of skeletal framework that will make your further reading faster, easier, and more meaningful. And if all you need is "just the facts, ma'am," your ability to *scan* a selection, chapter, or book will save you minutes, if not hours, every week.

Whether you're skimming or scanning, you will have equipped yourself with the ability to better digest what it is the author is trying to communicate.

CHAPTER 5

THE CHALLENGE OF TECHNICAL TEXTS

You've already learned a lot of ways to improve your reading. It's time to examine the unique challenges posed by highly technical texts. Physics, trigonometry, chemistry, calculus—you know, subjects that three-fourths of all students avoid like the plague. Even those students who manage to do well in such subjects wouldn't dare call them "Mickey Mouse" courses.

More than any other kind of reading, these subjects demand a logical, organized approach, a step-by-step reading method.

And they require a detection of the text's *organizational devices.*

Developing the skill to identify the basic sequence of the text will enable you to follow the progression of thought, a progression that is vital to your comprehension and retention.

Why? In most technical writing, each concept is like a building block of understanding—if you don't understand a particular section or concept, you won't be able to understand the *next* section, either.

Most technical books are saturated with ideas, terms, formulas, and theories. The chapters are dense with information, compressing a great wealth of ideas into a small space. They demand to be read very carefully.

In order to get as much as possible from such reading assignments, you can take advantage of some devices to make sense of the organization. Here are five basics to watch for:

1. Definitions and terms.
2. Examples.
3. Classifications and listings.
4. Use of contrast.
5. Cause-effect relationships.

As you read any text, but certainly a highly specialized one, identifying these devices will help you grasp the main idea, as well as any details that are essential to your thorough understanding of the material.

Definitions and terminology

In reading any specialized text, you must begin at the beginning—understanding the terms particular to that discipline. Familiar, everyday words have very precise definitions in technical writing.

What do I mean? Take the word *nice*. You may compliment your friend's new sweater, telling her it's *nice*, meaning attractive. You may find that the new chemistry teacher is *nice*, meaning he doesn't give too much homework. And when your friend uses the word *nice* to describe the blind date she's set up for you, it may mean something completely different—and insidious.

Everyday words can have a variety of meanings, some of them even contradictory, depending on the context in which they're used.

In contrast, in the sciences, terminology has fixed and specific meanings. For example, the definition of elasticity—*"the ability of a solid to regain its shape after a deforming force has been applied"*—is the same in Bangkok or Brooklyn. Such exact terminology enables scientists to communicate with the precision their discipline requires.

Definitions may vary in length. One term may require a one-sentence definition, others merit entire paragraphs. Some may even need a whole chapter to accurately communicate the definition.

Examples help clarify the abstract

A second communication tool is the example. Authors use examples to bridge abstract principles to concrete illustrations. These examples are essential to your ability to comprehend intricate and complicated theories.

Unlike other writing, technical writing places a very high premium on brevity. Economizing words is the key to covering a large volume of knowledge in a relatively small space. Few technical texts or articles include anecdotal matter or chatty stories of the author's experience.

This fact challenges the reader to pay particular attention to the examples that are included. Why? Technical writing often is filled with new or foreign ideas—many of which are not readily digestible. They are difficult in part because they are abstract. Examples work to clarify these concepts, hopefully in terms more easily understood.

For example, it may be difficult for you to make sense of the definition of symbiosis—"*the living together of two dissimilar organisms, especially when mutually beneficial*"—but the example of the bird that picks food from the crocodile's teeth, thereby feeding itself and keeping the crocodile cavity-free, helps bring it home.

Classification and listings

A third tool frequently utilized in texts is classification and listings. Classifying is the process by which common subjects are categorized under a general heading.

Some examples:

Matter may occur in three forms: solid, liquid, or gas.

Classification: Three forms of matter

Listing: Solid, liquid, gas

The social sciences are psychology, economics, and sociology.

Classification: Social sciences

Listing: Psychology, economics, sociology

Especially in technical writing, authors use classification to categorize extensive lists of detail. Such writings may have several categories and subcategories that organize these details in some manageable fashion.

Comparing/contrasting

A fourth tool used in communicating difficult information is that of comparing and contrasting. Texts use this tool to bring complicated material into focus by offering a similar or opposing picture.

Such devices are invaluable in grasping concepts that do not conjure up a picture in your mind. Gravity, for example, is not something that can be readily pictured—it's not a tangible object that can be described.

Through comparison, a text relates a concept to one that has been previously defined—or to one a reader may readily understand. Through contrast, the text concentrates on the differences and distinctions between two ideas. By focusing on distinguishing features, these ideas become clearer as one idea is held up against another.

Cause-effect relationships

A final tool that texts employ to communicate is the cause-effect relationship. This device is best defined in the context of science, where it is the fundamental quest of most scientific research.

Science begins with the observation of the effect—what is happening?

It is snowing.

The next step is to conduct research into the cause: *Why* is it snowing? Detailing this cause-effect relationship is often the essence of scientific and technical writing.

Cause-effect relationships may be written in many ways. The effect may be stated first, followed by the cause. An effect may be the result of several connected causes—a causal chain. And a cause may have numerous effects.

In your reading, it is vital that you recognize this relationship and its significance.

Read with a plan

More than any other type of writing, highly specialized, technical writing must be read with a plan. You can't approach your reading assignment merely with the goal of completing it. Such mindless reading will leave you confused and frustrated, drowning in an ocean of theory, concepts, terms, and examples.

Your plan should incorporate the following guidelines:

1. **Learn the terms** that are essential to understanding the concepts presented. Knowing the precise definitions that the author uses will enable you to follow his chain of thought through the text.
2. **Determine the structure or organization of the text.** Most chapters have a definite pattern that forms the skeleton of the material. A book may begin with a statement of a theory, give examples, provide sample problems, then summarize. Often this pattern can be discerned through a preview of the table of contents or the titles and subtitles.
3. **Skim the chapter** to get a sense of the author's viewpoint. Ask questions to define your purpose in reading. Use any summaries or review questions to guide your reading.
4. **Do a thorough analytical reading** of the text. Do not proceed from one section to the next until you have a clear understanding of the section you are reading—the concepts generally build upon each other. To proceed to a new section without understanding the ones that precede it is, at best, futile.
5. **Immediately upon concluding your thorough reading, review!** Write a summary of the concepts and theories you need to remember. Answer any questions raised when you skimmed the text. Do the problems. If possible, apply the formulas.

Technical material is saturated with ideas. When reading it, you must be convinced of one fact: Every individual word counts! You will want to read such material with the utmost concentration—it is not meant to be sped through.

Good readers know that such material demands a slow read that concentrates on achieving the greatest level of retention.

- ☞ Every definition has to be digested.
- ☞ Every formula must be committed to memory.
- ☞ Every example needs to be considered.

To improve your reading of such technical material, you will want to hone the skill of identifying the devices an author uses to communicate. In so doing, you will be able to connect the chain of thought that occurs. When reading such texts—or attempting to work out technical problems—try the following "tricks":

- ☞ Whenever you can, "translate" formulas and numbers into words. To test your understanding, try to put your translation into *different* words.
- ☞ Even if you're not particularly visual, pictures can often help. You should try translating a particularly vexing math problem into a drawing or diagram.
- ☞ Before you even get down to solving a problem, is there any way for you to estimate the answer or, at least, to estimate the range within which the answer should fall (greater than one, but less than 10)? This is the easy way to at least make sure you wind up in the right ballpark.

☞ Play around. There are often different paths to the same solution, or even equally valid solutions. If you've found *one*, look for others. This is a great way to increase your understanding of all the principles involved.

☞ When you are checking your calculations, try working *backwards*. I've found it an easier way to catch simple mathematical errors.

☞ Try to figure out what is being asked, what principles are involved, what information is important and what is not.

☞ Teach someone else. Trying to explain mathematical concepts to someone else will quickly pinpoint what you really know or don't know. It's virtually impossible to get someone else—especially someone who is slower than you at all this stuff—to understand if you don't!

CHAPTER 6

BECOMING A CRITICAL READER

After four years of undergraduate work, before my dear alma mater would award me the degree for which I felt my dollars, sweat, and blood had amply paid, I was made to endure a six-hour essay test. We literature majors were given one question—"Analyze and interpret the following:" (the "following" being a poem we had never seen before) and several blue books in which to write our erudite answers.

Unbelievable?

Hardly!

This test was given in much the same way that the Educational Testing Service gives its PSAT, SAT, ACT, LSAT, and GMAT verbal tests. In the notorious reading comprehension section, you are required to read a distilled passage—which, unless you've stolen a peek at the exam, you have never seen—and then given four to six questions to determine if you have any clue as to what you just read.

You will find that there are many times, particularly in comparative literature classes, when you will need to read something with great care in order to remember details and interpret meaning. Hester Prynne's red monogram, Poe's talking raven, and Samuel Beckett's mysterious friend all require a little more analysis than a superficial interpretation of props and plot.

Yet such detailed, analytical reading is not limited to literature. Political dissertations, historical analysis, and even scientific research may require more careful reading than the latest "space opera."

Such reading is often referred to as *critical reading,* a type of reading during which you seek to distinguish thoughts, ideas, or concepts—each demanding thorough study and evaluation.

Critical reading requires that you are able to identify the author's arguments, measure their worth and truth, and apply what is pertinent to your own experience. Unlike skimming, critical reading challenges the reader to concentrate at the highest level possible.

Prepare yourself to read critically

When preparing to read critically, you must lay the groundwork for concentration. Just as an athlete must ready himself mentally to achieve peak performance, you will want to ready yourself before you begin to read.

To prepare to read critically:

1. You must have a clearly defined purpose for reading. Make sure that you've identified your purpose before you begin.

2. Pay attention! Avoid letting your mind wander to that conversation you and your friend had today at lunch. Minimize distractions and interruptions, anything or anyone that causes you to break your focus.
3. Find your optimum study environment—a quiet corner in the library, your own room, wherever. In absolute silence, or with your new CD playing. (Be sure to read ***Manage Your Time*** or ***Get Organized***, two of the nine books in my ***How to Study Program***, for more tips on finding *your* perfect study environment.)
4. Do not concern yourself with how fast or slowly you read. Your goal should be to understand the material, not to find out how fast you can get it over with.
5. If it seems that you will need several hours to complete your reading, you might break the longer assignments into smaller, more manageable parts, then reward yourself at the end of each of these sections by taking brief breaks.

If you take these steps prior to reading any text that requires your utmost concentration, you will find that your mind is readied for the kind of focus necessary to read critically. Make a *habit* of such preparations and you will set yourself up to succeed.

Prereading is a must

Once you have prepared your mind to read, the next step is to understand the big picture—what is the author's thesis or main idea? Good comprehension is the consequence of your ability to grasp the main point of what the author is trying to communicate.

And grasping this message is accomplished through skimming the text, as we discussed in Chapter 4. Let's review the basic steps:

1. If there is a title or heading, rephrase it as a question. This will support your purpose for reading.
2. Examine all subheadings, illustrations, and graphics, as these will help you identify the significant matter within the text.
3. Read the introductory paragraphs, summary, and any questions at the end of the chapter.
4. Read the first sentence of every paragraph. In Chapter 3 you learned that this is generally where the main idea is found.
5. Evaluate what you have gained from this process: Can you answer the questions at the chapter's end? Could you intelligently participate in a class discussion of the material?
6. Write a brief summary of what you have learned from your skimming.

By beginning critical reading with a 20-minute skim of the text, you should be ready to answer three questions:

1. What is the text's principal message or viewpoint?
2. Is an obvious chain of thought or reasoning revealed?
3. What major points are addressed?

Now, read it

Once you identify and understand the basic skeleton of the material, your actual "read" of the material—following the details, reasoning, and chain of thought—is simply a matter of attaching meat to the bones.

This digestive process involves learning to interpret and evaluate what is written, what is directly stated, and what can be inferred from the context.

Effective analytical reading requires that you, the reader, distinguish the explicit, literal meaning of words *(denotation)* and what suggestions or intentions are intimated by the general content *(connotation)*.

Analyzing: what the words *connote*

Words and writing have two levels of meaning that are important to the reader's comprehension.

The first level is the literal or descriptive meaning. What a word expressly denotes means the specific, precise definition you'd find in Webster.

Connotation involves this second level of meaning—that which incorporates the total significance of the words.

What does that mean? Beyond a literal definition, words communicate emotion, bias, attitude, and perspective. Analyzing any text involves learning to interpret what is implied, just as much as what is expressly stated.

15 questions to help you

Beyond grasping the meaning of words and phrases, critical reading requires that you ask questions. Here are 15 questions that will help you effectively analyze and interpret most of what you read:

1. Is there a clear message communicated throughout?
2. Are the relationships between the points direct and clear?

3. Is there a relationship between your experience and the author's?
4. Are the details factual?
5. Are the examples and evidence relevant?
6. Is there consistency of thought?
7. What is the author's bias or slant?
8. What is the author's motive?
9. What does the author want you to believe?
10. Does this jibe with your own beliefs or experiences?
11. Is the author rational or subjective?
12. Is there a confusion between feelings and facts?
13. Are the main points logically ordered?
14. Are the arguments and conclusions consistent?
15. Are the explanations clear?

Obviously, this list of questions is not all-inclusive, but it will give you a jump start when critical reading is required. Remember, the essential ingredient to any effective analysis and interpretation is the questions you ask.

Summarizing: the final step

Nothing will be more important to your recall than learning to condense what you read into a clear and concise summary.

Many of you have learned to do this by excerpting entire segments or sentences from a text, certainly not a very efficient method for summarizing.

I recommend using the traditional outline (which is explained in detail in my book, ***Take Notes***).

Another suggestion is to use a two-step process called *diagramming,* which calls for the reader to *diagram* or illustrate the content he or she has just read, then write a brief synopsis of what he or she has learned.

Similar to outlining, diagramming helps the reader to visualize the relationships between various thoughts and ideas. Concept diagrams, or concept trees, are very useful visual aids for depicting the structure of a textbook.

Unless you have a photographic memory, you will find that recalling a picture of the main points will greatly increase what you remember. Beyond this, such diagrams require that you distill what is essential to the text and how it relates to the main message.

Suppose you read a chapter in your biology assignment about the parts of a cell. Your diagram might reduce your reading material to look like the following:

Parts of a Cell

Outside of Cell	Inside of Cell
cell wall	cytoplasm
cell membrane	vacuoles
nucleus chloroplasts	chlorophyll

More than a listing of main points, a diagram allows you to picture how parts fit together, which enhances your ability to recall the information you've read. This is especially true the more "visual" you are.

Distill it into a synopsis

The second step in the process of summarizing is to write a brief synopsis of what you've learned. When you need to review the material, diagrams will remind you of the significant elements in the text. Your synopsis will remind you of the main idea.

The goal here is to put in your own words what you gleaned from what you read. You will find this process an invaluable gauge of whether you have understood the message—and on what level.

Use this method one chapter at a time, and do not proceed to the *next* chapter until you have completed the following exercise:

1. Write definitions of any key terms you feel are essential to understanding the topic.
2. Write questions and answers you feel clarify the topic.
3. Write any questions for which you don't have answers—then make sure you find them through rereading, further research, or asking another student or your teacher.
4. Even if you still have unanswered questions, move on to the next section and complete numbers one to three for that section. (And so on, until your reading assignment is complete.) See if this method doesn't help you get a better handle on any assignment right from the start.

Critical reading is not easy. It requires a lot more concentration and effort than the quick-reference reading that you can get away with for much of your day-to-day class assignments. And I won't kid you—much of the reading you'll do in the latter years of high school and throughout college will be critical reading.

But if you follow the steps I've outlined for each critical reading assignment that you tackle—preparing yourself for the read, doing a preread skim, followed by an analytical reading, concluding with a summarization—you'll discover that critical reading can be a much smoother, even rewarding, experience!

The method you probably learned

If you were taught a specific reading method in school, it was probably the one developed back in the 1940s that is abbreviated "SQ3R." This stands for **S**urvey, **Q**uestion, **R**ead, **R**ecite, and **R**eview. Here's how the process works:

Survey. Preread the chapter, concentrating on topic sentences, subheads, and review questions, in order to get an overview of what's ahead.

Question. Once you've surveyed the chapter, ask yourself what information is contained in it. Consider turning the subheads into questions as an exercise.

Read. Now read the first section thoroughly, attempting to answer the questions you've posed. Take notes, highlight, underline, map.

Recite. Now answer the questions *without* looking at your notes or the text. When you're done, go on to the next section. Continue this detailed reading/reciting tandem until you finish the chapter (or the assignment).

Review. Go back over the entire assignment.

Does this sound familiar? I agree. I think this method is completely incorporated into the steps I've outlined in this and previous chapters, so I left it out of a previous edition of this book. Because some teachers have taken me to task for failing to mention it, here it is.

Frankly, I think the detailed method I've proposed—and the helpful advice along the way—covers far more ground.

CHAPTER 7

READING THE LITERATURE

"Will you walk a little faster?" said a whiting to a snail.
"There's a porpoise close behind us and he's treading on my tail!"
"If I'd been the whiting," said Alice, whose thoughts were still running on the song, "I'd have said to the porpoise, 'Keep back, please; we don't want you with us!'"
"They were obliged to have him with them," the Mock Turtle said. "No wise fish would go anywhere without a porpoise."
"Wouldn't it really?" said Alice in a tone of great surprise.
"Of course not," said the Mock Turtle. "Why, if a fish came to me, and told me he was going on a journey, I should say, 'With what porpoise?' "

"Don't you mean 'purpose?'" said Alice.

"I mean what I say," the Mock Turtle replied in an offended tone.

—Lewis Carroll, *Alice in Wonderland*

In this excerpt, you could enjoy the nonsensical picture of a porpoise pushing a snail and whiting to walk faster. You might laugh at the confusion of "porpoise" and "purpose" by the Mock Turtle. Or you could discern the *message*—that you need to have a purpose when you are on a journey...or reading.

In today's world of Sega, Mortal Kombat, and Green Day, literature often takes a back seat, so much so that many of your classmates (not *you*, of course) may not even know that *Alice in Wonderland* is an important piece of literature.

Why should you care about literature? Who needs to read the book when you can see the movie?

Although I didn't write this book to give you a lecture on the merits of the classics, please bear with me for a couple of paragraphs.

The greatest involvement device

Unlike anything else, literature *involves* the reader in the story. How? There are no joysticks to manipulate, no "sensurround" sound to engulf you. Your imagination is your only involvement device, but it far surpasses any high-tech computer gimmicks.

Your imagination makes reading the ultimate adventure. It allows you to immerse yourself in the story—identifying with the protagonist, fighting his battles, experiencing his fears, sharing his victories. You may become so involved, you end up staying up well past your bedtime, turning page after page late into the night!

Your imagination is the vehicle that allows you to explore a million different lives, from floating down the Mississippi River on a raft, to suffering through a star-crossed love affair, to having tea with the March Hare and the Mad Hatter, as our Alice did.

Creative writing may be serious or humorous or sublime...or all three. It is often subtle; meanings are elusive and delicate. Such writing, when done effectively, evokes emotional responses. You get angry. You shed a tear. You chuckle. An author's expression strikes a chord that moves you. You and the author communicate on a level that is far beyond an exchange of facts and information.

Enough said. Assuming that I have converted all you literature skeptics to avid library loiterers (and even if I haven't), I'll offer some advice to help you begin your journey to literary appreciation. It begins with understanding the basic roadmap.

Which reading method? Pleasure or critical?

Although I certainly encourage you to approach your reading with the enthusiasm and anticipation that would justify the pleasure-reading method (see Chapter 2), the demands of your teacher who assigns the reading will probably require the *critical* reading method.

Reading literature requires most of the skills we've discussed previously.

There are devices and clues to ferret out that will help you follow the story and understand its meaning better.

You will analyze and interpret what the author is saying and evaluate its worth.

But in addition, in literature, you will be able to appreciate the *words* themselves. In textbooks, you often must penetrate a thick jungle of tangled sentences and murky paragraphs to find the information you seek.

Great literature *is* its language. It's the flow and ebb of its words, the cadence of its sentences, as much as it is story and theme.

As you read more, you'll uncover the diversity of tapestries that different authors weave with words. You may discover similar themes coursing through the works of authors like Ernest Hemingway or Thomas Hardy, but their use of language is as different as desert and forest. The composition of the words themselves is an element you'll want to examine as you critically read literature.

Fiction: just another word for storytelling

Most fiction is an attempt to tell a story. There is a *beginning,* in which the characters and the setting are introduced. There is a *conflict or struggle* (middle) that advances the story to a *climax* (end)—where the conflict is resolved. A final *denouement* or "winding up" clarifies the conclusion of the story.

Your literature class will address all of these parts using literary terms that are often more confusing than helpful. The following are brief definitions of some of the more important ones:

Plot. The order or sequence of the story—how it proceeds from the opening through the climax. Your ability to understand and appreciate literature depends upon how well you follow the plot—the *story.*

Characterization. The personalities or characters central to the story—the heroes, heroines, and villains.

You will want to identify the main characters of the story and their relationship to the struggle or conflict. Pay particular attention as to whether the characters are three dimensional—are they real and believable?

Theme. The controlling message or subject of the story; the moral or idea that the author is using the plot and characters to communicate. Some examples: man's inhumanity to man; man's impotency in his environment; the corrupting influence of power, greed, and unrequited love. Just as with nonfiction, you need to discern this theme to really understand what it is the author wants to communicate.

Setting. The time and place in which the story takes place. This is especially important when reading a historical novel or one that takes you to another culture.

Point of view. Who is telling the story? Is it one of the central characters giving you flashbacks or a first-person perspective? Or is it a third-person narrator offering commentary and observations on the characters, the setting, and the plot? This person moves the story along and gives it an overall tone.

The first step in reading literature is to familiarize yourself with these concepts and then try to recognize them in each novel or short story you read.

The second step is the same as for reading nonfiction—to identify your purpose for reading.

Allow your purpose to define how you will read. If you are reading to be entertained, then a pleasure read is the way to go. If you're reading for a class and will be required to participate in discussions or be tested on the material, you'll want to do a critical read.

How long should it take?

As a general rule, fiction is not meant to be read over a period of months—or even weeks. Try to read it as quickly as possible to get a full appreciation of the author's plot, character, and theme. You should read fast enough to progress through the plot, get a sense of the characters and their struggles, and hear the author's message or theme.

It's helpful to set a goal as to when you want to finish your reading. Frequently, of course, this will already be set for you, if your reading is a class assignment.

You should, however, set daily goals. Set aside one or two hours to read, or set a goal of reading three chapters a day until you finish. Reading sporadically—10 minutes one day, a half-hour the next, then not picking up the book until several days later—means that you'll lose track of the plot and characters and just as quickly lose interest.

Too often when students do not establish a regular schedule, their reading becomes fragmented, making it very difficult to piece together the whole story. A reasonable goal is to try to read a novel in less than a week, a short story in one sitting. To achieve this goal, once you begin, you should read every day until you finish. By doing this, the story and characters will stay fresh in your mind.

If you try to read fiction more rapidly, you will greatly increase your enjoyment of it. It is vitally important that as you try to read faster, you give the story your full attention. By doing this you will be surprised by how improved your understanding and appreciation are.

To speed your reading of fiction, try this experiment:

1. Find a novel or short story that interests you and is relatively easy to read. Tomes like *Ulysses or The Naked Lunch* shouldn't be candidates.

2. Set aside two or three hours to invest in reading the book. If at all possible, finish it in one sitting. If you can't, then allocate the same amount of time each day until you do.

By trying this experiment, you will discover that fiction is *intended* to be read this way—whenever possible, in one sitting. It is as if you are sitting at a master storyteller's feet as he spins his tale. You want to know how the story ends and what happens to the hero.

Will the villain get his comeuppance? Will the hero get the girl? Or will he (or she) ride off on Old Paint?

You'll find that you appreciate the story far more at the end than anywhere in the middle.

Some other tips for reading fiction:

1. Understand the plot and maintain awareness of its progression.
2. Take breaks to review what has occurred and who is involved.
3. Vary your reading method—from skimming transitional bridge material to carefully reading description and narration.
4. Question the story's theme. What is the message?

You're allowed to enjoy it

A final recommendation: Give yourself permission to *enjoy* what you are reading. You will be amazed at the difference this will make. Fiction, unlike any other reading, can take you on an adventure. Through your mind, you can journey to faraway lands, pretend you are someone else, feel emotions you may never otherwise experience.

All of this happens as you build an appreciation of literature, as you learn to understand fiction and allow yourself to enjoy great stories.

CHAPTER 8

FOCUSING YOUR MIND

Concentration: It's one of the biggest challenges facing any reader.

Why? Unlike other activities, reading requires an *active* mind and a *passive* body. This is a deadly combination, especially when you have spent the day in classes and haven't had a chance to burn off that excess energy with a tennis match, a game of hoops, or a quick run around campus.

Concentration-wise, reading can be more demanding than class lectures, homework assignments, or note-taking. In class, you at least have vocal variety and the threat of being called on to keep you focused. And writing, although a sedentary activity, still requires some hand-eye coordination to keep your brain working.

Keep your mind on one thing

Concentration begins with the ability to keep your mind focused on one thing—your reading assignment. This is not an innate talent, but a learned discipline. Much like an athlete must learn to be so focused that she is completely unaffected by the screaming crowds, a good reader absorbs himself in what he's reading.

How does *your* mind discipline "rate"? Answer these questions to find out:

1. When I read, do I often allow random thoughts to steal my focus?
2. As I read, am I easily distracted by noises or other activities?
3. Am I watching the clock to see how long I have been reading?

There is no simple, magic formula for conjuring up concentration—especially when you're faced with a critical reading assignment you're not particularly looking forward to. But if you follow the preparatory steps I've discussed in previous chapters—define your purpose, skim for a preread, identify questions for which you will seek answers—you should find it a bit easier to stay focused.

Steps to better concentration

Here are some other practical steps I recommend to increase your ability to concentrate:

1. **Get some exercise before you begin your reading.** A game of racquetball, an exercise class, a workout at the gym, even a brisk walk, will help burn off *physical* energy so you'll be able to direct all of your *mental* energy to your reading.

2. **Read in the right place.** No, it's not in front of the TV, nor in your room if your roommate is hosting a pizza party. Reading is a solitary activity. Find a quiet corner, preferably in a place designated for study only—at your desk, in the library. Although tempting, reading on your bed can be dangerous if you're struggling to concentrate. You just may lose the battle and find yourself in the perfect place to doze off.
3. **Eliminate distractions.** If you've properly scheduled your reading time (see ***Manage Your Time***), you won't be distracted by other pending assignments. If you're trying to read one assignment while worrying about another, your concentration—and comprehension—will inevitably suffer.

   Make sure there's nothing else in sight to vie for your attention. Are there letters on your desk that you need to answer? Put them away and schedule some time to write back. Sirens and screams from the TV show in the other room? Turn it off, turn it down, or close your door.
4. **Plan breaks.** If you have three hours or more of reading ahead of you, the mere thought of it may be so discouraging that you'll lose your concentration before you even pick up the book. Schedule short 5- or 10-minute breaks after each hour of reading. Get up. Listen to some music. Stretch. If you must break more frequently, keep your breaks shorter. By breaking up your reading into smaller, more digestible bites, you'll be able to concentrate more effectively.

Wait! Don't start reading yet.

Have you defined your purpose for reading? Once again, you must have a clearly defined purpose or goal. What are you reading for? (We have addressed this numerous times, but spaced repetition is a very effective way to make a point.)

The point is that reading without purpose is the greatest means to getting nowhere, which is where you'll find your mind after about a half-hour.

Know why you are reading. If your teacher or professor has given you questions to answer, then you know what you're looking for. If not, ask your *own* questions, using the clues in your book (as discussed in Chapter 2).

An effective preread of the material should help you define your purpose and stimulate some interest in finding out more—which will result in increased concentration.

Motivation: crucial to concentration

Motivation is key to your success in just about any endeavor, whether it's graduating with honors, maintaining an effective time-management program, or improving your reading. You can utilize all the tricks and steps I've mentioned in this chapter, but if you lack the motivation to read, you'll still find it a struggle to concentrate on your assignments.

There are two types of motivation—intrinsic and extrinsic. What's the difference?

An avid murder mystery fan, you buy stacks of paperbacks at the used bookstore and spend your free time with your nose buried in them. You love the challenge of figuring out "who did it" before you reach the end. In fact, you'd spend all weekend reading mysteries if you didn't have to complete a reading assignment for your physics class.

You're not particularly interested in physics, but your efforts on this assignment could secure you an A for the term, so you're determined to read the material and "ace" the exam.

Your motivation for reading the mysteries is intrinsic—you do it because you enjoy it. You don't get any awards. You don't get paid for it.

The physics reading, on the other hand, requires external motivation. You're reading it because you want to earn a high grade in class. Your reward is external—beyond the reading itself.

Whether you are intrinsically motivated to read or doing it for some external reward doesn't matter as much as the fact that you are motivated by something! If you find it difficult to get excited about reading your economics assignment, remind yourself of how this exercise will help your grade—get yourself externally motivated.

If *that* doesn't get you motivated enough to read for three hours, there's nothing wrong with a little bribery. Reward yourself with something more immediate. Promise yourself that if you stay focused on your reading until it's completed, you can watch that video afterward. Or you can buy that new CD. (Be careful, though. If you need *lots* of extrinsic motivation, you could run out of money!)

The value of concentration can be summed up in one statement: Concentration is essential to comprehension. Where there is failure to focus, there will be little or no understanding.

Without concentration, you will see only words on a page.

CHAPTER 9

RETAINING THE INFORMATION

The ultimate test of your comprehension is what you remember *after* you have finished your reading—what you walk away with.

As a student, most of your reading will be for classes in which, sooner or later, you'll be required to regurgitate the information you've read in some type of format—essay test, term paper, multiple-choice, true-false, or fill-in-the-blank final.

So, beyond just being able to *complete* your reading assignments, you want to be sure you *remember* what you read.

All of you have probably had the experience of forgetting that important fact that made the difference between an A- and a B+ (or a B- and a C+). It was sitting right there, on the tip of your brain. But you couldn't quite remember it.

Memory *can* be improved

You probably know people with photographic (or near-photographic) memories. They know all the words to all the songs in *Rolling Stone's* Top 50, remind you of things you said to them three years ago, and never forget anyone's birthday (or anniversary or "day we met," or "first kiss day," *ad infinitum*).

Some people seem to be able to retain information naturally, but a good memory—like good concentration—*can* be learned. You can control what stays in your mind and what is forgotten. The key to this control is to learn and tap into the essential elements of good memory.

Some people remember with relative ease and have no problem retaining large volumes of information. Others often are aggravated by a faulty memory that seems to lose more than it retains. Several factors contribute to your capability to recall information you take in:

Intelligence, age, and experience all play a role in how well you remember. Not everyone remembers the same way. You need to identify how these factors affect your memory and learn to maximize your strengths.

Laying a strong foundation is important to good memory. Most learning is an addition to something you already know. If you never grasped basic chemistry, then mastering organic chemistry will be virtually impossible. By developing a broad base of knowledge, you will enhance your ability to recall new information.

Motivation is key to improving your memory. A friend of mine, the consummate baseball fan, seems to know every baseball statistic from the beginning of time. He can spout off batting averages and ERAs from any decade for virtually any player, his favorite team's season schedule...and most of the other teams', too! Although I wouldn't say he is the most intelligent guy I've ever met, he obviously loves baseball and is highly motivated to memorize as much as possible about his favorite subject.

You probably have a pet interest, too. Whether it's movies, music, or sports, you've filled your brain with a mountain of information. Now, if you can learn that much about one subject, you are obviously capable of retaining information about other subjects—even chemistry. You just have to learn how to motivate yourself.

A method, system, or process for retaining information is crucial to increasing your recall. This may include organizing your thinking, good study habits, or mnemonic devices—some means that you utilize when you have to remember.

Using what you learn, soon after you learn it, is important to recall. It's fine to memorize a vocabulary list for a quick quiz, but if you wish to retain information for the long haul, you must reinforce your learning by using this knowledge. For example, you will add a new word to your permanent vocabulary if you make a point to use it, correctly, in a conversation.

The study of foreign languages, for many, proves frustrating when there are no opportunities outside of class to practice speaking the language. That's why foreign-language students often join conversation groups or study abroad—to reinforce retention of what they have learned by using it.

Why we forget

As you think about the elements of developing good memory, you can use them to address why you *forget.* The root of poor memory is usually found in one of these areas:

1. We fail to make the material meaningful.
2. We did not learn prerequisite material.
3. We fail to grasp what is to be remembered.
4. We do not have the desire to remember.
5. We allow apathy or boredom to dictate how we learn.
6. We have no set habit for learning.
7. We are disorganized and inefficient in our use of study time.
8. We do not use the knowledge we have gained.

All of us are inundated with information every day, bombarded with facts, concepts, and opinion. We are capable of absorbing some information simply because the media drench us with it. (I've never read Nancy Reagan's notorious unauthorized biography, nor do I intend to, but how could I not be aware of her reputation for recycling Christmas gifts?)

In order to retain most information, we have to make a concerted effort to do so. We must make this same effort with the material we read.

How to remember

There are some basic tools that will help you remember what you read:

Understanding. You will remember only what you understand. When you read something and grasp the message, you have begun the process of retention. The way to test this is to state the message in your own words. Can you summarize the main idea? Unless you understand what is being said, you won't be able to decide whether it is to be remembered or discarded.

Desire. Let me repeat: You remember what you *choose* to remember. If you do not want to retain some piece of information or don't believe you *can,* then you *won't*! To remember the material, you must *want* to remember it and be convinced that you *will* remember it.

Overlearn. To insure that you retain material, you need to go beyond simply doing the assignment. To really remember what you learn, you should learn material thoroughly, or *over*learn. This involves prereading the text, doing a critical read, and having some definite means of review that reinforces what you should have learned.

Systematize. It's more difficult to remember random thoughts or numbers than those organized in some pattern. For example, which phone number is easier to remember: 538-6284 or 678-1234? Once you recognize the pattern in the second number, it takes much less effort to remember than the first. You should develop the ability to discern the structure that exists and recall it when you try to remember. Have a system to help you recall how information is organized and connected.

Association. It's helpful to attach or associate what you are trying to recall to something you already have in your memory. Mentally link new material to existing knowledge so that you are giving this new thought some context in your mind.

If we take these principles and apply them to your reading assignment, we can develop a procedure that will increase what you take with you from your reading.

A procedure to improve recall

Each time you attempt to read something that you must recall, use this six-step process:

1. **Evaluate the material and define your purpose** for reading. Identify your interest level and get a sense of how difficult the material is.
2. **Choose appropriate reading techniques** for the purpose of your reading. If you are reading to grasp the main idea, that is what you will recall.
3. **Identify the important facts.** Remember what you need to. Identify associations that connect the details you must recall.
4. **Take notes.** Use your own words to give a synopsis of the main ideas. Use an outline, diagram or concept tree to show relationship and pattern. Your notes provide an important backup to your memory. Writing down key points will further reinforce your ability to remember.
5. **Review.** Quiz yourself on those things you must remember. Develop some system by which you review notes at least three times before you are required to recall. The first review should be shortly after you've read, the second should come a few days later, and the final should take place just before you are expected to recall. This process will help you avoid cram sessions.
6. **Implement.** Find opportunities to *use* the knowledge you have gained. Study groups and class discussions are invaluable opportunities to implement what you've learned.

CHAPTER 10

LET'S READ UP ON ADD

No one endorses illegal drugs. But we must face and deal with what's happening to the three million-plus who are on a *legal* drug—Ritalin, the prescribed drug of choice for kids diagnosed with Attention Deficit Disorder (ADD), hyperactivity, or the combination of the two (ADHD). I could write a book on ADD, which seems to be the "diagnosis of choice" for school kids these days.

Luckily, I don't have to. Thom Hartmann has already written an excellent one—*Attention Deficit Disorder: A Different Perception* (Underwood Books, 1997)—from which I have freely and liberally borrowed (with his permission) for this chapter.

Some definitions, please

What is ADD? It is probably easiest to describe as a person's difficulty in focusing on a single thing for any significant duration of time. People with ADD are described as easily distracted, impatient, impulsive, and often seeking immediate gratification. They have poor listening skills and trouble doing "boring" jobs (such as sitting quietly in class or, as adults, balancing a checkbook). "Disorganized" and "messy" are words that also come up often.

Hyperactivity, however, is more clearly defined as restlessness, resulting in excessive activity. Hyperactives are usually described as having "ants in their pants." ADHD, the first category recognized in medicine some 75 years ago, is a combination of hyperactivity and ADD.

According to the American Psychiatric Association, a person has ADHD if he or she meets eight or more of the following paraphrased criteria:

1. Can't remain seated if required to do so.
2. Easily distracted by extraneous stimuli.
3. Can't easily focus on a single task.
4. Frequently begins another activity without completing the first.
5. Fidgets or squirms (or feels restless mentally).
6. Can't (or doesn't want to) wait for his turn during group activities.
7. Will often interrupt with an answer before a question is completed.
8. Has problems with chore or job follow-through.
9. Has difficulty playing quietly.
10. Impulsively jumps into physically dangerous activities without weighing the consequences.
11. Easily loses things (pencils, tools, papers) necessary to complete school or work projects.

12. Interrupts others inappropriately.
13. Talks impulsively or excessively.
14. Doesn't seem to listen when spoken to.

Three caveats to keep in mind: The behaviors must have started before age 7, not represent some other form of classifiable mental illness, and occur more frequently than in the average person of the same age.

Characteristics of people with ADD

Let's look at the characteristics generally ascribed to people with ADD in more detail:

Easily distracted. Because ADD people are constantly "scoping out" everything around them, focusing on a single item is difficult. Just try having a conversation with an ADD person while a television is on.

Short, but very intense, attention span. Though it can't be defined in terms of minutes or hours, anything ADD people find boring immediately loses their attention. Other projects may hold their rapt and extraordinarily intense attention for hours or days.

Disorganization. ADD children are often chronically disorganized—their rooms are messy, their desks are a shambles, their files incoherent. Although people without ADD can be equally messy and disorganized, they can usually find what they are looking for; ADDers *can't*.

Distortions of time-sense. ADDers have an exaggerated sense of urgency when they're working on something and an exaggerated sense of boredom when they have nothing interesting to do.

Difficulty following directions. A new theory on this aspect holds that ADDers have difficulty processing auditory or verbal information. A major aspect of this difficulty involves the very-common reports of parents of ADD kids who say their kids love to watch TV and hate to read.

Daydreaming, falling into depressions, or having mood swings.

Take risks. ADDers seem to make faster decisions than non-ADDers. This is why Wilson Harrell and Thom Hartmann, former publisher of *Inc.* magazine and author of *For Entrepreneurs Only*, conclude that the vast majority of successful entrepreneurs probably have ADD! They call them "Hunters," as opposed to the more staid "Farmer" types.

Easily frustrated and impatient. ADDers do not beat around the bush or suffer fools gladly. They are direct and to the point. When things aren't working, "Do something!" is the ADD rallying cry, even if that something is a bad idea.

Why ADD kids have trouble in school

First and foremost, says Thom Hartmann, it's because schools are set up for "Farmers"—sit at a desk, do what you're told, watch and listen to the teacher. This is hell for "Hunters" with ADD. The bigger the class size, the worse it becomes. Kids with ADD, remember, are easily distracted, easily bored, easily turned off, always ready to move on.

What should you look for in a school setting to make it more palatable to an ADDer? What can you do at home to help your child (or yourself)? Hartmann has some solid answers.

☞ **Learning must be project- and experience-based**, providing more opportunities for creativity and smaller "bites" of information. Many "gifted" programs offer exactly such opportunities. The problem for many kids with ADD is that they've spent years in non-gifted, Farmer-type classroom settings and may be labeled with underachieving behavior problems, effectively shut out of the programs virtually designed for them! Many parents report that children diagnosed as ADD, who failed miserably in public school, thrived in private school. Hartmann attributes this to the smaller classrooms, more individual attention with specific goal-setting, project-based learning, and similar methods common in such schools. These factors are just what make ADD kids thrive!

☞ **Create a weekly performance template** on which *both* teacher and parent chart the child's performance, positive and negative. "Creating such a larger-than-the-child system," claims Hartmann, "will help keep ADD children on task and on time."

☞ **Encourage special projects for extra credit.** Projects give ADDers the chance to learn in the mode that's most appropriate to them. They will also give such kids the chance to make up for the "boring" homework they sometimes simply can't make themselves do.

☞ **Stop labeling them "disordered."** Kids react to labels, especially negative ones, even more than adults. Saying "you have a deficit and a disorder" may be more destructive than useful.

☞ **Think twice about medication**, but don't discard it as an option. Hartmann has a very real concern about the long-term side effects of the drugs normally prescribed for ADDers. He also notes that they may well be more at risk to be substance abusers as adults, so starting them on medication at a young age sends a very mixed message. On the other hand, if an ADD child cannot have his or her special needs met in a classroom, *not* medicating him or her may be a disaster. "The relatively unknown long-term risks of drug therapy," says Hartmann, "may be more than offset by the short-term benefits of improved classroom performance."

Specific suggestions about reading

☞ **Practice, practice, practice.** ADDers will tend to have trouble reading, preferring visual stimulation to the "boring" words. Turn off the TV. Minimize the time spent with the Gameboy or with Nintendo. ADDers may well be extraordinarily focused on such visual input and stimulating games, but only to the detriment of their schoolwork. Where possible, though, utilize videos, computers, interactive multimedia, and other forms of communication more attuned to ADDers to help them learn. There is a tremendous amount of educational software and CD-ROM material that may work better for ADDers than traditional printed books.

However, ADDers must obviously learn to read and practice reading. I would suggest finding a professional or a program to deal with your or your child's probable reading problems. Anything you can do to make reading more fun and interesting should be explored.

☞ **Break everything into specific goal units.** ADDers are very goal-oriented; as soon as they reach one, it's on to the next. Reestablishing very short-term, "bite-size" goals is essential. Make goals specific, definable, and measurable, and stick to only one priority at a time.

☞ **Create distraction-free zones.** Henry David Thoreau (who evidently suffered from ADD, by the way) was so desperate to escape distraction he moved to isolated Walden Pond. Organize your time and workspace to create your own "Walden Pond," especially when you have to read, write, take notes, or study. ADDers need silence, so consider the library. Another tip: Clean your work area thoroughly at the end of each day.

☞ **Train your attention span.** ADDers will probably never be able to train themselves to ignore distractions totally, but a variety of meditation techniques might help them stay focused longer.

☞ **Utilize short-term rewards.** ADD salespeople don't do well when a sales contest lasts for six months, even if the reward is, say, a 10-day cruise. But stick a $100 bill on the wall and watch them focus! Those with ADD are not motivated by rewards that are too ephemeral or too far in the future. They live for the here and now and need to be rewarded immediately.

CHAPTER 11

BUILD YOUR OWN LIBRARY

"The reading of all good books is like conversation with the finest men of past centuries."

—Descartes

If you are ever to become an active, avid reader, access to books will do much to cultivate the habit. I suggest you "build" your own library. Your selections can and should reflect your own tastes and interests, but try to make them wide and varied. Include some of the classics, contemporary fiction, poetry, and biography.

Save your high school and college texts—you'll be amazed at how some of the material retains its relevance. And try to read a good newspaper every day so as to keep current and informed.

Your local librarian can refer you to any number of lists of the "great books," most of which are available in inexpensive paperback editions. Here are four more lists—compiled by yours truly—of the "great" classical authors; the "great" not-so-classical authors, poets, and playwrights; some contemporary "pretty greats," and my own selection of "great" books.

You may want to incorporate these on your buy list, especially if you're planning a summer reading program.

I'm sure that I have left off someone's favorite author or "important" title from these lists. So be it. They are not meant to be comprehensive, just relatively representative. I doubt anyone would disagree that a person familiar with the majority of authors and works listed would be considered well-read!

Who are Derek Walcott, Nadine Gor-dimer, Kenzaburo Oe, Octavio Paz, and Camilo Jose Cela? All winners of the Nobel Prize for Literature (1989 to 1994, plus Toni Morrison in 1993). I'm willing to bet a year's royalties not one of you reading this has heard of more than one of them (with the exception of Ms. Morrison). So how do *you* define great if these award-winners are so anonymous? I include this merely to dissuade another 200 or so letters castigating me for those authors or works I *did* include here.

Some "great" classical authors

Aeschylus
Aesop
Aquinas
Aristophanes
Aristotle
Balzac
Boccaccio
Burke
Cervantes
Chaucer
Cicero
Confucius
Dante
Descartes
Dewey
Emerson
Erasmus
Flaubert
Goethe
Hegel
Homer
Horace
J. Caesar
Kant
Machiavelli
Milton
Montaigne
Nietzsche
Ovid
Pindar
Plato
Plutarch
Rousseau
S. Johnson
Santayana
Shakespeare
Spinoza
Swift
Vergil
Voltaire

Some other "great" authors

Sherwood Anderson
W.H. Auden
Samuel Beckett
Brandan Behan
William Blake
Bertolt Brecht
Charlotte Bronte
Emily Bronte
Pearl Buck
Lord Byron
Albert Camus
Lewis Carroll
Joseph Conrad
e.e. cummings
Daniel Defoe
Charles Dickens
Emily Dickinson
Feodor Dostoevski
Arthur Conan Doyle
Theodore Dreiser
Alexandre Dumas
George Eliot
T.S. Eliot
William Faulkner
Edna Ferber
F. Scott Fitzgerald
E.M. Forster
Robert Frost
John Galsworthy
Jose Ortega y Gasset
Nikolai Gogol
Maxim Gorki
Thomas Hardy
Nathaniel Hawthorne
Ernest Hemingway
Hermann Hesse
Victor Hugo
Aldous Huxley
Washington Irving
William James
James Joyce
Franz Kafka
M.M. Kaye
John Keats
Rudyard Kipling
D.H. Lawrence
H.W. Longfellow
James Russell Lowell
Thomas Mann
W. Somerset Maugham
Herman Melville
H.L. Mencken
Henry Miller
H.H. Munro (Saki)
Vladimir Nabokov
O. Henry
Eugene O'Neill
George Orwell
Dorothy Parker
Edgar Allan Poe
Ezra Pound
Marcel Proust
Ellery Queen
Ayn Rand
Erich Maria Remarque
Bertrand Russell

J.D. Salinger
George Sand
Carl Sandburg
William Saroyan
Jean Paul Sartre
George Bernard Shaw
Percy Bysshe Shelley
Upton Sinclair
Aleksandr I. Solzhenitsyn
Gertrude Stein
Robert Louis Stevenson
Dylan Thomas
James Thurber
J.R.R. Tolkien
Leo Tolstoy
Ivan Turgenev
Mark Twain
Robert Penn Warren
Evelyn Waugh
H.G. Wells
Walt Whitman
Oscar Wilde
Thornton Wilder
Tennessee Williams
P.G. Wodehouse
Thomas Wolfe
William Wordworth
William Butler Yeats
Emile Zola

Some "pretty great" contemporary authors

Edward Albee
Isaac Asimov
John Barth
Saul Bellow
T. Coraghessan Boyle
Anthony Burgess
Truman Capote
John Cheever
Don DeLillo
Pete Dexter
E.L. Doctorow
William Gaddis
William Golding
Robert Heinlein
Joseph Heller
Lillian Hellman
John Hersey
Oscar Hijuelos
Jerzy Kozinski
Norman Mailer
Bernard Malamud
Gabriel Garcia Marquez
Cormac McCarthy
Toni Morrison
Joyce Carol Oates
Flannery O'Connor
Thomas Pynchon
Philip Roth
Isaac Bashevis Singer
Jane Smiley

Wallace Stegner
Rex Stout
William Styron
Anne Tyler
John Updike
Alice Walker
Eudora Welty

Some "great" works

The Adventures of Huckleberry Finn
The Adventures of Tom Sawyer
The Aeneid
Aesop's Fables
Alice In Wonderland
All Quiet On the Western Front
An American Tragedy
Animal Farm
Anna Karenina
Arrowsmith
Atlas Shrugged
As I Lay Dying
Babbitt
The Bell Jar
Beloved
The Bonfire of the Vanities
Brave New World
The Brothers Karamazov
The Canterbury Tales
Catch-22
The Catcher In the Rye
Chimera
Confessions of an English Opium Eater
The Confessions of Nat Turner
The Count of Monte Cristo
Crime and Punishment
David Copperfield
Death Crimes for the Archbishop
Death of a Salesman
The Deerslayer
Demian
Don Juan
Don Quixote
Ethan Fromme
Far From the Maddening Crowd
A Farewell to Arms
The Federalist Papers
The Fixer
For Whom the Bell Tolls
The Foundation
A Good Scent From a Strange Mountain
The Good Earth
The Grapes of Wrath
Gravity's Rainbow

The Great Gatsby
Gulliver's Travels
Hamlet
Heart of Darkness
The Hound of Baskervilles
I, Claudius
The Idiot
The Iliad
The Immortalist
The Invisible Man
Jane Eyre
JR
Julius Caesar
Kim
King Lear
Lady Chatterley's Lover
"Leaves of Grass"
The Legend of Sleepy Hollow
Les Miserables
A Lesson Before Dying
A Long Day's Journey Into Night
Look Homeward, Angel
Lord Jim
The Lord of the Rings
MacBeth
The Magic Mountain
Main Street
Man and Superman
The Merchant of Venice
The Metamorphosis
Moby Dick
Mother Courage
Native Son
1984
Of Human Bondage
Of Mice and Men
The Old Man and the Sea
Oliver Twist
One Flew Over the Cuckoo's Nest
The Optimist's Daughter
Othello
Our Town
Paradise Lost
The Pickwick Papers
The Picture of Dorian Gray
A Portrait of the Artist as a Young Man
Portrait of a Lady
Pride and Prejudice
The Prophet
Ragtime
"The Raven"
The Red Badge of Courage
The Remembrance of Things Past
The Return of the Native
"The Road Not Taken"
Robinson Crusoe
Romeo and Juliet
The Scarlet Letter
The Shipping News
Siddhartha
Silas Marner

Sister Carrie
Sophie's Choice
The Sound and the Fury
Steppenwolf
A Streetcar Named Desire
The Sun Also Rises
The Tale of Genji
A Tale of Two Cities
Tender Is the Night
The Thin Red Line
The Time Machine
A Thousand Acres
Tom Jones
The Trial
Ulysses
Vanity Fair
Walden
War and Peace
"The Wasteland"
Winesburg, Ohio
Wuthering Heights

Reading every one of these books will undoubtedly make you a better reader; it will certainly make you well-read. The added bonus to establishing such a reading program is an appreciation of certain authors, books, cultural events, and the like that separates the cultured from the merely educated and the undereducated.

Read on and enjoy!

Chapter 12

Reading: A Lifelong Activity

And further, by these, my son, be admonished: of making many books there is no end...

—Solomon (*Ecclesiastes* 12:12)

Well, you made it through another book. I hope you found the motivation—whether intrinsic or extrinsic—to define your purpose, discern the important details, grasp the main idea, and retain what you read. I promised not to preach about the joys of reading. And I haven't...too much.

Your need to read—and comprehend and retain what you read—will not end when you graduate from school.

Planning on working? From the very first week, when you're handed the company policy guide, you'll be expected to seek out the facts—like what happens if you're late more than twice.

You'll be required to read critically—and know what statements like, "Our dress code requires professional attire at all times," mean.

Business proposals, annual reports, patient charts, corporate profiles, product reports, sales reports, budget proposals, business plans, resumes, complaint letters, interoffice memos—no matter what type of work you do, you won't be able to avoid the avalanche of paper and required reading that accompanies it.

Not only will your job require the ability to read and comprehend, but so will other facets of your life. If you plan to own your home, wait until you see the pile of paperwork you'll have to wade through.

Credit card applications? Better read the fine print to make sure you know when your payment is due...and how much interest you're paying on that brand-new TV.

Insurance policies, appliance warranties, local ordinances, newspapers, membership applications, and tax forms—it seems like any goal you pursue in your life will require you to scale mountains of reading material.

For your own best interest, you must be prepared to read—and understand.

I wish you the greatest possible success in your future reading pursuits, of which there will be many...throughout your life.

Book 3

Improve Your Memory

CHAPTER 1

THANK YOU, ZBIGNIEW

Which do you think you're more likely to remember—your first date with your future spouse (even if it was decades ago) or what you had for breakfast last Thursday?

Probably the former (though not if last Thursday was your first experiment with yak butter).

Which event conjures up the most memories—the Blizzard of 1996 or the last time it rained (unless, of course, it *really* poured cats and dogs)?

Which name would you find difficult to forget—Joe Smith or Zbigniew Brzezinski? We'll deal with how to remember *spelling* old Zbig later.

What do all the "memorable" names, dates, places, and events have in common? The fact that they're *different*. What makes something memorable is its *extra*ordinariness, how much it differs from our normal experiences.

The reason so many of us forget where we put the car keys or our eyeglasses is that putting these objects down is the most ordinary of occurrences, part and parcel of the most humdrum aspects of our lives. We have trouble remembering facts and formulas from books and classroom lectures for the same reason. To be schooled is to be bombarded with facts day in and day out. How do you make those facts memorable? (By the way, has anyone seen my glasses?)

Beef up your RAM

In order to understand how to make the important facts memorable, how to keep them stored safely at least until final exams, let's first take a look at how the brain and, more specifically, memory works.

I'm going to call upon a rather useful, and for that reason somewhat overused analogy, and ask you to think of your brain as that computer you typed your last paper on—an organic computer, wired with nerves, hooked up to various INPUT devices (your five senses), and possessed of both ROM (read-only memory) and RAM (random access memory).

The ROM is the data you can't touch—the disk operating system, the information that tells your heart to pump and your lungs to breathe.

RAM, on the other hand, is much more accessible. Like most PCs nowadays, your brain stores RAM in two places: *short-term* memory (those old 1.44 mb disks you've been meaning to trash) and *long-term* memory (that 20-gigabyte baby on the hard drive).

Okay, so what happens to INPUT in this system?

A matter of choice

Given the bombardment of data we receive every day, our brains constantly are making choices. Data either goes in one ear and out the other, or it stops in short-term memory. But when that old floppy disk gets full, the brain is left with a choice—jettison some old information or pass it on to the hard drive.

How does it make a decision *which* information to pass on and *where* to store it?

Well, scientists aren't positive about this yet, but, of course, they have theories.

The most readily stored and accessed is data that's been *rehearsed*—gone over again and again. Most of us readily access our knowledge of how to read, how to drive, the year Columbus "discovered" America, the name of the first President of the United States and other basics without any difficulty at all. (At worst, you remember "Columbus sailed the ocean blue in 1492.") We've worn familiar paths through our memory banks accessing this type of information or skill.

Why, then, can some people recite the names, symbols, and atomic weights of the elements of the periodic table—while they're playing (and winning) *Trivial Pursuit*—as easily as they can the date of Columbus's dubious achievement?

To return to our computer analogy, this information has gotten "tagged" or "coded" in some way so that it can be easily retrieved by the user. For instance, before storing a file in your computer's long-term RAM, you give it a name, one that will easily conjure what exactly that file is. In other words, you make the file *stand out* in some way from the host of other files you've stored on your disk drive.

For some people, myriad bits of data are almost automatically tagged so that they can be quite easily and handily stored and retrieved. But most of us, if we are to have exceptional memories, must make a special effort.

Twist and shout...and remember

First and foremost, there are three very different kinds of memory—visual, verbal, and kinesthetic, *each* of which can be strong or weak and only the first two of which are associated with your *brain.*

Most people have the easiest time strengthening their *visual* memories, which is why so many memory techniques involve forming "mental pictures."

To strengthen our verbal memories, we use rhymes, songs, letter substitutions, and other mnemonic gimmicks.

Finally, don't underestimate the importance of kinesthetic memory, or what your *body* remembers. Athletes and dancers certainly don't have to be convinced that the muscles, joints, and tendons of their bodies seem to have their own memories. Neither does anyone who's ever remembered a phone number by moving his fingers and "remembering" how it's dialed.

The next time you have to remember a list, any list, say each item out loud and move some part of your body at the same time. A dancer can do the time step and remember her history lecture. A baseball pitcher can associate each movement of his wind up with another item in a list he has to memorize. Even random body movements will do. For example, if you have to memorize a list of countries, just associate each one with a specific movement. For "Burundi," lift your right index finger while saying it. For "Zimbabwe," rotate your neck. Bend a knee for "Equador" and raise your left hand for "San Marino." Kick "Latvia" in the shins and twirl your hair for "Guinea-Bissau." When you have to remember this list of countries, just start moving! It may look a little strange—especially if you make your movements a little too exotic or dramatic in the middle of geography class—but if it works better than anything else for *you*, who cares?

You can also use this new-found memory as a backup to your brain. You may still memorize key phone numbers, for example, but you may also accompany each recitation with the hand movements necessary to actually dial the number. You'll probably find that even if you forget the "mental" tricks you used, your "body memory" will run (or lift or squat or bend or shake!) to the rescue!

Woe unto the poor memorizer

Students, of course, must possess or develop good memories or they risk mediocrity or failure. The mere act of getting by in school means remembering a lot of dates, mathematical and scientific formulas, historical events, characters and plots, sometimes entire poems. (I had a whacko biology teacher who made us memorize the 52 parts of a frog's body. All of which, of course, have been absolutely essential to my subsequent career success. Not.)

There are two practical plans of attack. The most familiar is rehearsal or repetition. By any name, it is the process of reading or pronouncing something over and over until you've learned it "by heart." (I really didn't want to hold the parts of a frog *too* close to my heart, though.)

But a much easier way—getting back to our computer analogy—is to tag or code things we are trying to remember and to do so with images and words that are either outrageous or very familiar.

For instance, have you ever wondered how, in the days before index cards, ballpoint pens, or TelePrompTers, troubadours memorized song cycles and politicians memorized lengthy speeches? Well, in the case of the great Roman orator Cicero, it was a matter of associating the parts of his speeches with the most familiar objects in his life—the rooms of his home. Perhaps the opening of a speech would be linked to his bed chamber, the next part to his yard. As he progressed through the speech, he would, in essence, mentally take his usual morning stroll passing through the rooms of his home.

In other cases, more outrageous associations work much better. The more ridiculous or impossible the association, the more memorable it is. Absent-mindedness is not one of the problems we will try to solve in this book, but a common cure for it illustrates my point.

If you frequently have trouble remembering, say, where you put down your pen, get into the habit of conjuring up some startling image *linking* (a key word later on in this book) the pen and the place. For example, as you're putting your pen down on the kitchen table, think about eating peas off a plate with it or of the pen sticking straight up in a pile of mashed potatoes. Even days later, when you think, "Hmm, where did I leave that ballpoint?" the peas and plate (or mashed potatoes) will come to mind, reminding you of the kitchen table.

The rest is easy

These are the essential principles of memory for which the computer analogy is particularly apt. After all, when dealing with the mind, as with the machine, the GIGO (garbage in, garbage out) rule applies. If you passively allow your brain's process to decide what and how items are stored, you will have a jumbled memory, from which it is difficult to extract even essential bits of knowledge.

On the other hand, if you are selective and careful about assigning useful tags to the items headed for the long-term memory banks, you are on the way to being able to memorize the Manhattan telephone directory!

CHAPTER 2

AND NOW FOR A LITTLE QUIZ

I know what you're thinking. You bought this book so you could improve your memory and perform better on exams and those darned pop quizzes, and now I turn around and throw some *more* tests your way. I could note that "them's the breaks!"

Or as one of my high school teachers used to say, I could encourage you to think of tests as your best friends (no, it wasn't the crazy biology teacher I told you about in Chapter 1). In this book, and throughout your academic career, tests will give you the measure of how far you've come...and how far you've got to go. Follow the advice in this book and your score on similar tests in the last chapter should be 25 percent higher.

Test 1: Numbers

Look at the number directly following this paragraph for no more than 10 seconds. Then, cover the page (or better yet, close the book and put it aside) and write down as much of it—in order—as you can.

674216899411539273

Test 2: Words and definitions

Following are 15 obscure words along with their definitions. Study this list for 60 seconds. Then, cover it up and take the test directly below the list. Allow yourself no more than 90 seconds to complete the quiz...and no peeking.

Dorp	A village.
Ridley	A gray or olive-colored sea turtle.
Afflatus	Inspiration, especially as a result of divine communication.
Baize	A soft feltlike fabric, usually dyed green, commonly used for the tops of game tables.
Wittol	A man who knows of and tolerates his wife's infidelity.
Incult	Rude; unrefined.
Nidation	Implantation of an embryo in the lining of the uterus.
Pecky	(Of timber) Spotted with fungi.
Sclaff	In golf, to scrape the ground with the head of the club just before impact with the ball.

Linguica A highly spiced Portuguese garlic sausage.

Venatic Of or pertaining to hunting.

Falcate Curved like a scythe or sickle; hooked.

Guerdon A reward; recompense.

Kegler A participant in a bowling game.

Zymurgy The branch of applied chemistry dealing with fermentation, as in winemaking or brewing.

Have you studied the words diligently? Okay, no cheating now, fill in the blanks:

1. Nobody understood why the________remained married to his adulterous wife.
2. Winemaking requires a knowledge of_______.
3. ________means "curved."
4. A Portuguese food is_________.
5. Something pertaining to hunting is_________.
6. Another word for rude is___________.
7. Even professional golfers tend to___________.
8. Would you like to be a_______in the bowling match tomorrow?
9. Joe did such a good job on his assignment that his teacher offered him a___________.
10. Which turtle can be gray-colored?___________.
11. The bark of a log can be_____________.
12. The pool table was covered with___________.
13. Nidation occurs where?____________.
14. The worshipper was seeking________in his time of need.
15. I come from a quiet and traditional_________.

Test 3: Names

Take three minutes to memorize the names of the following authors and their Pulitzer Prize-winning books:

Ironweed / William Kennedy
Lonesome Dove / Larry McMurtry
A Thousand Acres / Jane Smiley
The Shipping News / E. Annie Proulx
The Killer Angels / Michael Shaara
Humboldt's Gift / Saul Bellow
The Optimist's Daughter / Eudora Welty
The Fixer / Bernard Malamud
The Executioner's Song / Norman Mailer
Beloved / Toni Morrison
Elbow Room / James Alan McPherson
House Made of Dawn / N. Scott Momaday

Time's up! Okay, cover the list and fill in as many of the blanks as you can. If you get last names only, that's fine. Take another three minutes to complete the quiz:

1. *Lonesome Dove*____________________
2. *Ironweed*____________________________
3. James Alan McPherson__________________
4. *A Thousand Acres*______________________
5. *House Made of Dawn*____________________
6. *The Shipping News*_____________________
7. Saul Bellow___________________________
8. *The Fixer*____________________________
9. *The Killer Angels*______________________
10. Eudora Welty_________________________
11. *The Executioner's Song*__________________
12. Toni Morrison_________________________

Test 4: Dates

Here are the dates of 12 historical events. Take up to three minutes to memorize them, then cover the page and take the quiz below.

1958	Khrushchev assumed sole power in USSR.
1888	Playwright Maxwell Anderson born.
1940	Arthur Koestler published *Darkness at Noon.*
1977	Republic of Djibouti became independent.
1771	Gustavus III became king of Sweden.
1118	Approximately when Knights Templar order was founded.
1967	Folksinger Woody Guthrie died.
1844	Kierkegaard published *Philosophical Fragments.*
1942	Sir Alexander Korda became first filmmaker ever knighted.
1969	King Idris I overthrown in Libya.
1975	Khalid Ibn Abdul-Aziz acceded to Saudi Arabian throne.
1763	French and Indian Wars ended.

1. Woody Guthrie died in ____________.
2. The Republic of ____________ became independent in ______.
3. The Knights ________ order was founded around _______.
4. _______ Anderson was born in ______.
5. Khrushchev assumed sole power in the USSR in ______.

6. *Philosophical Fragments* by ________was published in ________.
7. Gustavus III became king of ________in ____.
8. The first filmmaker ever knighted was Sir ______________, in __________.
9. The ______and Indian Wars ended in ________.
10. King Idris I was overthrown in _____.
11. Arthur _______published his book in ______.
12. Khalid Ibn __________acceded to the throne in _____.

Test 5: Reading retention

Read the text below, then answer the questions following. Give yourself two minutes to read the text and two minutes to answer the questions *without referring back to the paragraph*!

> Although William Sheridan Allen asserts that only one resident of Norheim in 100 would have joined the Nazi Party if they knew of Hitler's ultimate plans, the National Socialist German Worker's Party nevertheless managed to gain more popular support in the early 1930s than any of the other political parties struggling for power in the turmoil left by World War I.
>
> The social conditions of this period made the people of Norheim, Germany, ready to accept Nazi ideals. By 1930, Norheim was beginning to reel from the growing depression that had blanketed Germany. The middle class's bank accounts were already nearly wiped out after years of increased taxes, tight credit, and mass inflation. Unemployment was increasing every month. Financial

dependence on the government was at an all-time high; the government's ability to take care of its citizenry at an all-time low. Norheim and many of the hundreds of other towns and cities just like it were soon ready to follow any leader or party they believed could deliver a dose of economic stability.

The NSDAP, however, faced serious obstacles in its rise to dominance. Neither the Communists (KDP) nor Social Democrats (SPD) were willing to cede their power to the upstart Nazis. But the Nazis skillfully exploited both the biases of the citizenry and the weaknesses of the other parties. Masking their real intentions, the Nazis started slowly, using religion and nationalism to recruit new members. In Norheim, recruiting speeches were often given by local ministers and the Party featured weekly cultural events.

In Norheim, however, the biggest attraction of the upstarts was their anti-Marxist rhetoric; its citizens generally distrusted the SPD because of their "insistent class consciousness." As problems in Russia developed through 1930 and 1931, this distrust only accelerated Norheimers' move to the more radical Nazis.

But no analysis of the rise of Nazism can fail to give large credit to their mastery of propaganda. In this regard, the local party's recruitment methods in Norheim could serve as a paradigm for the rest of Germany. Speeches were always carefully targeted to the particular audience; Nazi leaders had no problems shouting exactly what their listeners wanted to hear. Admission prices to Nazi events were even adjusted according to that particular audience's ability to pay, and small halls were always rented to heighten the illusion that large numbers of people were always in attendance at Nazi events. From 1925 to 1928, for example, the targeted workers heard mainly anti-Semitic propaganda. The middle class in 1929 and the unemployed, Lutherans, and small businesspeople added as "targeted classes" in 1930 all received different targeted messages and different treatment. The threat of boycotts, for example, was especially effective with small farmers and businessmen.

Public displays played a major role in convincing the people of Norheim that the NSDAP was the party of the future. Public exhibitions—parades, torchlight processions, and open-air speeches (declared illegal by the Prussian government)—made the Nazis seem larger and more popular than they actually were, at least in 1930. Dues-paying members were always significantly outnumbered by supporters, sympathizers, and hangers-on, so that the perceived Nazi movement was always far larger than the real one.

Questions

1. The writer's primary purpose in this selection is to:

A. Describe social conditions in Norheim, Germany.
B. Explain causes for the rise of Nazism.
C. Discuss the emphasis of anti-Semitism in Nazi propaganda.
D. Discuss types of propaganda employed in Europe.
E. Compare the Social Democrat party to the Nazi party.

2. The author asserts that the Nazis:

A. Worked alongside the other political parties to provide economic stability.
B. Pioneered many social reforms and created jobs.
C. Tried to make themselves seem lesser in number than they were, to promote a feeling of intimacy.
D. Were responsible for the depression after WWI.
E. Were masters of propaganda.

3. Which of the following ideas *cannot* be inferred from the passage?

A. NSDAP are the German initials of the Nazi party.
B. Norheim was in Prussia.
C. Citizens sought religion and nationalism.
D. The Nazi party's exploitation of weaknesses of the other parties caused them to become unpopular.
E. All of the above.

4. The phrase "insistent class consciousness" refers directly to:

A. The KDP.
B. Unemployed businesspeople.
C. The SPD.
D. The NSDAP.
E. Lutherans.

5. The passage states that the Nazi party offered:

A. Weekly cultural events.
B. Decreased taxes.
C. The same type of propaganda to all social classes.
D. Long-established traditions.
E. Financial support.

To check how you did in this last test section, see the answers at the end of this chapter. Go back and check the passage itself to figure out the answers to the others.

How did you do?

Take a piece of paper and write down the scores you got on each of these exercises. This will indicate how much improvement you need to successfully recall the material you learn in school. It will also provide a benchmark so that you can see how far you've come when you take similar quizzes in the last chapter.

The emphasis of these tests was not arbitrary. It corresponds exactly to the skills you will be learning throughout this book: memorizing chains of information (such as the book/author and the date/event pairings), developing a sense for numbers, remembering what you read, and getting a better grasp on vocabulary.

Answers to Test 5: 1. B, 2. E, 3. D, 4. C, 5. A

CHAPTER 3

ROY G. BIV AND FRIENDS

In Chapter 1, we talked about the need to establish tags or codes for items we wish to remember so our minds will have relatively little difficulty retrieving them from long-term memory.

In this chapter, we will begin talking about one of the methods used for "tagging" items *before they enter* that morass of memory.

The "chain-link" method will help you remember items that appear in sequence, whether it's the association of a date with an event, a scientific term with its meaning, or other facts or objects that are supposed to "go together."

The basis for the chain-link system is that memory works best when you associate the unfamiliar with the familiar, though sometimes the association may be very odd. But to really make it effective, the odder the better.

Our boy Roy

One of the simplest methods is to try to remember just the first letter of a sequence. That's how "Roy G. Biv" (the colors of the spectrum, in order from left to right—red, orange, yellow, green, blue, indigo, violet) got famous. Or "Every Good Boy Does Fine," to remember the notes on a musical staff. Or perhaps the simplest of all, "FACE," to remember the notes in between. (The latter two work opposite of old Roy—using *words* to remember *letters.*) Of course, not many sequences work out so nicely. If you tried to memorize the signs of the zodiac with this method, you'd wind up with (A)ries, (T)aurus, (G)emini, (C)ancer, (L)eo, (V)irgo, (L)ibra, (S)corpio, (S)agittarius, (C)apricorn, (A)quarius, (P)isces. Now maybe you can make a name or a place or something out of ATGCLVLSSCAP, but I can't!

One solution is to make up a simple sentence that uses the first letters of the list you're trying to remember as the first letters of each word. For example, "**A** **T**all **G**iraffe **C**hewed **L**eaves **V**ery **L**ow, **S**ome **S**low **C**ows **A**t **P**lay."

Wait a minute! It's the same number of words. Why not just figure out some way to memorize the first set of words? What's better about the second set? A couple of things. First of all, it's easier to picture the giraffe and cow and what they're doing. As we'll soon see, creating such mental images is a very powerful way to remember almost anything. Second, because the words in our sentence bear some relationship to each other, they're much easier to remember. Go ahead, try it. See how long it takes you to memorize the sentence vs. all the signs. This method is especially easy when you remember some or all of the items but *don't* remember their *order*.

Remember: Make your sentence(s) memorable to *you*. *Any* sentence or series of words that helps you remember these letters will do. Here are just two more I created in a few seconds: "**A** **T**all **G**irl **C**alled **L**ively **V**era **L**oved to **S**ip **S**odas from **C**ans **A**nd **P**lates. **A**ny **T**iny **G**erbil **C**ould **L**ove **V**enus. **L**ong **S**illy **S**nakes **C**ould **A**ll **P**ray." Isn't it easy to make up memorably silly pictures in your head for these?

The rain in Spain

Let's say that I was a literature major who wanted to remember that Vladimir Nabakov published *Lolita,* his most famous novel, in 1958.

The usual way for me to do this would be to repeat over and over again, "*Lolita,* 1958, *Lolita,* 1958..." *ad nauseam.* How much easier it would be to just say, "Lolita was my date in '58"! I've established a link between Lolita, the coquettish girl of Nabakov's novel, the date of publication, and some imaginary Saturday night special date. (You'll learn more about how to remember dates in Chapter 8).

In addition, I was able to use another terrific memory technique—rhyming. Rhyme schemes, no matter how silly or banal, can help us remember things for years. For instance, who can forget that it's "*i* before *e* except after *c*, or when it sounds like *a* as in *neighbor* and *weigh*"?

The stranger the better

Let's step away from schoolwork for a moment to consider the case of a woman who can't remember where she puts anything—car keys, wallet, her month-old baby (just kidding!).

Using the chain-link method would ensure that she would never forget. For instance, let's say she puts her car keys down on her kitchen counter and, as she does, thinks of a car plowing right into the kitchen and through the countertop. Will that woman be able to forget what she did with her keys? Would you?

Or, to pick an example more germane to academic life, let's say that you wanted to remember that *mitosis* is the process whereby one cell divides itself into two. Instead of repeating word and definition countless times, why not think, "My toes is dividing," and form a mental picture of two of your toes separating? Much easier, isn't it?

Where in the world is...?

The best way to teach this technique is by example, so let's take another one. Suppose you wanted to remember the following list of 10 relatively obscure world capitals (and, of course, the countries they go with): Tirana (Algeria), Belmopan (Belize), Thimphu (Bhutan), Suva (Fiji), Brazzaville (Congo), Moroni (The Comoros), Accra (Ghana), Muscat (Oman), Valletta (Malta), Funafuti (Tuvalu).

Study the list for no more than two minutes, cover up the page, and try to write down as many combinations as you remember. Heck, you don't even have to do them in order (but you get serious extra credit if you do!).

Time's up

How did you do? Did you get them all right? How long do you think you'd have to study this list to be able to recite it perfectly? I guarantee you it would take a lot less time if you established a chain link that you could just reel in out of your memory bank.

Following are the associations and pictures I would use to remember this list (and remember, make your pictures memorable to *you*!):

Tirana (Algeria): Being a New Yorker, the thing that immediately came to mind was the *Tawana* Brawley case in which Rev. *Al* Sharpton was involved. I'd remember a picture of the Reverend being *jeered* when it was discovered the whole thing was a hoax.

Belmopan (Belize): Picture *Elmo* from *Sesame Street* wearing a big *B* on his chest (hence *Belmo*) while holding a pan and begging you to take it (*Puleeze*!).

Thimphu (Bhutan): Thimphu is a *thimble* trying on a *tan boot*. Picture it on the pan Elmo is holding to make it really memorable!

Suva (Fiji): I'd remember the Indian god *Siva* being very nervous (*fidgeting*).

Brazzaville (Congo): So happens I once worked with an author named Jerry *Braza*. I'd picture him in his *villa* playing his *bongo*.

Moroni (The Comoros): The *Commodores* (an old singing group for those of you under 30!) eating *macaroni*.

Accra (Ghana): "The water (*agua*) is *gone*."

Muscat (Oman): *Muskrat! Oh, my*! You can always combine these last two, picturing yourself looking for water, finding none, then seeing a fat muskrat grinning with water rolling down his cheeks. (Remember, I *said* strange.)

Valetta (Malta)—To make it really weird, the muskrat's *valet, Walter* is standing at attention, waiting to dress him. (See the next one; it's gets better.)

Funafuti (Tuvalu)—That's right, he's dressing him in that *fun* and *fruity* vest from *True Value* hardware stores!

Got all that? Okay, let's put it all together into a single string. Now it really gets strange:

So you're standing on a street corner watching Reverend Al getting jeered while he talks about Tawana. Elmo runs in front of him, carrying a pan that holds a thimble trying on a tan boot. To the right, there's Siva fidgeting in front of Jerry Braza's villa, where he's playing the bongos to accompany the Commodores while they sing and eat macaroni. (This has all made me very thirsty, so...) I look for some water, only to find it's gone. The muskrat drank it. And there he is (oh my!) while his valet, Walter, stands by, waiting to dress him in his fun and fruity vest from True Value.

Is this efficient?

You're probably wondering just how much time it took me to construct these ridiculous associations and the even more bizarre story to go with them. The answer: about three minutes. I'll bet it will take you a lot longer to memorize the list of capitals and countries. And my way of doing this is so much more fun! Not only that, but I'd be willing to bet that you'll remember "that muskrat and his valet" a lot longer than "Muscat" and "Valetta."

The reason is that you use so much more of your brain when you employ techniques like this. Reciting a list of facts over and over to yourself uses only three of your faculties—sight (as you read them from the page), speech, and hearing—in carving the memory trail. Constructing a bizarre story like the one we just did also puts to work your imagination, perhaps the most powerful of your mind's many powers.

How the French do it

Let's try another example, one with which I doubt you are at all familiar—the French Revolutionary calendar: Brumaire, Floréal, Frimaire, Fructidore, Germinal, Messidor, Nivôse, Pluviôse, Prairiel, Thermidor, Vendémiaire, Ventôse.

Here's the way I would remember: There'd be a big *broom* sweeping through the *air* across a field of *flowers*. That's the first picture—two down (Brumaire, Floréal).

Now the broom would turn into a *frying pan* flying through the *air* (Frimaire).

Suddenly a refrigerator (naturally a Frigidaire) would open (Fructidore) and out would pop my friends Germ and Al (Germinal). They'd yell at me, "Hey, why have you got such a *messy door*?" (Messidor).

Well, people yelling at me make me *nervous* (Nivôse) so I'd stammer, "*Pl*ease, *you've* t*oas*ted me!" (Pluviôse).

So I got down on some *rail*road tracks to *pray* (Prairiel) until a giant Lobster *Thermidor* came tumbling down in a *vend*ing machine, right out of the *air* (Vendémiaire).

The smell went right to my nose (Ventôse).

Immediately after making up this story, I turned away from the computer and, without even trying, recited the words I was supposed to have just memorized. It's that easy.

Now you try. How would you remember another obscure list, like this longer one of alphabets? Chalcidan, cuneiform, Cyrillic, devanagari, entrangelo, futhark, Glagol, Glossic, Greek, Gurmukhi, hieroglyphs, hiragana, ideograph, kana, katakanam Kuffic, linear A, linear B, logograph, nagari, naskhi, ogham, pictograph, Roman, runic, syllabary.

Time yourself. When you can construct a series of pictures to remember a list like this—and remember it—all in less than five minutes, you are well on your way to mastering this powerful memory technique.

Hear my song

Observations of people who have been in accidents or suffered other types of severe brain trauma have yielded many interesting insights into the ways our minds and memories work. For instance, people who have had the left side of their brains damaged might lose their ability to speak and remember words and facts, but often are still able to sing songs perfectly.

Current thinking on this is that the faculty for speech resides in the left hemisphere of the brain, while the ability to sing can be found in the right.

The greater the proportion of your mind's power you devote to remembering, the more (and more easily) I think you'll remember, so I'd like to suggest song as another great way to remember strings of information.

For instance, I remember few things from chemistry class in my junior year of high school (not having had memory training at that time). But one thing I'll never forget is that ionization is a dissociative reaction; it is the result of electrons becoming separated from their nuclei.

The reason I remember this is that Mr. Scott, my crazy chemistry teacher, came into class singing (to the main theme from the opera "Grenada") "I-, I-, I-onization. I-, I-, I-onization. Oh, this is, oh, this is a dissociative reaction in chemistry."

Or there's the case of one of Robert Frost's most loved poems, "Stopping by Woods On a Snowy Evening." Did you ever realize that you could sing the entire poem to the music of "Hernando's Hideaway" by Xavier Cugat?

Try it with the last four lines—"The woods are lovely dark and deep, but I have promises to keep, and miles to go before I sleep. And miles to go before I sleep." Trust me: It works for the whole poem. Unfortunately, that beautiful poem, one of my favorites, may now be ruined forever!

Just do it

Music is one of the ways that you can create a chain link to improve your memory. As the examples we've already discussed show, there are many others:

Unusual. To the extent possible, make the chain-link scenarios you construct highly unusual.

Active. Don't think of an object just sitting there. Have it do something! Remember Mom and her car smashing through the kitchen counter earlier in the chapter? How can such an image be forgotten?

Emotional. Conjure up a scenario in establishing your chain link that elicits an emotional reaction—joy, sorrow, physical pain, whatever.

Rhyming. Many lessons for preschoolers and those just in 1st and 2nd grade are done with rhymes. If it works for them, it should work for you, right?

Acronyms. If you've taken trigonometry, you've probably come across good old Chief *SOH-CAH-TOA*. If you've been lucky enough to evade trig (or didn't have Mr. Oldehoff in 7th grade), you've missed one of the easiest way to remember trigonometric functions: *S*ine equals *O*pposite/*H*ypotenuse; *C*osine equals *A*djacent/*H*ypotenuse; *T*angent equals *O*pposite/*A*djacent.

Relax and have fun

You're probably thinking that all of this doesn't sound like it will make your life any easier. I know it *seems* like a lot of work to think of the sound-alikes and construct crazy scenarios or songs using them. Trust me: If you start applying these tips *routinely*, they will quickly become second nature and make you a more efficient student.

There's the rub

The only problem with this method is that you might occasionally have trouble remembering what your sound-alike signified in the first place. But the process of forming the link will, more often than not, obviate the problem because the link to the original item is made stronger by the act of forming these crazy associations. Again, the crazier they are, the more *memorable* they are.

In the next chapter, we'll get away from straight factual memory for a little while and talk about how we can get a better grasp of material as we read through it the first time.

Chapter 4

One Chapter to a Better Vocabulary

William F. Buckley, watch out.

The whole demeanor of Mr. Buckley, star moderator of *Firing Line*—all pursed lips and raised eyebrows—implies that becoming a master of vocabulary is more difficult than it actually is. (Unless, of course, you currently attend or graduated from Yale, in which case it may well *be* a difficult task—at least, that's one Princetonian's erudite opinion.)

No, the way to a great vocabulary is at your fingertips, and it has absolutely nothing to do with those Word-A-Day calendars.

In this chapter, I will show you two ways to improve your memory for sesquipedalian (having many syllables) and small, obscure words.

The building blocks method

Whenever possible, try to remember *concepts* rather than memorizing random data. For instance, if someone told you to memorize a long string of numbers—for example, 147101316192225—it would be far better if you recognize that each number is three higher than the one before, then simply remember that rule (1-4-7-10-13-16-19-22-25).

Similarly, it is far better to absorb the way words are constructed—to memorize a relatively small number of prefixes, suffixes, and roots—than to try cramming the contents of *Webster's Dictionary* into your already overloaded brain.

A note on English

Our borrowed mother tongue, English, is perhaps the most democratic of all languages. Built on a Celtic base, it has freely admitted a multitude of words from other languages, particularly French, Latin, Greek, German, and a rich body of slang (from anywhere we could get it).

The oldest branches in this diverse family tree, Celtic and Old English, are the least amenable to some of the techniques we are about to learn. These are basically simple words, not built in complicated fashion as are Latinate and Greek terms.

However, as any crossword puzzle addict can tell you, our language is replete with myriad Romance words (those from French, Italian, and Spanish) that often can be dissected into rather simple elements.

The roots of language

Here are two dozen or so roots from Latin and Greek that contribute to thousands of English words:

Root	Meaning	Example
annu	year	annual
aqua	water	aquarium
arch	chief	archenemy
bio	life	biology
cap, capt	take, seize	capture
chron	time	chronological
dic, dict	say	indicate
duc, duct	lead	induction
fact, fect	do, make	effective
fer	carry, bear	infer
graph	write	graphics
homo	same, identical	homonym
logos	word	logical
manu	hand	manufacture
mitt, miss	send	remittance
path	feel, feeling	apathy
ped, pod	foot	pedal
plico	fold	implication
pon, posit	place, put	imposition
port	carry	export
psyche	mind	psychopathic
scrib	write	scribe
spec	observe, see	speculative
tend, tent	stretch	intention
tene	have, hold	tenacious
vert, vers	turn	introverted

The cart before the horse

As the preceding examples suggest, knowing the definition of a root alone is usually not enough. Prefixes, the fragments added to the beginning of a word, can greatly change the message conveyed by the root. Here are some examples of common prefixes:

Prefix	Meaning	Example
a-, ab-	from, away	aberration
a-, an-	without, not	amoral
ad-, af-, at-, ag-	to, toward	admonition affection aggressor
ant-, anti-	against	antidote
ante-	before	antecedent
bi-	two	bicycle
con-, com-	with, together	commitment
de-	away from	deviant
dis-	apart, opposite	disrespect
e-, ex-	out of, over	exorbitant
en-	in	envelope
extra-	beyond	extraordinary
hyper-	above, over	hyperthermia
hypo-	under	hypoglycemic
il-, im-, in-	not	illicit impeccable
inter-	between	intercept
intra-	within	intrauterine
mal-	evil	maladjusted
multi-	many	multiply

ob-, op-	toward, against	obdurate, opposite
per-	through	perspicacious
peri-	around	peripatetic
post-	after	posthumous
pre-	before	premonition
pro-	for, forth	production
re-	again, back	regression
sub-, sup-	under	substantiate
sym-, syn-	with, together	sympathetic synergy
tri-	three	triangle
un-	not	uncool

The tail that wags the dog

The last, but certainly not the least important building block of words is the suffix, which quite often indicates how the word is being used. Suffixes can be used to turn an adjective into an adverb (the "-ly" ending), to compare things (smallER, smallEST) or even to modify other suffixes (liveLIEST). Some suffixes with which you should be familiar are:

Suffix	Meaning	Example
-able, -ible	capable of	pliable
-ac, -al, -ial	pertaining to	hypochondriac remedial
-acy	quality of	fallacy, legacy
-age	quality of	outage
-ance, -ence	state of being	abundance
-ant, -ent	one who...	student

-ary	devoted to	secretary
-cy	state of	lunacy
-dom	quality of, state of	martyrdom kingdom
-en	made of	wooden
-er, -or	one who...	perpetrator
-ful	full of	woeful
-hood	state of	neighborhood
-ic	pertaining to	pedantic
-ine	like	leonine
-ion	act of	extermination
-ish, -ity	quality of	purplish, enmity
-ist	one who practices	novelist
-ive	disposition of	active
-less	lacking	penniless
-ly	like	cowardly
-ment	process of	enlightenment
-ness	state of	holiness
-ory	pertaining to	memory
-ose	full of	grandiose
-ous	like	porous
-ry	state of	ribaldry
-some	full of	toothsome

Practice those prefixes

I don't expect that you'll memorize these lists, of course. But if you read them over a few times, paying particular attention to the examples, you'll absorb the roots, prefixes, and suffixes fairly quickly.

Here's a list of 20 words. Write the definition in the blank space using what you remember of the building blocks of words above. Then, check to see how you did using the lists above.

1. Perspicacious ______________________
2. Psychographic ______________________
3. Introspective ______________________
4. Subjudice ______________________
5. Contentious ______________________
6. Transponder ______________________
7. Complected ______________________
8. Contravene ______________________
9. Presentiment ______________________
10. Ductile ______________________
11. Neologism ______________________
12. Implicit ______________________
13. Replicate ______________________
14. Subtend ______________________
15. Intermittent ______________________
16. Transubstantiate ______________________
17. Conurbation ______________________
18. Hyperthermia ______________________
19. Realottment______________________
20. Antipathy ______________________

Method with madness in it

How did you do on the quiz? I'll bet a lot better than you thought, simply because of this rather brief introduction to etymology.

Now let's examine another way of remembering so that you can have powerful words at your disposal—the sound-alike method. As we saw in Chapter 3, forming your own associations—sometimes wildly outrageous ones—can be quite helpful in carving easy-access roads to the long-term memory banks.

In order to use this method, create a scenario using the sound-alike of the word or parts of the word and the definition of the word.

Consider this example: Let's say that you've seen the word "ostracize" countless times, but can never quite remember that it means "to cast out from a group." You could then create this nonsense thought: "The ostrich's eyes are so big, no one wants to look at him."

In such an example, you would be using the size of the ostrich and creating an absurd reason he might be a cast out. Or I could have made the phrase: "The ostrich's size was so big he was thrown out of his hole."

Sure, you're saying, that's an easy example. But let's take another one. Because we're in a chapter on vocabulary, let's consider "sesquipedalian," which means "having many syllables" or "tending to use long words." Our sound-alike association could be: "She says quit peddling those big words."

Or one picture might be worthy of a particular vocabulary word. You might associate the difficult-to-remember word not with a phrase, but with an outrageous picture.

For instance, to remember that the word "flambe" means a food covered with flames, think of a plate of food with bees whose wings are ablaze flying from it.

Again, as we learned in Chapter 3, this sort of exercise is not a lot of work, but it is a great deal of fun. It'll help your mind hold onto words, even those you use infrequently, forever.

Here's a list of "50-cent words" with sound-alikes that will make them easy to learn:

Cutaneous (pertaining to or affecting the skin): "Cute skin, ain't it just?"

Necromancy (a method of divination through invocation of the dead): "Nancy, dig up Phil Niekro."

Hoosegow (slang for a jail): "Who's cow is in jail?"

Welter (to toss or heave): "Toss it here, Walter!"

Sullage (sewage or waste): "Sully, age is a waste."

Hieromonk (an Eastern monk who was also a priest): "Need a priest? Hire a monk."

Avouch (to declare or assert): " 'Ouch!' he vowed."

Cognomen (a nickname or epithet): "No man was named Cog."

Dikdik (a tiny antelope): "Did did you you see see that that antelope antelope?"

Guayabera (a kind of Cuban sport skirt or jacket): "Put on your shirt and buy me a beer, Fidel."

Liatigo (strap on a Western saddle): "Let that strap go, horsey!"

Petiole (the stalk by which a leaf is attached to a stem): "Pet my old leaf?"

Mizzle (to rain in fine drops): "It's drizzling, Ma."

Jaguarundi (a tropical American wildcat): "Help! There's Jaguar undies on top!"

Frutescent (shrubby): "Smelly fruits grew on the shrub."

Refrangible (capable of being refracted, like rays of light): "Hey, Ray, ball the light for Angie."

Osteophyte (an abnormal outgrowth of bone): "Two bones were fighting, Ossie."

Icosahedron (a solid having 20 faces): "I guess he'd run 20."

Euclase (rare green or blue mineral): "That green gem you got sure is classy."

With this tool, you can become a horribly pedantic conversationalist and never have to run to the dictionary while you're reading *Finnegan's Wake.*

Try a sample

Still another method that works quite well—and is relatively easy to employ for some words—is to associate a word with a very particular example. If you're reading an English grammar textbook and you come across the term "oxymoron," which is defined as "a figure of speech combining seemingly contradictory words or phrases," think how much easier it would be to remember if your notes looked like this:

Oxymoron	jumbo shrimp, cruel kindness
Onomatopoeia	PLOP, PLOP, FIZZ, FIZZ
Metaphor	food for thought
Simile	this is *like* that

CHAPTER 5

REMBRING HOW TOO SPEL GUD

Every time I have my daughter read to me, I become aware of the difficulties of spelling in English. What's that "k" doing on the edge of the knife, and why didn't someone put the lights out on that "gh" in night? How come graffiti has two "f"s and one "t" while spaghetti doubles the "t" (and pronounces the "gh" as a hard "g"!)?

Well, one way to win the spelling bee in your town is to have a great vocabulary, using some of the suggestions mentioned in Chapter 4. Another way is to learn the rules of English spelling, then make special note of the rather frequent exceptions to those rules.

Double or nothing

Many people make mistakes on words with doubled consonants. The most common quick-repeating consonants are "l," "n," "p," and "s", but "t" and "r" repeat fairly often, too. The incidence of these doubles might seem accidental or arbitrary, but they usually follow these rules:

Double "l": Usually results from adding suffixes ending in "l" to roots beginning with the letter, vice versa for suffixes (examples: *alliterative, unusually*). However, alien does *not* have a double "l" because it is itself a root.

Double "n": A similar rule applies to "n"s. Double "n"s usually result from adding a suffix that turns an adjective ending in "n" into a noun (*wantonness* or *thinness*) or "-ny," which turns a noun ending in "n" into an adjective (*funny*).

Double "p"s, "r"s, and "s"s don't generally have a hard-and-fast rule, so you'll usually have to rely on other tricks of memory. For instance, I've always had trouble spelling *embarrassment* (double "r" *and* double "s") because it certainly doesn't seem to follow the same rule as *harassment* (double "s" only).

In these cases, you'll have to associate some rule with the word. When I worked as a reporter, you'd often hear people answer questions about spelling in such codes. "Four 's's and two 'p's" is the answer to "How do you spell Mississippi?" I remember the rule for the word *harassment* by imagining someone pushing away (or harassing) the "r" some part of my brain insists should be there.

Double "r"s and double "t"s and other doubles occurring (note the double "r"!) before "-ed":

☞ If the word ends in a single consonant (occuR, omiT).

☞ If the word is accented on the last syllable (comPEL, reMIT).

Is it "i" before "e" or…?

The general rule is: "i" before "e" except after "c" or when it sounds like "a," as in "neighbor" and "weigh." This rule holds, with some exceptions: *seize*, *leisure*, *caffeine*, and the names of other chemical compounds.

Honest "-able"

Many people get thrown over words ending in "e" that have "-able" or "-ible" added to them. What to do with that final "e"? Well, here are some rules:

☞ **Keep the final "e"** for words ending in "-ice," "-ace" or "-ge." Someone is embracEABLE and situations are managEABLE.

☞ **Drop that final "e"** when it is preceded by any consonant other than "c" or "g" (*unlovable*).

Other rules for adding suffixes to words ending in "e":

☞ Retain the "e" when adding "-ly" and "-ment" (unless the word ends in "-dge." It's *judgment*, *not* judgEment).

☞ Drop the "e" before adding "y" as a suffix (*phony*).

☞ Drop the final "e" and add "-ible" to words ending in "-nce," "-uce" or "-rce" (*producible*, *unconvincible*).

☞ Use "-ible" for words ending in "-miss" (*dismissible*).

Rules are meant to be broken

The English language is based on Celtic, Norwegian, German, Latin, French, and several other languages. As a result, it veers from the rules fairly often. So, while these guidelines certainly will help you a great deal, sometimes you will have to rely on association and some of the other methods we spoke of in other chapters to remember all the *exceptions* to them.

Chapter 6

Remembering Numbers the Mnemonic Way

Up until now, we've been dealing in the rich world of words. Anything having to do with words is a relatively easy task for the memory because words always can be associated with *things*, which, because they can be seen, touched, heard, and smelled, can carry more than one association and, therefore, be easier to remember.

But a number is an abstraction. Unless associated with something, it is relatively difficult to remember. For instance, most people have tremendous difficulty remembering telephone numbers that they've only heard once. The reason is that a phone number doesn't usually conjure up an image or a sensation. It is merely seven or 10 digits without a relationship to one another or to you.

The trick, then, is to establish more associations for numbers.

But how? After all, they can be so abstract. It would be like trying to remember colors without having the benefit of *things* associated with those colors.

Making friends with numbers

Numbers are infinite, but the system we use to designate them is even more user-friendly than the alphabet. It consists of 10 digits that all of you should know by now (just follow the bouncing ball): 0, 1, 2, 3, 4, 5, 6, 7, 8, and 9.

The trick to the mnemonic alphabet—a rather popular technique for remembering numbers—is turning those numbers into the equivalent of letters, symbols that represent sounds. The pioneer of this concept is Harry Lorayne, author of many books on memory. His method calls for associating the 10 familiar Arabic numerals with a sound or a related group of sounds.

Here's how this brilliantly simple scheme works:

1 = T, D
2 = N
3 = M
4 = R
5 = L
6 = J, soft G, CH, SH, DG, TCH
7 = K, hard C, hard G, Q
8 = F, V, PH
9 = P, B
0 = Z, soft C, S

You're probably thinking, "What sense does this all make, and how in heck am I supposed to remember it?"

Well, though this seems like madness, believe me, there's some extraordinarily wonderful method in it.

The number one is a single downstroke, as is the letter "T." "D" is a suitable substitute because it is pronounced almost the same way as "T"—by touching the tongue to the front of the roof of the mouth.

"N" represents two because "N" has two downstrokes.

"M" is a stand-in for three because, you guessed it, it has three downstrokes.

Four is represented by "R" because the dominant sound in the word *four* is the "-RRRRRR" at the end.

The Romans used "L" to represent 50. Also, if you fan out the fingers of your left hand as if to say, "It's 5 o'clock," your index finger and thumb form the letter "L."

Hold a mirror up to a six and you get a "J," particularly if you write as badly as I do. Therefore, all letters pronounced like "J"—by touching your tongue to the inside of your lower teeth—are acceptable substitutes for six.

Place two sevens back to back, turning one upside down, and what do you have? Right, a "K." All of those letter sounds formed in the back of the mouth, as is "K," are therefore potential substitutes for the lucky seven.

Draw a line parallel to the ground through a handwritten eight and you will create a symbol that resembles a script, lower case "F." Therefore, all sounds formed by placing the top teeth on the lower lip can represent eight.

Once again, I invoke my mirror, mirror on the wall to show that a nine and a capital "P" are virtually identical. "B," also formed by putting your lips together, is a substitute for nine anytime.

Zero is an easy one. Zero begins with a "Z," so any sound formed by hissing through the space between flat tongue and roof of mouth is acceptable.

Now what?

Believe me, this device, which probably seems very ungainly to you now, is a terrific way to remember numbers. Go over the preceding list a few more times, cover it up, and take the little quiz below, matching numbers with appropriate sounds and vice-versa:

6 ______________________________

B ______________________________

F ______________________________

2 ______________________________

L ______________________________

Q ______________________________

9 ______________________________

S ______________________________

J ______________________________

7 ______________________________

Consonantal divide

Have you noticed that all of the sounds used in the mnemonic alphabet are consonants? That's because users of the system should be free to use vowels however they please around these consonants to form words or memorable sounds. Therefore the number 15 can be "QueeN." Or the number of that wonderful person you met in the Rathskeller today and would so like to see again could be "vasectomy to go," or 806-1316 (VSCTMTG).

How about trying to remember pi to seven places. You could try to memorize 3.141592 or just think, "MeTRic TalL PeNny."

Is it easier to remember your social security number (say, 152-40-1821) or "TelL NoRa SaDie PHoNeD"?

A great date

One of the most useful applications of this method is remembering dates and tying them to events. If you wanted to remember, for example, "William the Conqueror invaded England in 1066," you could endlessly repeat that sentence, or you could remember, "Bill THiS eGG." Combining these methods with the chain-link technique we discussed in earlier chapters, you could imagine an egg rolling off the white cliffs of Dover, where William first landed. (Alternately, you can make up a ridiculous but simple rhyme like, "In 1066, Billy C ate fish and chips" that would also work just fine.)

Now you try it. Make up phrases using the mnemonic alphabet equivalents for your Social Security number, the first three phone numbers in your little black book, or the times for high and low tide tomorrow. Then try the quiz, writing in first the letter equivalents for the numbers, then a brief word, phrase, or sentence that would help you remember it. I've done the first one for you.

844941	FRRPRT	FuRRy PoRT (or FuRRy PRiDe)
671024	________	________
95776002	________	________
84712457	________	________
746603201	________	________
1234567890	________	________
0967854213	________	________

What about even longer numbers? How do you remember 20-, 30-, even 50-digit numbers without trying too hard? Well, you could make your "story sentences" longer. But you can also group the numbers into a series of pictures. For example, let's say you had to remember the number 289477500938199101550—that's 21 digits! Try grouping it into smaller number combinations, creating a picture for each. In this case, I've managed with only three pictures:

> 289477 can be represented by NVPRGK or a picture of a sailor (NaVy) PouRing GunK.
>
> 500938 is LZZBMV. How is the sailor standing? LaZily. Where is he standing? Right By a MoVie theatre. (See it in your head.)
>
> 199101550. What is playing at the theatre? DeBBie DoeS DaLLaS. (Now you know why he wasn't paying attention to the gunk!)

Can you see how you could easily memorize a 50-digit number with just four or five pictures? Try it yourself. You'll see how easy it is.

Everybody loves them dead presidents

Or so sang bluesman Willie Dixon, referring to the presidential portraits that grace our folding money. But he could just as easily have been referring to your least favorite history professor—you know, the one who expects you to know who was the 23rd president of the United States? By the way, that was Harrison, and the way we will remember that is "No ('N' represents 2), My ('M' is for 3) hairy son."

Now you try it. Here are the dozen most recent U.S. vice presidents. How are you going to remember them?

34. Harry Truman
35. Alben Barkley
36. Richard Nixon
37. Lyndon Johnson
38. Hubert Humphrey
39. Spiro Agnew
40. Gerald Ford
41. Nelson Rockefeller
42. Walter Mondale
43. George Bush
44. Dan Quayle
45. Al Gore

How did you do?

Here's how I would use mnemonics to establish a chain link between names and numbers:

Truman: "Meet MR (34) true, man."
Quayle: Picture a RoaRing (44) quail.
Mondale: Picture a Jamaican Ayrdale (mon) RuNning (42)
Ford: Picture a brand-new Ford RiSing (40) in the air.

Get the idea? This is an absolutely invaluable tool. It will empower you to remember phone numbers without resorting to writing on wet cocktail napkins. Perhaps more important, it will help you remember dates and facts without incessantly repeating them.

CHAPTER 7

REMEMBERING NAMES AND FACES

Like it or not, you're not going to be in school for the rest of your life. Soon, you will begin to look for a job, to string together a network of acquaintances and contacts that will help lift you onto that first rung of the corporate ladder.

You'll participate in that horrible convention called the cocktail party and other social events where you'll be expected to be charming.

Every once in a while, I go to a cocktail party, if only to remind myself why I don't do it more often. But seriously, cocktail parties give me a chance to practice a skill that I consider one of the key reasons for my earlier success as an advertising salesperson: remembering the names (and some of the other pertinent personal data) that went with the faces.

In fact, one of the principal reasons I became interested in the subject of memory improvement was that I was tired of calling people "pal" and "buddy" when I could *not* remember their names after they said to *me,* "Hey, Ron, how have you been?"

You can avoid those embarrassing moments forever by memorizing these key steps to link a person's face and name in your memory forever.

Take a good look

Whenever you meet someone, look him or her in the face and make special note of some outstanding feature. Does the person have a big nose? Huge earlobes? Dimples? Big, beautiful blue eyes? A cleft in the chin? A mole? It doesn't have to be a particularly ugly or beautiful feature—just something that sets the person apart from the rest of the people in the room.

Once you've locked in on a feature, do *not* stare at it, but *do* get your imagination working—make that feature truly outstanding by embellishing it. If it's a big nose, make it as big as a toucan's beak in your mind's eye. Dimples should be as large as craters; big earlobes should dangle on the person's shoulders.

Make sure you got it

I remember once introducing my friend Tony to three people who, along with him, were the first to arrive at my house for a little dinner party. One minute later, I went into the kitchen to fix drinks for everybody and Tony was right at my heels. "What was the name of that brunette in the miniskirt?" he asked in a hushed voice. "Monique," I said. "How 'bout the bald guy?" asked Tony. "That's Joe."

Finally, very embarrassed, Tony asked, "And what about the other woman?"

There are fleas with longer memories. But now Tony prides himself on being able to remember the names of 30 or 40 people in a room after being introduced only once.

The first thing he taught himself was to *repeat the person's name*, looking right at him or her as he did so. Tony, being a very charming guy, doesn't do this as if he's trying out for a lead role in the remake of *Being There*. He repeats the name back as part of a greeting—"Nice to meet you, Monique." "Hi Joe, I've heard a lot about you. You're Ron's partner, right?"

Using such a technique, you will not only be noting the person's name, you will be making sure that you got it right.

Think of a link

Once you've done that, it's time to come up with some sort of link between the name and the feature that you've already exaggerated out of proportion.

I saw the most obvious example of this as a kid when a memorist appeared on a Sunday morning TV show. He was introduced to the 100 or so youngsters in the audience and repeated all of their names back to them at the end of the show. Asked how he had done it, he used the example of a boy named Tommy Fox. The boy had a dimple, said the memorist, so he imagined a bare meadow with a hole in the middle. A fox bounded through the hedge followed by hunters shouting, "Tommy Ho!"

Bingo! The name and the face were linked forever.

Too easy, you say?

There are much *easier* ones. Before you go too far afield creating a memorable mental picture, don't overlook the obvious. Some names are so memorable you shouldn't have to work too hard—try "Boomer" Esiason (okay, you *might* have to work on "Esiason") or Chip Dale (gotta love those chipmunks). Other first or last names should *automatically* trigger specific pictures—a flower (Rose, Daisy, Hyacinth), a piece of jewelry (Amber, Ruby, Jasper, Opal, Pearl, Jade, Ivory), an object (Gates, Ford, Bentley, Royce, Zipper, Glass, Cross, Brook, River, Pen, Pack, Beam, Tent, *ad infinitum*), a profession (Tinker, Taylor, Soldier, Spy), a city or town (Clifton, Springfield, Austin, Houston, Dallas, Savannah, York), a familiar street, the name of your favorite team, a breed of dog or cat.

Some names differing by only a letter could use such objects as links—Pack to remember Gregory *Peck*, Pen for Sean *Penn*, Tent for *Trent*, Road for Rhodes or, for a little more stretch, Tombs for *Thomas*, Cow for *Cowher* (Go, Steelers!).

Your associations could take advantage of your own particular knowledge. Small for *Klein*, if you know German; tie-ins to your favorite sports figure or movie star or author; an association with terms endemic to your profession. The list of possible tie-ins is absolutely endless.

If you *still* can't think of such a link, you can always rhyme: Wallets for *Wallace*, Georgie Porgie, Bad Chad, Freaky Frank, Ron Ron weighs a ton.

Once you've come up with these sound-alikes or pictures, find some way to link them with the image you've formed of the person's chief facial features.

For instance, once I was introduced to a man named Vince Dolce (pronounced Dole-see). As I was walking toward him, I noticed some rather dark circles under his eyes. In my imagination, because I'm so accustomed to using the technique outlined above, the circles became bigger than a raccoon's. When I heard that his name was

Dolce, I immediately thought, “dull sheep” and pictured tired, sleepy sheep grazing on those now even bigger circles below Vince’s eyes. The sheep, of course, were bothering him, and this made him *wince* (for Vince).

That’s all there is to turning a room full of strangers into people who—for better or worse—you’ll never forget!

CHAPTER 8

REMEMBERING A SPEECH OR ORAL REPORT

The English poet John Donne wrote, "Death be not proud," and no wonder: In many public opinion polls in which respondents were asked to rate their biggest fears, public speaking—not the grim reaper—won...hands down.

The reasons for this are many, but undoubtedly heading the list is the horrible idea that in mid-sentence we will go blank, completely unable to recall the brilliant speech we'd stayed up writing late the night before.

We'll return to our seat in a muddled silence. Feeling like a naked person in a spotlight.

To make sure that doesn't happen to you, I'll teach you how to use chain links, association, and all of the other tricks we've discussed in this book to help you remember speeches or oral class presentations.

Take note

The way to go about preparing a speech is to outline it, write it, *re*outline it, and then use the outline as your key to remembering it. Why should you bother when you went through the trouble of writing the speech in the first place?

Well, because there are two kinds of speakers: good and dull. The good ones *talk* to you. The bad ones *read* to you. In order to be a *speaker*, rather than a *reader*, you should know your speech by heart.

A tasty toastmaster

Let's step aside from the memory issue and talk about how you should organize your speech (after all, it will be the key to remembering it well).

I've done so much public speaking throughout my career that I've actually grown to enjoy it—in fact, I look *forward* to talking to a room full of strangers. I don't think that would be the case at all were it not for a piece of valuable advice I acquired quite a few years ago. There is only one best way to organize a speech: Tell them what you are going to say; say it; then, tell them what you said.

Let's say you were assigned to take one side of an argument in a debate and your topic is, "The solution to the drug problem: Legalize all drugs." Your outline might look something like this:

The Opening

I. Drugs should be legalized

II. This will help solve, not deepen, the drug crisis in this country

III. Keeping drugs illegal assures that criminals get rich and government funds get wasted

The Middle

I. The reasons to legalize drugs
   A. Artificially inflated prices
      1. Costs are inflated 2,500 percent
   B. Public funds are being wasted
      1. Law enforcement is not working
      2. Funds for rehabilitation are paltry
      3. Education funds are inadequate

II. Control would be easier
   A. It has worked in other countries
   B. Licensing would increase revenues
   C. Harsh penalties would curb sales to minors
   D. Drug addicts would be known and available for counseling

III. Prohibition doesn't work
   A. Statistics to support statement
   B. Parallels with Roaring Twenties

The Closing

I. The costly, ineffective War on Drugs

II. Legalization sounds radical, but it would work

III. The alternative is far more dangerous

Commit it to memory

Once you have the outline, use the chain link method to remember the flow of your speech.

Here's how it might work for the outline above: First, you'd remember your opening by picturing yourself at an opening—a doorway, or maybe opening night of a play titled, *Drug Free America.* Imagine yourself walking inside the theater and seeing three scenes set from left to right:

I. Congress enacting a law
II. People emerging from hospital beds and saying they don't need drugs anymore
III. Criminal types having piles of money taken from them by police

Next, you imagine yourself sitting in the *middle* section of the theater.

I. You look at your *Playbill* and it reads
   A. "2,500 percent"
   B. On the stage you see
      1. Police in handcuffs
      2. A nurse in a clinic begging for money
      3. A schoolroom with no teacher
II. Imagine some sort of control to remember this part of your exposition section, perhaps your foot on a gas pedal
   A. Your foot is on the gas pedal because you're driving past an Amsterdam street or a windmill (because Holland has a model program of legalization and control)
   B. You reach for your driver's license, which has a big dollar sign on it
   C. Out the window you see a seedy character being dragged from a schoolyard by the police
   D. You see that nurse in the clinic helping someone

Then, all of a sudden, you car is cut off by gangsters being chased by police as if in a classic car chase from *The*

Untouchables. Then, imagine yourself closing your car door and hearing:

I. The sounds of war. You look up and you see huge dollar signs suspended on parachutes coming down from the sky.

II. You see Karl Marx (or another "radical") in an army outfit and then,

III. A mushroom cloud or some other apocalyptic image.

Once you've conjured up a set of hooks like this, read your speech several times, mentally flipping through the appropriate images as you do so. In that way your words and ideas will become *linked* to pictures, making them so much easier to remember.

Get the picture?

The whole key to a good memory is establishing tags, links, associations—anything that will help your mind reel the memories in from the deep abyss of your memory banks.

The point of this chapter and all the others in this book is to show you how simple this can be. The rest is up to you. Developing a good memory requires you to practice the techniques I've discussed throughout this book.

After you've done so, you'll be more likely to get higher grades on exams that test your knowledge of facts. What's more, you might never forget where your keys, wallet, or glasses are again.

Good luck!

CHAPTER 9

TEST YOUR PROGRESS

As promised, I'm going to give you a chance to check your progress. If you've studied the contents of this book thoroughly and have made an effort to put some of its advice to work, you should score much higher now than you did on the quiz in Chapter 2.

Test #1: The mnemonic alphabet

Study this number for 30 seconds. Then cover it up and replicate as much as you can, taking only another 20 seconds or so.

62889124732451827096 4

Test #2: A better vocabulary

Here are a number of obscure vocabulary words and their meanings. Study them for no more than three minutes, then answer the questions below.

1. **Roux:** A cooked mixture of butter or other fat and flour used to thicken soups, sauces, etc.
2. **Bregma:** The place on the top of the skull where the frontal bone and parietal bones join.
3. **Crimple:** To wrinkle or curl; crinkle.
4. **Litmus:** A blue coloring matter obtained from certain lichens.
5. **Longicorn:** Having long antennae.
6. **Naos:** A temple or shrine.
7. **Resplendent:** Shining brilliantly; gleaming.
8. **Serry:** To crowd closely together.
9. **Withershins:** Counterclockwise.
10. **Decuple:** 10 times as great.
11. **Brock:** European badger.
12. **Adscititious:** Derived from an external source; additional.
13. **Epizoic:** Living on the surface of an animal.
14. **Tantara:** A blast of a trumpet or horn.
15. **Ophiology:** The study of snakes.
16. **Cognoscenti:** Well-informed persons, especially those who have superior knowledge of a particular field, particularly the arts.
17. **Divagate:** To wander; stray.
18. **Marplot:** A person who spoils a plot, design, or project by meddling.
19. **Vespine:** Pertaining to wasps.
20. **Mome:** A fool; blockhead.

Okay, cover them up and take this test:

1. Something 10 times as great is called ______.
2. Did you see that cute _______ poking his face out of the ground?
3. _______ is another word for counterclockwise.
4. The meeting had a tendency to ___________ from the agenda.
5. Something is "epizoic" if it can live on ______.
6. The extra money must have come from an ______________ source.
7. Let's all ____________ together under the awning until it stops raining.
8. A mome is A) a fool or B) a genius?
9. Everybody went to the ____________ on the night before the holy festival.
10. The look in her eyes was as ________ as the diamond he presented to her.
11. _______ is a blue coloring matter from certain lichens.
12. New Orleans cooks use a lot of ____________ in their recipes.
13. A creature with long antennae is __________.
14. Be very careful when handling the baby; the _______ is a very sensitive spot on the head.
15. Studying the ________ world is fascinating; I never realized how different wasps are from bees.
16. It seemed like the panel of _________ enjoyed his performance, although he was only an amateur.
17. The new fabric is delicate and may ________.

18. My boyfriend is studying __________, but I have to admit, I'm afraid of reptiles.
19. A blast from the ___________ awakened everyone in the village.
20. Someone who meddles, spoiling plans, can be called a ______.

Test #3: Dates and events

Study the following dates, events, and facts. Then take the test that follows.

1967: London Bridge is moved to Arizona.

1876: Alexander Graham Bell invents the telephone.

Harvard, oldest university in the United States, was founded in 1636.

With an annual rainfall of 3.73 inches, Nevada is the driest state in the Union.

President McKinley was assassinated in 1901.

Congress passed the Tonkin Gulf Resolution, increasing American involvement in the Vietnam War, in 1964.

George Washington was inaugurated in Philadelphia in 1789.

The horrific battle of Gettysburg was fought in 1863.

30,000 people work in the Pentagon building.

Eli Whitney invented the cotton gin in 1793.

Jamestown, the first permanent European settlement in the New World, was founded in 1607.

The Korean War, though never officially declared, raged from 1950 to 1953.

Pilgrims signed the Mayflower Compact in 1620.

Thomas Jefferson purchased the Louisiana Territory from Napoleon in 1803.

Now answer the following questions:

1. The cotton gin was invented when and by whom?
2. The Battle of Gettysburg raged in what year?
3. How many people live in California?
4. In what year was Jamestown founded?
5. How many inches of rain fall on the driest state of the Union? What state is it?
6. What is the name and founding date of the oldest university in the United States?
7. George Washington was inaugurated in Philadelphia. In what year did it occur?
8. When and by whom was the telephone invented?
9. When and to what state was the London Bridge moved?
10. How many people work in the Pentagon?
11. When did America enter into full-scale conflict in Vietnam?
12. When did Teddy Roosevelt succeed McKinley?
13. America became the proud owner of New Orleans in what year?
14. When did the Korean War take place?
15. When did the Pilgrims sign the Mayflower Compact?

Test #4: Reading retention

Scan the following paragraphs excerpted from *Taking the Mystery Out of TQM* (Career Press, 1995), in order to answer the questions that follow (which you may read first). The answers are at the end of Test 4. This should take you no more than two minutes:

> The Taguchi Loss Function demonstrates a formula to determine the cost of a lack of quality. According to the Loss Function, for each deviation there is an incremental economic loss of some geometric proportion. The cumulative impact can be great for a number of parts deviating just a little. This differs from the traditional view which states that there is no real detrimental impact as long as parts are produced within engineering tolerances or specifications.
>
> Think of this concept in the management of a company. Consider the interrelationships and interdependence among finance, marketing, sales, and information systems. Each group has developed procedures to achieve its goals. In order for each to perform optimally, all work from other departments must be understood and integrated into a flow chart to reflect the integrity of the whole.
>
> According to Taguchi, if all systems and schedules are off only slightly, there is probably little impact on any one individual or even one department. Taken collectively, however, the toll will be far greater. Even if each department missed each of its deadlines by only a single day, the impact could well be a product that is too late for the customer who ordered it.

1. If each department misses its deadline by one day, the result could be:
A. Increased productivity
B. Grand scale layoffs
C. The product is too late
D. Unnoticeable

2. The Taguchi Loss Function demonstrates a formula to determine:
A. Employee attitudes
B. The effects of poor quality
C. Praise or insults
D. Office partnerships

3. The author compares the Taguchi Loss Function to:
A. Group dynamics
B. Geometry
C. Scheduling
D. Company management

4. The traditional view states that:
A. The cumulative impact can be great for a number of parts deviating just a little.
B. Each group has developed procedures to achieve its goals.
C. There is no detrimental impact so long as parts are produced with engineering tolerances or specifications.
D. For each deviation, there is an incremental loss of some geometric proportion.

Now read the following passage and answer the questions that follow (but do not look at the questions first). Give yourself four minutes for this exercise:

Five major scandals tainted the administration of President Ulysses S. Grant. Although the hero of Vicksburg was the first president to encounter charges of substantial wrongdoing during his administration, it was never proved that he was directly involved in any criminal acts nor that he profited from any of the acts of others.

The first incident occurred in 1869, the first year of his presidency. Known as Black Friday, it involved speculators James Fisk and Jay Gould and their attempt to corner the gold market. By involving Grant's brother-in-law, they hoped to prevent the government from "dumping" its gold onto the market, which would make it impossible for their scheme to succeed. Grant was not directly involved in Fisk's and Gould's machinations, but he gave the appearance of complicity, allowing himself to be entertained lavishly and publicly on Fisk's yacht. However, when the pair's aggressive gold purchases sent its price skyrocketing in a matter of days, Grant acted swiftly, ordering the Treasury Department to sell off $4 million in gold reserves. While this ended Fisk's and Gould's attempt, this step brought ruin to a number of individuals and businesses that were "riding the wave" of gold fever and resulted in a national economic shock not matched until the 1929 stock market crash.

The second major scandal involved the embezzlement of massive amounts of money by the Credit Mobilier holding company, which was involved with the construction of the Union Pacific railway. To avoid being discovered, the conspirators heavily bribed members of Congress and officials of the Republican Party, of which Grant was the nominal head. Although this scandal erupted during a heated reelection campaign against newspaper publisher Horace Greeley, Grant was evidently completely uninvolved and was reelected handily.

Two other scandals involved taxes and officials appointed to collect them. One tax collector, John Sanborn, managed to keep nearly half of the delinquent taxes he collected, a total that exceeded $200,000. That paled in comparison to the fraud discovered by Treasury Secretary Benjamin H. Bristow among liquor distillers and the officials charged with collecting taxes from them. Although Grant called for swift action against the conspirators, his fervor flagged when his trusted personal secretary, Orville Babcock, was implicated in the scheme. Grant then slowed the investigation, but 110 conspirators were eventually found guilty.

In the final year of Grant's second term, evidence mounted that Secretary of War W.W. Belknap had been taking bribes from white traders at Indian trading posts. Because Grant had made much of his earlier attempts to institute a fair and nonabusive set of policies toward the Indians, the scandal was a personal embarrassment, though, again, Grant was in no way directly involved. Faced with certain impeachment, Belknap resigned.

1. In what year did the Credit Mobilier embezzlement become public?
2. In what year did Belknap resign?
3. Approximately how much tax revenue did John D. Sanborn collect before he was caught?

None of these answers are directly stated in the selection, though all can be easily inferred from it. The answers are: 1) 1872 (If the first year of Grant's presidency was 1869, then the reelection campaign was 1872, so the previous election occurred in 1868. Election years are always divisible by four.); 2) 1876, the final year of Grant's second term. (See above for reasoning.); 3) $400,000 (He kept "nearly half of the taxes he collected, for a total that exceeded $200,000.")

Answers to the first part of Test 4:

1. C **3. D**
2. B **4. C**

Test #5: Remembering lists

Study the first two lists for one minute each, then close the book and recite them back. Do the same for the third and fourth lists, except allow three minutes for the third, five minutes for the fourth:

Dances: Farruca, carol, jota, redowa, hoolachan, malaguena, tarantella, valeta, bourree, allemande.

Alcoholic drinks: oloroso, fino, bingo, sack, geropiga, catawba, demerara, arak, zythum, usquebaugh, twankay.

Cheeses: Derby, Gloucester, stracchino, Red Windsor, Bel Paese, Esrom, Feta, Vacherin, Wexford, Caerphilly, sapsago, Gammelost, Crowdie, Chevrotin, Lymeswold, Pultost, Raclette, Blarney, Edam, Havarti, Mysost, Islay.

Ships or vessels: Monoxylon, drake, whiff, packet, lymphad, galley, carrack, bawley, praam, randan, sub, razee, geordie, felucca, bireme, coracle, dinghy, skiff, sloop, grab, coaster, brigantine, saic, tub, tug, fore-and-after, masoolah, puteli, shallop, patamar, gallivat, dogger, gondola, tern, budgerow, butty.

Test #6: The rules of English spelling

Identify the misspelled words in the following list:

Dissatisfied
Immediately
Stoney
Likeable
Receeve
Measurement
Liesure
Commited
Occurence

Compeling
Harrasment
Embarassment
Drunkeness
Unconvincible
Regretible
Mistake
Mistatement

How did you do? (See the bottom of this page for the spelling solutions.)

I hope that you scored well and are confident that you can approach your schoolwork—and the rest of your life, inside and outside of school—with the assurance that your memory will be an ally rather than a foil.

In the above list, the following are the only words spelled *correctly*: stoney (though stony is preferred), likeable, mistake, dissatisfied, unconvincible, immediately, and measurement.

Book 4

Improve Your Writing

INTRODUCTION

THE GOOD NEWS ABOUT WRITING PAPERS

It's going to happen.

There you'll be, sitting quietly in class, contemplating the weekend to come, minding your own business.

Suddenly, without even a warning, your teacher will announce that your next assignment is...to write a Research Paper.

Nothing strikes more fear in the hearts of students everywhere. The thought of spending hours in the library digging up information; writing a long, detailed report; typing footnotes. For heaven's sake—if it's not enough to bring on actual terror, it certainly qualifies for mild panic!

"How will I get it all done?" you think. "Where do I start?" And, no doubt, "Why *me*?"

Let me reassure you right off: You *will* get it done. You will get a *great* grade on it. You will even *learn* a few things along the way. How? With the help of this book. I've been there. (And because I'm still writing after all these years, I'm *still* here!) I'll show you my "tricks of the trade," every step of the way.

Nibbles are better than gobbles

A Buddhist saying proclaims: "The journey of a thousand miles begins with a single step." Well, so does the process of writing your research paper. The secret is to take things one step at a time. By breaking your assignment—no matter how huge or time-consuming a project—into a series of small steps, you'll turn a conceivably immense undertaking into a series of very manageable jobs.

First, in Chapter 1, you'll learn about the different elements that make up a research paper. I'll show you how to put together a work schedule *and* give you some tips on time management.

In Chapter 2, I'll help you decide on a specific topic...and show you the kinds of topics to avoid like sour milk. I'll also show you how to develop a specific research angle or research argument—your *thesis*—and produce a preliminary outline for your paper.

Then, in Chapters 3, 4, and 5, we'll spend some time in the library. You'll learn where to look for reference materials, a great system for keeping track of those you use, and a special note-taking system. You'll quickly be transformed into a more efficient, organized researcher—and get *more* done in *less* time.

There are now tremendous research opportunities available online via the Internet, and some excellent software programs that will help you organize and write any report or paper. All of these are covered extensively in ***Use Your Computer***. Because of space limitations, I have *not* reproduced most of that information in this book but I urge you to consult ***Use Your Computer*** for it.

In Chapters 6 and 7, you'll begin the actual writing of your paper. I'll show you some tricks that will help you organize it, some tips on overcoming writer's block, and a checklist to make sure you avoid plagiarizing. By the end of Chapter 7, you'll already have written a rough draft.

In Chapter 8, we'll discuss the various methods you can use to document your sources of information—*when* you must document a source and *how* to do it.

Next, in Chapter 9, we'll edit your rough draft. You'll learn special strategies that will make your writing better, smoother, clearer.

You will learn the ins and outs of putting together a bibliography—a list of the reference materials you used to write your paper—in Chapter 10. I'll give you the lowdown on all the rules you need to follow.

In Chapter 11, you'll learn some super proofreading tricks so you catch *every* typographical error and spelling mistake in your paper. And *voilà!* You'll be on your way to class, finished masterpiece in hand!

In Chapter 12, I've summarized the advice from ***"Ace" Any Test*** regarding essay tests. Because my advice for such a test is to "treat it like writing a paper," a short section on essays seemed appropriate to this book. You'll also learn to prepare oral reports in this chapter.

You'll thank them later—really!

Doing a research paper requires a lot of work. But the payoff is great, too. In addition to the obvious benefit—learning a lot about your research subject—you'll develop important skills every step of the way. You will learn, for example:

1. How to track down information about *any* subject.
2. How to sort through that information and come to a conclusion about your subject.
3. How to prepare an organized, in-depth report.
4. How to communicate your ideas clearly and effectively.

Once you've developed these skills, you will *own* them.

You'll be able to apply them in *all* your high school or college classes. They'll come in handy not only when you prepare other research papers, but also when you tackle smaller writing assignments, such as essays and oral reports.

When you graduate, these same skills will help you get ahead in the work world; the ability to analyze a subject and communicate through the written word are keys to success, no matter what career you choose.

Your teacher really didn't ask you to write a research paper just to make your life miserable. Of all the things you'll learn in school, the skills you acquire as we produce your research paper will be among the most valuable.

How to use this book

The steps I outline throughout this book are somewhat flexible. After you've "notched your pen" with one or two papers, you may want to adapt these steps a bit to fit your personal work style.

That's fine, just *don't skip any step altogether.* You may not understand the benefits of a particular step until you're further along in the process. So don't skip.

Let's get started

Writing a research paper takes time, serious thought, and effort. It is *not* easy. I can't change that any more than I can change your teacher's mind about assigning the paper in the first place.

But I *can* tell you that if you follow the steps outlined in this book, you'll write a better paper than you ever dreamed of. I can also guarantee that you will learn some things along the way that will stay with you for the rest of your life.

It won't be painless, but at least the operation will be a success!

CHAPTER 1

GETTING READY FOR ACTION

You may be only writing *one* paper, but there are actually *three* different jobs ahead of you:

First, you must be an *objective reporter*. You'll dig up all the facts you can about your subject, gathering statistics, historical data, first-person accounts, and more.

You will read reference books, newspaper stories, magazine articles, scholarly journals and other materials, watch relevant videos or films, check out online resources, even interview a live expert or two.

Your job is to find out the truth, to gather data with an unbiased eye. You can't discard or ignore information just because it doesn't fit into the neat framework your personal opinions and expectations have constructed.

Second, you must be a *detective*. Like a scientist evaluating the results of an experiment, you must review the evidence, decide what it does and doesn't mean, and draw the obvious (and, perhaps, not-so-obvious) conclusions.

Third, you must be an *author,* ready to share your new-found knowledge. Having sifted through reams of information, you will write a cogent, well-thought-out, in-depth report, telling your readers what you have learned.

This is an exciting process—where else can you play three such different roles in a matter of weeks?—but one that demands some organization and adherence to a short, but vitally important, list of rules.

5 fundamental rules

Let's start with the fundamental rules that need to be emblazoned on your mind:

1. *Always* follow your teacher's directions to the letter.
2. *Always* hand in your paper on time.
3. *Always* hand in a clean and clear copy of your paper.
4. *Always* keep at least one copy of every paper you write.
5. *Never* allow a single spelling or grammatical error in your papers.

You wanted it typewritten?

Your teacher's directions may include:

☞ A general subject area from which topics should be chosen—"some aspect of Kennedy's presidency," "an 18th-century invention," "a short story by Washington Irving," etc.

- ☞ Specific requirements regarding format—typed, double-spaced, include title page, do not include title page, etc.
- ☞ Suggested length—10 to 15 typewritten pages.
- ☞ Other requirements—turn in general outline before topic is approved; get verbal okay on topic before proceeding; don't include quotes (from other works) longer than a single paragraph; other idiosyncrasies of your own teachers.

Whatever his or her directions, *follow them to the letter*. Some high school teachers may forgive you your trespasses, but I have known college professors who simply refused to accept a paper that was not prepared as they instructed—and gave the poor but wiser student an F for it (without even *reading* it).

If you are unsure of a specific requirement or if the suggested area of topics is unclear, it is *your* responsibility to talk to your teacher and clarify whatever points are confusing you.

It is not a bad idea to choose two or three topics you'd like to write about and seek preliminary approval, especially if the assignment seems particularly vague.

Excuses: Nice try, bad grade

There is certainly no reason or excuse, short of catastrophic illness or life-threatening emergency, for you to *ever* be late with an assignment. Some teachers will simply refuse to accept a paper that is late and give you an F for your efforts. At best, they will accept it but mark you down, perhaps turning an A paper into a B...or worse.

Teachers don't read tea stains

Teachers have to read a lot of papers and shouldn't be faulted for being human if, after hundreds of pages, they come upon your wrinkled, tea-stained, pencil-written tome and get a bit discouraged. Nor should you be surprised if you get a lower grade than the content might merit *just because the presentation was so poor.*

I am not advocating that you emphasize form over substance. Far from it—the content is what the teacher is looking for, and he or she will primarily be basing your grade on *what* you write. But presentation *is* important, teachers are only human (really!) and you can't fault them for trying to teach you to take pride in your work. So follow these simple rules:

☞ Never handwrite your paper.

☞ If you're using a computer, put a new ribbon in your dot matrix printer and/or check the toner cartridge in your laser printer. If you type (or have someone else type) your paper, use clean white bond and (preferably) a new carbon ribbon so the images are crisp and clear.

☞ Unless otherwise instructed, always double-space your paper. Leave adequate margins all around.

☞ Use a simple typeface that is clear and easy-to-read; avoid those that are too big—stretching a five-page paper to 10—or too small and hard to read.

☞ Never use a fancy italic, modern, or any other ornate or hard-to-read typeface for the entire paper.

Recycling isn't just for cans

There should be a number of helpful messages in your returned papers, which is why it's so important to retain them. What did your teacher have to say? Are her comments applicable to the paper you're writing now—poor writing, lack of organization, lack of research, bad transitions between paragraphs, poor grammar or punctuation, misspellings? The more such comments—and, one would expect, the lower the grade—the more extensive the "map" your teacher has given you for your *next* paper, showing you right where to "locate" your A+.

If you got a low grade but there weren't any comments, ask the teacher why you got such a poor grade. You may get the comments you need to make the next paper better. This also shows the teacher you actually care, which could help your grade the next time around.

Teachers don't like bad speling

Many employers merrily use resumes and cover letters with grammatical and/or spelling errors for hoops practice. Don't expect your teachers to be any more forgiving—there are definitely a few out there who will award an F without even noticing that the rest of the paper is great; too bad you misspelled "Constantinople" or left a participle twisting slowly in the wind.

Paper writing 101

Here are the steps that, with some minor variations along the way, are common to virtually any written report or paper:

1. Research potential topics.
2. Finalize topic.

3. Carry out initial library research.
4. Prepare general outline.
5. Do detailed library research.
6. Prepare detailed outline (from note cards).
7. Write first draft.
8. Do additional research (if necessary).
9. Write second draft.
10. Spell-check and proofread.
11. Have someone *else* proofread.
12. Produce final draft.
13. Proofread one last time.
14. Turn it in and collect your A+.

Doing all these tasks efficiently and effectively requires careful timing and planning. After all, this isn't the only assignment, and may not even be the only paper, you have to get done in a short amount of time.

So get out your calendar and mark the date your paper is due. How many weeks till then? Four? Six? 10? Plan to spend from one-half to three-quarters of your entire schedule for a paper on research, the rest on writing.

Block out set periods of time during each week to work on your paper. Try to schedule large chunks of time—two, three hours or more each time—rather than many short periods. Otherwise, you'll spend too much time reviewing where you left off and repeating steps unnecessarily.

As you make up your work schedule, set deadlines for completing the general steps of your paper-writing process. For example:

Week 1: Decide on topic and "angle" of your paper.

Week 2: Make list of reference materials.

Weeks 3/4:	Read reference materials; take notes.
Weeks 5/6:	Do detailed outline; write first draft.
Week 7:	Edit paper; prepare bibliography.
Week 8:	Proofread paper; type final copy.

Of course, I can't tell you exactly how much time to set aside for each step, because I don't know any of the specifics about your paper—how long it's supposed to be, how complex the topic, etc.—or how fast you work. I *can* tell you that you should plan on consulting and/or taking notes from at least five or six different books, articles, or other reference materials. (Your teacher or subject or grade level may demand *more;* I doubt you'll need fewer, even in junior high or middle school.) And plan on writing two or three drafts of your paper before you arrive at the final copy.

Refer to your work schedule often, and adjust your pace if you find yourself lagging behind.

The more time you have to complete a project, the easier it is to procrastinate about dealing with it, even to putting off identifying the steps and working them into your regular schedule. If you find yourself leaving such long-term projects to the last week, schedule the projects furthest away—the term paper due in three months, the oral exam 10 weeks from now—*first.* Then, trick yourself—schedule the completion date at least seven days prior to the actual turn-in date, giving yourself a one-week cushion for life's inevitable surprises. (Just try to forget you've used this trick. Otherwise, you'll be like the perennial latecomer who set his watch 15 minutes fast in an effort to finally get somewhere on time. Except that he always reminded himself to add 15 minutes to the time on his wrist, defeating the whole purpose.)

If you only had the time...

Mastering time management does not require the brain of a rocket scientist—it just means *making the most of your time.* And that means planning ahead—for example, instead of making 15 short trips to the library, plan five or six extended research periods. You'll save travel time and footwork and get a lot more done in the same period of time.

Be prepared. Stock up on pencils, typewriter ribbons, computer disks, and any other supplies you need. Otherwise, you may end up running to the store at midnight in search of an elusive printer ribbon or laser cartridge.

One great way to maximize your time is to have (or have immediate access to) a current reading assignment, your calendar, notes for a project, or all three with you *at all times.* You'll be amazed at the amount of work you get done waiting in line, between classes, or any time you have a few minutes to spare. And if you actually get snowbound for a couple of days, wouldn't it be nice to have some work with you to finish up?

And *stay* organized. Keep all materials related to your paper in a separate notebook or file. No messy piles of work scattered here and there, just waiting to be lost or thrown away by mistake.

Don't procrastinate!

Do not, I repeat, do *not* put off doing your research paper until the last minute—or even until the last week! If you do, you will make your task much more difficult. And probably wind up with a lousy paper, too. Start working on your assignment now. *Right* now.

Presuming you ignore this command, you might want to find a copy of my book—*Last Minute Study Tips*—to figure out how to write a good paper when there's little or no time to spare!

CHAPTER 2

DEVELOPING YOUR BATTLE PLAN

You're ready to take the first and conceivably most important step on the road to you're A+ research paper: deciding on a subject.

Once you've chosen a *general* area of study, you must target a *specific* topic or question. Then, you need to come up with a general outline—a basic blueprint of your paper.

In this chapter, I'll help you complete all three tasks.

Choosing your topic

In some cases, your teacher will assign your topic. In others, your teacher will assign a general area of study, and you'll have the freedom to pick a specific topic.

With freedom sometimes comes danger—give this decision long and careful thought. Pick the wrong topic, and you can write yourself right into disaster.

I'm not implying that you should pick the simplest topic you can find—simple topics often lead to simply awful papers—but there are definitely pitfalls you must avoid.

Danger #1: Thinking too big

You need to write a 15-page paper for your religion class and decide your topic will be "Catholicism Through the Ages."

Whoa, Nelly! Think about it: Can you really cover a topic that broad in 15 pages? Not unless you simply rehash the high points. You could write volumes on the subject (people have) and still have plenty left to say!

Instead, you need to focus on a particular, limited aspect of such a broad subject or attack it from a specific angle. Rather than "Catholicism Through the Ages," how about "A Study of the Catholic Reformation in the 16th Century"?

Remember, your job is to prepare an *in-depth* report about your subject. Be sure you can do that in the number of pages your teacher has requested.

Danger #2: Thinking too small

By the same token, you must not focus too narrowly. Choose a subject that's too limited, and you might run out of things to say on the second page of your paper. "A Day in the Life of a Trappist Monk" might make an interesting one- or two-page story, but it won't fill 10 or 15 pages... even with *really* wide margins.

Hint: If you can't find a single *book* on your supposed topic, rethink it! Although there's nothing wrong with choosing a topic that can be researched via magazine articles, the newspaper, monographs, and the like, why make your research so difficult if you don't have to?

Danger #3: Trodding the lonesome trail

Pick a topic that's too obscure, and you may find that little or no information has been written about it. In which case, you will have to conduct your own experiments, interview your own research subjects, and come up with your own, original data. That is, of course, how scientists forge new pathways into the unknown. But I'm guessing that you have neither the time, desire, nor experience to take a similar start-from-scratch approach.

Take it from someone who's done this more than once—it may be wonderfully creative and a lot of fun to work in such original areas, but it can also be frustrating and stressful. And don't underestimate the reaction of your teacher, who may well wish for something a little easier to grade than some far-reaching new theory he or she really needs to think about. I got a C on the best paper I think I ever wrote. The grad student grading it came right out and told me that because he couldn't "check" my ideas—there was nothing published to support my interpretation—he couldn't give me a better grade. I think that attitude is absurd—and that the C was, too—but I suggest you keep it in mind.

The point is: Make sure that there is enough research material available about your topic. And make sure that there are enough *different* sources of material—different authors, different books, etc.—so you can get a well-rounded view of your subject (and not be forced for lack of other material to find ways to make somebody else's points sound like your own).

Make a possibilities list

Taking all of the above into consideration, do a little brainstorming now about possible topics for your paper.

Don't stop with the first idea—come up with several different possibilities.

In fact, put this book down and go make a list of three or four potential topics right now.

(If you really want a special Fry award for forward-thinking, how about trying to get two or more papers for two or more classes *out of the same research?* The paper we just discussed about 16th century Catholicism might also satisfy—*with little or no changes*—your history assignment. At the very least, you should be able to do a little extra research—not *nearly* as much as you would expect to do for an entirely different paper—and utilize a good portion of the first paper as the basis for a second. What a great way to maximize your library time!)

Do some preliminary research

Got your list? Then get thee to a library. You need to do a little advance research.

Scan your library's card-catalog index or computer listings, the *Readers' Guide to Periodical Literature,* and other publication indexes. How many books and articles have been written about each topic on your "possibilities" list? Read a short background article or encyclopedia entry about each topic.

By the time you leave the library, you should have a general understanding of each of your potential subjects. You also should know whether you'll have trouble finding information about any topic on your list. If so, eliminate it.

And the winner is (drum roll, please)...

With any luck at all, you should be left with at least one topic that looks like a good research subject. If two or more topics passed your preliminary-research test, pick the one that interests you most.

You're going to spend a lot of time learning about your subject. There's no rule that says you can't enjoy it!

Develop a temporary thesis

Once you have chosen the topic for your paper, you must develop a *temporary thesis.*

What's a *thesis,* you ask? The word "thesis" is a relative of "hypothesis"—and means about the same thing: The central argument you will attempt to prove or disprove in your paper. It's the conclusion—based upon your research—you draw about your subject.

A thesis is not the same thing as a *topic.* Your topic is what you study; your thesis is the conclusion you draw from that study.

A *thesis statement* is a one- to two-sentence summary of your thesis, summing up the main point of your paper.

Suppose you decided that the topic of your research paper will be "Changes in 16th Century Catholicism: Catholic Reformation or Counter Reformation?" At the end of your research, you conclude that a case can be made for *both.* Your thesis statement, then, might be something like this one:

> *Catholicism in the 16th century changed significantly in structure, doctrine, and personal meaning. These changes can be seen as both a strong reaction to combat the Protestant threat (Counter Reformation) and a spontaneous reform from within (Catholic Reformation).*

In your paper, you would try to show why both aspects of your thesis are true, marshaling proofs and arguments to illustrate how both perspectives (a spontaneous reform vs. a reaction spurred by the rise of Protestantism) could explain the changes that occurred.

Temporary means just that

Note that word *temporary*. No matter how good it looks to you now, your temporary thesis may *not* wind up being your final thesis. Because you haven't completed all your research yet, you can only come up with a "best-guess" thesis at this point.

You may find out during your research that your temporary thesis is all wet. If that's the case, you will revise it, perhaps even settling on a thesis that's the exact opposite of your first! In fact, you may revise your thesis *several* times during the course of your research.

If a temporary thesis doesn't spring easily to mind—and it probably won't—sit back, and do some more brainstorming. Ask yourself questions like:

- ☞ "What's special or unusual about ____?" (Fill in the blank with your topic.)
- ☞ "How is ____ related to events in the past?"
- ☞ "What impact has ____ made on society?"
- ☞ "What do I want the world to know about ____?"
- ☞ "What questions do I have about ____?"

The answers to these and similar questions should lead to several good thesis ideas. If you find yourself needing more information about your topic to answer these questions, go to the library and do more reading.

Ask your instructor

Some teachers require you to submit your thesis statement for their approval prior to beginning your paper. Even if this is *not* required, getting your instructor's opinion is always a good idea. He or she will help you determine whether your thesis argument is on target, and, if not, perhaps how to fix it.

Create a temporary outline

Once you have developed your temporary thesis, think about how you might approach the subject in your paper. Jot down the various issues you plan to investigate. Then, come up with a brief, temporary outline of your paper, showing the order in which you might discuss those issues.

Back to your 16th century Catholicism thesis. Based on your preliminary research, your general, temporary outline might look like this:

A. Definitions of Catholic Reformation, Counter Reformation
B. Acceptance that Christendom would never reunite under one church hierarchy
C. Changes seen as a reaction to clergy abuses
D. Council of Trent
E. Reform movements within the Church
F. St. Teresa of Avila
G. Radical shifts in Catholic positions on social issues (usury, prostitution)
H. Rise of strength of local parish
I. Ignatius Loyola

Don't worry too much about this outline—it will be brief, at best. It's simply a starting point for your research, a plan of attack.

But don't skip this step, either. As you'll find out in later chapters, it will be a big help in organizing your research findings.

Chapter 3

Research: The Hunt for Materials

You've accomplished a lot so far: You've determined your topic of study. You've developed a temporary thesis. And you've created a temporary outline for your paper. Congratulations!

Now it's time to begin your research in earnest.

We're going to tackle this initial information hunt in two phases. First, you'll come up with a list of all the books, magazines, and other research materials you want to consult.

Then, you'll sit down and do the actual reading and note-taking.

In Chapter 4, I'll show you a time-saving way to compile and organize your reading list. And in Chapter 5, I'll teach you an efficient way to take notes.

But first, you need to learn where and how to locate the many different kinds of research materials you can consult.

Into the library

The obvious place to begin your hunt for research materials is the library. Today's libraries offer an amazing variety of resources—learn how to tap into their gold mine of information and you'll be much richer. If you have gotten this far in life *without* being introduced to library basics, just ask your librarian for help. (As a matter of fact, even if you consider yourself something of a library expert, always ask your librarian for help!) Make the information desk a regular hangout. Tell the librarians what you're working on—they'll invariably know the best sources of information and where to find them.

Most libraries are divided into reading rooms, restricted collections, and unrestricted book stacks. Unrestricted book stacks are those through which anyone using the library can wander, choosing books to use while in the library or, if allowed, to take home. Restricted areas generally include any special collections of rare books, those open only to scholars or to those with particular credentials, either by library rule or by order of whoever donated the collection (and, often, the room housing it) to the library. In some libraries, *all* book stacks are closed, and *all* books must be obtained from a librarian.

Most libraries contain both *circulating materials*—those books and other items you may check out and take home with you—and *noncirculating materials*—those that must be used only in the library. All fiction, general nonfiction, and even most "scholarly" titles will usually be found in the first group. Reference material, periodicals, and books in special collections are usually in the second.

At most libraries, many of those old, familiar library tools—such as the trusty card catalog—have been replaced by computerized systems. These can be a little intimidating for first-time users, but they are great time-savers. Again, don't be shy about asking for help. Your librarian will be happy to show you how to operate the computers.

As you'll discover in ***Use Your Computer***, you don't even have to leave home anymore to have access to some of the greatest libraries in the world via the Internet, including, within the next three to four years, the entire Library of Congress. Yep. Everything currently housed on 500 miles of shelves will be available on the Internet. A lot of information is already on the Net, including early films of New York, hundreds of Mathew Brady's Civil War photos, special exhibitions from the Vatican Library and Dead Sea Scrolls, and much, much more. (Even so, I'd still recommend a trip to the *non*-virtual Library of Congress. How else can you view—up close and personal—a Gutenberg bible, Lincoln's handwritten draft of the Gettysburg Address, and, most important of all—to my daughter Lindsay, anyway—the very first Barbie doll, among hundreds of other treasures?)

How your library is organized

To provide organization and facilitate access, most small and academic libraries utilize the Dewey decimal classification system, which uses numbers from 000 to 999 to classify all material by subject matter. It begins by organizing all books into 10 major groupings.

Given the millions of books available in major libraries, just dividing them into these 10 groups would still make it quite difficult to find a specific title. So each of the 10 major groupings is further divided into 10 and each of these now 100 groups is assigned to more specific subjects within each large group. For example, within the philosophy classification (100), 150 is psychology and 170 is ethics. Within the history classification (900), 910 is travel and 930 is ancient history.

000 – 099	General
100 – 199	Philosophy
200 – 299	Religion
300 – 399	Social Sciences
400 – 499	Language
500 – 599	Science
600 – 699	Useful Arts
700 – 799	Fine Arts
800 – 899	Literature
900 – 999	History

There is even further subdivision. Mathematics is given its own number in the 500 (science) series—510. But specific subjects within mathematics are further classified: 511 is arithmetic, 512 is algebra.

Finally, to simplify your task even more, the last two digits in the Dewey code signify the type of book:

01	Philosophy of
02	Outlines of
03	Dictionary of
04	Essays about
05	Periodicals on
06	Society transactions and proceedings
07	Study or teaching of
08	Collections
09	History of

If your library doesn't use the Dewey system, it probably is organized according to the Library of Congress system, which uses letters instead of numbers to denote major categories:

A	General works (encyclopedias and other reference)
B	Philosophy, Psychology, and Religion
C	History: Auxiliary sciences (archeology, genealogy, etc.)
D	History: General, non-American
E	American history (general)
F	American history (local)
G	Geography/Anthropology
H	Social sciences (sociology, business, economics)
J	Political sciences
K	Law
L	Education
M	Music
N	Fine arts (art and architecture)
P	Language/Literature
Q	Sciences
R	Medicine
S	Agriculture
T	Technology
U	Military science
V	Naval science
Z	Bibliography/Library science

Beyond the encyclopedia

When you were younger, you probably relied solely on the encyclopedias in your school library when you had to write a report. Sorry, but those simpler, easier days are gone for good.

Yes, you may want to read encyclopedias to get a general overview of your topic. But you need to turn to other sources for more detailed information. You need to read books written by experts in the field you're researching, and magazine and newspaper articles about every aspect of your subject.

Why stop there? Pamphlets, anthologies, brochures, government documents, films, and videos are just some other possible sources of information for your paper.

Where to look for materials

How do you find out whether anyone has written a magazine or newspaper article about your topic? How do you know if there are any government documents or pamphlets that might be of help? How do you locate those written-by-the-experts reference books?

You look in your library's publication indexes, which list all of the articles, books, and other materials that have been published and/or are available in your library. Most are arranged alphabetically by subject.

Some of the major publication indexes are listed below. There are others—ask your librarian for suggestions.

1. **The card catalog.** This is a list of all the books in your library. (Although most libraries now store it on computer, it's still often called a card catalog because it used to be kept on index cards.) Books are indexed in three different ways: by subject, author, and title.

2. **Newspaper indexes.** Several large-city newspapers provide an indexed list of all articles they have published. Your library may even have past issues of one or more available on microfiche.
3. **Periodical indexes.** To find out if any magazine articles have been published on your subject, go to a periodical index. *The Readers' Guide to Periodical Literature,* which indexes articles published in the most popular American magazines, may be one with which you're familiar.
4. **Vertical file.** Here's where you'll find pamphlets and brochures.
5. ***U.S. Documents* monthly catalog.** Useful for locating government publications.

Your approach to research

All of us who have become familiar with the wonders of the library have probably developed our own approach to enjoying them and using them most efficiently. My own experience emphasizes what may be the obvious: Getting the right start is all-important. Because I try to keep from being overwhelmed with too much material, I begin any research working with the broadest outlines or topics (and the broadest resources) and wind my way down the ladder, getting more and more specific in topic and sources as I go along.

Let's assume you needed to prepare a report on the current state of affairs in Bosnia (providing it remained stable for a whole day!). Here's how you might approach the task:

1. Consult any one of the numerous leading **encyclopedias** you will find in your library—*World Book, Britannica, Americana, Collier's,* etc. Here you'll find an overview and historical perspective on the area. Encyclopedic entries are usually the most comprehensive and concise you will find. They cover so much territory and are so (relatively) up-to-date that they are an ideal "big-picture" resource. Of course, when you're dealing with a relatively late-breaking news story such as Bosnia, you may find *any* encyclopedia woefully out-of-date. (Did you guess to look up "Yugoslavia" instead to get some historical perspective? Good for you!)

2. With overview in hand, you can start consulting the **major indexes and directories** that your library has to develop a list of more specific resources. Obviously, the entries in these major resources can then be consulted directly —specific issues of *The New York Times* on microfilm, periodicals at the periodicals desk, etc. In no time at all, you'll develop a long list of names and places to check out, leading you to a number of potential topics and sources. Here's just a brief list of those you could cull from a single magazine or newspaper article, all relating to Bosnia: Alija Izaetbegovic, Bosnia and Herzegovina, Croatia, Franjo Tudjman, Serbia, Slobodan Milosevic, Montenegro, Radovan Karadzic, Bosnian Serbs, Bosnian Croats, Ratko Mladic, Posavina Corridor, Eastern Slavonia, Muslims, Sarajevo, Belgrade, Dayton, OH. Think you'll run out of research materials?

In one brief tour of your library's resources, you'll easily discover and know how to obtain more material than you would need to write a book on virtually any one of the subtopics, let alone a report encompassing all of them.

What if you're uncomfortable in the library? An infrequent user? Or simply find it a confusing place that's more trouble than it's worth?

As I've emphasized, developing *any* habit is just a matter of practice. The more you use the library, the more comfortable you will become using it. And, of course, the more books you will become comfortable with. In a very short time, you will have your own personal list of resources that you start with whenever you receive an assignment.

If you want the library to become like a second home, its every shelf a familiar friend, why not go to work there? Many libraries, smaller ones in particular, often offer opportunities for paid and volunteer work. Even if you work for free, this is an excellent way to learn the ins and outs of your library.

Many of you might not use the library as much as you should (or even would like) because it's just a confusing series of catacombs. The more comfortable you are—the more you know about the materials it contains and how to locate and use them—the more you will *want* to be there.

And the more help you will be able to obtain from this great resource that's just waiting to welcome you!

CHAPTER 4

CREATING A WORKING BIBLIOGRAPHY

Working bibliography? "Ugh," you think, "sounds complicated. Sounds like *work*!"

Relax. Remember what I told you in Chapter 3—the first step of your research is to put together a list of books, magazines, pamphlets, etc., you want to read. "Working bibliography" is simply a fancy name for that list.

There are two steps involved. First, you'll create bibliography cards for each source you want to review. Then, you'll transfer all the information from your bibliography cards to a single list—your working bibliography.

This two-step method has been around since someone wrote the first research paper, and with good reason: It works! It helps you conduct your research in an organized, efficient manner *and* makes preparing your final bibliography easier.

In other words, this is one of those great time-saving tools that I promised to show you!

This is not a complicated job, but it is an important one, so follow my instructions to the letter.

Essential ingredients: 3 x 5 index cards

To create your bibliography, you'll need a good supply of 3 x 5 index cards. You can buy these for next to nothing at most dime stores, bookstores, and office supply stores. (You'll also use index cards when you take notes for your paper, so buy a big batch now. A few hundred cards ought to suffice.)

While you're stocking up on index cards, pick up one of those little boxes designed to hold the cards. Put your name, address, and phone number on the box. If you lose it, some kind stranger may return it. If not, after you duplicate all your work, I guarantee you'll never lose one again.

Step 1: Create your bibliography cards

You'll complete the first step of the bibliography two-step at the library. Take your index cards, a couple of pens or pencils—and this book, of course.

Start a systematic search for any materials that might have information related to your paper. Look through the indexes we covered in Chapter 3 and any other indexes your librarian recommends.

When you find a book, article, or other resource that looks promising, take out a blank note card. On the front of the card, write down the following information:

In the upper right-hand corner of the card: Write the library call number (Dewey decimal number or Library of Congress number), if there is one. Add any other detail that will help you locate the material on the library shelves (for example, "Science Reading Room," "Reference Room," "Microfiche Periodicals Room").

On the main part of the card: Write the author's name, if given—last name first, first name, middle name or initial. Then the title of the article, if applicable, in quotation marks. Then the name of the book, magazine, newspaper, or other publication—underlined.

Add any details you will need if you have to find the book or article again, for example:

☞ Date of publication.

☞ Edition—for example, "third (1990) edition" for a book; "morning edition" for a newspaper.

☞ Volume number.

☞ Page numbers on which the article or information appears.

In the upper left-hand corner of the card: Number it. The first card you write will be #1, the second, #2, and so on. If you happen to mess up and skip a number somewhere along the line, don't worry. It's only important that you assign a different number to each card.

At the bottom of the card: If you're going to do research in more than one library, write the name of the library. Also write down the name of the index in which you found the resource, in case you need to refer to it again.

Do this for *each* potential source of information you find, *and put only one resource on each card.*

Some experts in the research-paper business have different ideas about what goes where on bibliography cards. It's not really important—if you prefer to put the elements of your card in some different order, it's okay.

Just be sure that you're consistent, so you'll know what's what later on. And leave some room on the card—you'll be adding more information when you actually get the reference material in your hands.

Sample Bibliography Card for a Book

(1) 315.6
Main Reading Room

Halloran, Sally

The Life and Times of Bob Smith.
(see esp. pp. 43-48)

Card Catalog
Main Street Library

Sample Bibliography Card for a Magazine Article

(2) Periodical Room

Arenas, George
"The Life and Times of Bob Smith"
Smith Magazine
(April 24, 1989; pp. 22-26)

Readers' Guide
University Library

Sample Bibliography Card for a Newspaper Article

(3) Microfiche Room

Ellen, Terry

"Bob Smith: The New Widget Spinner"
The New York Times
(June 16, 1976, late edition, p. A12)

New York Times Index
Main Street Library

Citing online information

Because students are increasingly using online sources, the MLA, which publishes style guides for research papers, has integrated electronic citations into its latest edition. Xia Li's and Nancy Crane's guide, *Electronic Style: A Guide to Citing Electronic Information* (Meckler Media) is another good reference. Sample online citation:

Terhune, Alan J. "Sensationalism." Reporting News.
http://www.ccs.syr.edu/home/lbp/reporting-news.html
(22 May 1995)

Evaluating resources

You may find so many potential resources that you won't have time to read them all. Concentrate on those that have been published most recently or written by the most respected sources. However, don't limit yourself *too* much—gather information from a wide range of sources. Otherwise, you may learn only one side of the story.

Primary vs. secondary resources

There are two types of resources: *primary* and *secondary.*

Primary resources are written by people who *actually witnessed or participated in an event.* When you read a scientist's report about an experiment he has conducted, you are consulting a primary resource.

Secondary resources are written by people *who were not actually present at an event,* but have studied the subject. When you read a book about the 1950s written by someone who was born in 1960, you are learning from a secondary resource.

Primary resources are likely to be more reliable sources of information. But depending upon your subject, there may not *be* any primary resources available to you.

Step 2: Prepare your working bibliography

When you get home, copy the information from each of your bibliography cards onto a single list. As you do this, follow the bibliography style rules outlined in Chapter 10. (These rules cover bibliographic minutiae—where to put periods, how many spaces to indent lines, etc.) When you have finished your list—your working bibliography—make a photocopy or two. Keep one copy with your research file, another in a safe place in your room or desk.

Although you'll work from your bibliography cards as you conduct your research, your working bibliography is important for two reasons:

1. You'll have a separate record of all the potential resources you found. If you lose any of your bibliography cards, you will still have all the information about the source.

2. You'll be able to use your working bibliography as the basis for your final one.

The final bibliography, a required part of your paper, lists resources from which you gathered information. Your *working* bibliography contains all the resources from which you *might* gather information.

Looks like extra work to me!

Why bother to create all those bibliography cards if you're just going to transfer the information to another piece of paper? Can I possibly be wasting your time? Of course not. It's a matter of convenience and organization.

With index cards, you can organize your list of resources in different ways, just by shuffling the deck.

For example, you might want to start by organizing your cards by resource: magazine articles, encyclopedias, books, newspapers, etc. Then, when you're in the magazine room of the library, you will have a quick and easy way to make sure you read all your magazine articles at the same time. Ditto for your trip to the newspaper reading room, the reference shelf, and so on.

But at some point, you might want to have your list of resources organized in alphabetical order. Or separated into piles of resources you've checked and those you haven't. No problem: Just shuffle your cards again.

This is one of the few cases where computer literacy can lead you to grief. Do *not* try to keep your notes—or just your bibliography cards—on your computer, even if you're using computer-created note cards (such as Apple's Hypercard). It is simply *not* as easy, neat, or efficient. Trust me. Been there. Done that. Not good.

CHAPTER 5

DIGGING IN: RESEARCHING IN DETAIL

If you ever fantasized about being a detective or investigative reporter, get ready to enjoy yourself! It's time to follow up all of those research leads you found, track down the evidence, and uncover the truth, the whole truth, and nothing but the truth.

In other words, it's time to start taking notes.

When you write your paper, you'll work from your notes, not the original reference materials. Why? Because it's easier to turn a few cards than flip through hundreds of pages in search of the information you need. Because it's easier than lugging home stacks of heavy books from the library. And because sometimes you don't have a choice—many of the materials you may need to consult can't be taken *out* of the library!

In this chapter, I'm going to show you my own special system for taking notes. Master it—it will be a huge help when you sit down to organize and write your paper.

Send for information/schedule interviews

Before you do anything else, send away for anything you want to review that isn't available in your library. If you want to get a brochure from a particular association, for example, order it now. It may take a few weeks for such materials to arrive. (Check the online services and the Internet to see if any needed material can be easily downloaded. The more skilled Web browsers among you may spend little on postage, even for obscure material from Zimbabwe.)

If you're going to interview any experts, schedule interview dates with them. Make up a list of good questions and buy or borrow a quality tape recorder so you can accurately record your interviewee's comments.

Then hit the books

Set aside solid blocks of time for your library work. And remember: It's better to schedule a handful of extended trips to the library than 15 or 20 brief visits.

When you go to the library, take your bibliography cards, a good supply of blank index cards, your preliminary outline, and several pens or pencils.

Your bibliography cards are the map for your information treasure hunt. When you arrive at the library, pull out the first five or six cards, locate the materials listed on them, pick a secluded desk or table and get to work.

When you write your paper, you will get all the information you need from your notes, rather than from the original sources. Therefore, it's vital that you take careful and complete notes.

What sort of information should you put in your notes? Anything related to your subject and especially to your thesis. This includes:

1. General background information—names, dates, historical data, etc.
2. Research statistics.
3. Quotes by experts.
4. Definitions of technical terms.

You may be used to keeping your notes in a three-ring binder or notepad. I'm going to show you a note-taking system I think is better—you'll record all of your notes on your blank index cards.

As was the case with your bibliography cards, you must follow some specific guidelines to make this method work. You'll want to refer to the guidelines in this chapter often during your first few note-taking sessions. After that, the system will become second nature to you.

Step #1: Complete the bibliography card

Let's say that you have found a reference book that contains some information about your subject. Before you begin taking notes, get out the bibliography card for that book.

First, check that all of the information on your card is correct. Is the title exactly as printed on the book? Is the author's name spelled correctly?

Next, add any other information you will need to include in your final bibliography. The type of information you need to put on your bibliography card depends on two factors: 1) the type of reference material and 2) the bibliography format you are required to use.

Various authorities have set forth a bewildering array of bibliography rules. Although none of them are inherently right or wrong, your individual instructor may not agree with me, so be sure to ask her which rules she wants you to follow.

In this book, we'll cover the bibliography gospel according to the Modern Language Association of America (MLA), one of the most widely accepted authorities on such matters.

Unfortunately, even when using only one set of rules, there are different instructions for different types of materials. You handle a bibliography listing for a magazine article differently than you do for a book, for instance. If I were to show you how to handle all the different types of materials you might encounter, this book would easily be three times as large.

And it would be a waste of time and paper, because there are several books already on the market that *do* show every type of listing under the sun. (The MLA, for example, puts out its own very thorough reference manual.) You may want to consult one of these books if you're working with out-of-the-ordinary types of reference materials. Just make sure that the book you consult follows the bibliography format your teacher requires.

Because most students rely heavily on books, magazine articles, and newspaper articles for research, I'll give you the rules for those materials here.

Bibliography listings typically include three categories of information: the author's name, the title of the work, and the publishing information. However, there are lots of little pieces of data that fall within those three categories.

Include on your card the following information, in the following order:

For a book:

1. Name(s) of the author(s).
2. Title of the part of the book used (if the entire book does not deal with your subject), in quotes.
3. Title of the book, underlined.
4. Name of the editor, translator, or compiler.
5. Edition used, if more than one edition has been published. (If you don't see any information about an edition, assume it's the first.)
6. Number of volume(s) used, if more than one.
7. Name of the series, if the book is part of one.
8. Place of publication, name of the publisher, date of publication.
9. If pertinent information appears in only a small portion of the book, the page numbers on which it appears.
10. Supplementary information—any other details needed to identify the exact book you used (for example, "Spanish language translation").

You generally will find all this information on the book's cover, title page, and/or copyright page.

For an article in a magazine or newspaper:

1. Name(s) of the author(s).
2. Title of the article, in quotation marks.
3. Name of the periodical, underlined. (If you are working with a newspaper that is not widely known or nationally published, put the name of the city or town in which it is published. For example: The Herald [Lawrence, NJ]).

4. Series number or name, if one is given.
5. Volume number. Include this only if you are working with a scholarly journal. If you're not sure whether a periodical is considered a "scholarly journal," ask your librarian or include the volume number just in case.
6. Date of publication. Include the edition of a newspaper, if there's more than one (morning or evening edition, early or late edition).
7. The page numbers on which the article appears. Include the section letter or number for a newspaper: A8, B12, etc.

For a magazine, look for this information on the masthead near the front and within the article itself. For a newspaper, look at the front page and within the article.

Of course, not every bibliography card will include all of these details. Some books may not have an editor, for example. You don't need to write "no editor" on the card; simply move on to the next applicable piece of information.

Step #2: Fill out your note cards

Once your first bibliography card is finished, set it aside. Get out some blank index cards and start taking notes from your reference source. Follow these guidelines:

☞ **Write one thought, idea, quote, or fact on each card.** If you encounter a very long quote or string of data, you can write on both the front and back of a card, if necessary. *But never carry over a note to a second card.*

What if you *can't* fit the piece of information on one card? You're dealing with too much information at once. Break it into two or more smaller pieces, then put each on a separate card.

- ☞ **Write in your own words.** Summarize key points about a paragraph or section, or restate the material in your own words. Avoid copying things word for word.
- ☞ **Put quotation marks around any material copied verbatim.** It's okay to include in your paper a sentence or paragraph written by someone else to emphasize a particular point (providing you do so on a limited basis). But you must copy such statements *exactly as written* in the original—every word, every comma, every period. You also must *always* put such direct quotes within quotation marks.

Add organizational details

As you finish each note card, do the following:

- ☞ **In the upper left-hand corner of the card,** write down the resource number of the corresponding bibliography card (from its left-hand corner). This will remind you where you got the information.
- ☞ **Below the resource number,** write the page number(s) on which the information appeared.
- ☞ **Get out your preliminary outline.** Under which outline topic heading does the information on your card seem to fit? Under your "A" heading? Under "C"? Jot the appropriate topic letter in the upper right-hand corner of your note card.

If you're not sure where the information fits into your outline, put an asterisk (*) instead of a topic letter. Later, when you do a more detailed outline, you can try to fit these "miscellaneous" note cards into specific areas.

☞ **Next to the topic letter,** jot down a one- or two-word "headline" that describes the information on the card.

☞ **When you've finished taking notes from a particular resource,** put a check mark on the bibliography card. This will let you know that you're done with that resource, at least for now.

Be sure that you transfer information accurately to your note cards.

Double-check names, dates and other statistics.

As with your bibliography cards, it's *not* vital that you put each of these elements in the exact places I've outlined above. You just need to be consistent: Always put the page number in the same place, in the same manner. Ditto with the resource number, the topic heading and the headline.

Here's a sample of a completed note card to which you can refer.

Sample Completed Note Card

(2)	C
p. 22	Education—Degrees
Smith awarded honorary degrees in law from both Harvard & Princeton.	

Add your personal notes

Throughout your note-taking process, you may want to create some "personal" note cards—your own thoughts, ideas, or impressions about your subject or your thesis.

Perhaps you've thought of a great introduction for your paper. Put it on a card. Or maybe you've thought of a personal experience that relates to your topic. Put it on a card.

Write each thought on a separate note card, just as you have with information you've taken from other resources. Assign your note card a topic heading and mini-headline, too. In the space where you would normally put the number of the resource, put your own initials or some other symbol. This will remind you that *you* were the source of the information or thought.

Keep an eye out for new resources

When you look up information in one reference book, you'll often find leads to additional resources. Check to see if these resources are on your working bibliography. If not, and you think they are worth consulting, add them. Make up a bibliography card for each new source, too.

Throw away unprofitable leads

If a particular resource doesn't yield any useful information, take the bibliography card for that resource out of your stack. Stick it away in your card file, just in case you want it later.

Or if you're certain that you won't want to refer back to the resource, throw the bibliography card away altogether. Then scratch the listing from your working bibliography. Don't waste precious time renumbering your remaining cards—it doesn't matter if a number is missing.

Why are you doing all this?

Of all the tips you'll learn in this book, this note-taking system is undoubtedly one of the most valuable. In fact, many *professional* writers swear by it (including me).

When you go to write your final bibliography, you'll have all the information you need on your bibliography cards. No trips back to the library to look up bibliography details! Just put your cards in the order that they will appear in your bibliography and copy the information.

But the biggest benefit of the system is that it helps you organize your findings and makes your writing job easier.

You'll find out *how* easy in the next chapter.

CHAPTER 6

ORGANIZING YOUR RESEARCH

Your research is done.

Which means—if you managed your time as I suggested earlier—that at least *one-half* of your *paper*, perhaps as much as *three-quarters* of it—is *done,* even though you've yet to write one word of the first draft. (And you'll soon find you have done that already, too!)

You've finished going through all of those reference materials listed in your working bibliography. You've completed your bibliography cards. You've uncovered a lot of information about your subject. And you've taken extensive notes. It's time to organize your data.

You need to decide if your temporary thesis is still on target, determine how you will organize your paper, and create a detailed outline.

Review your thesis statement

Take a close look at your temporary thesis statement. Does it still make sense, given all the information your research has revealed? If it doesn't, revise it.

Your research should have led you to *some* conclusion about your subject. This, in turn, should lead you to the final thesis of your paper.

Sort your note cards

Once you have your final thesis, begin thinking about how you will organize your paper. This is where the note-card system you learned in Chapter 5 really pays off. Get out all of your note cards, then:

- ☞ Group together all of the cards that share the same outline topic letter (in the upper right-hand corner of each card).
- ☞ Put those different groups in order, according to your temporary outline—topic "A" cards on top, followed by topic "B" cards, then topic "C" cards.
- ☞ Within each topic group, sort the cards further. Put together all of the cards that share the same "headline"—the two-word title in the upper-right hand corner.
- ☞ Go through your miscellaneous topic cards—those marked with an asterisk. Can you fit any of them into your existing topic groups? If so, replace the asterisk with the topic letter. If not, put the card at the very back of your stack.

Decide on the order of your paper

Your note cards now should be organized according to your preliminary outline. Take a few minutes to read through your note cards, beginning at the front of the stack and moving through to the back. *What you are reading is a rough sketch of your paper*—the information you collected in the order you (temporarily) plan to present it.

Now, consider: Does that order still make sense? Or would another arrangement work better? Let's say, for example, that you had planned to organize your paper chronologically—to tell readers what happened, in the *order* that it happened. After reviewing your note cards, you may decide that it would be better to take a cause/effect approach—to discuss, one by one, a series of different events and explain the impact of each.

Here are some of the different organizational approaches you might consider for your paper:

1. **Chronological.** Discuss events in the order in which they happened (by time of occurrence).
2. **Spatial.** Present information in geographical or physical order (from north to south, largest to smallest, etc.).
3. **Cause/effect.** One by one, discuss the effects of a series of individual events or actions.
4. **Problem/solution.** Present a series of problems and possible solutions.
5. **Compare/contrast.** Discuss similarities and differences between people, things, or events.
6. **Order of importance.** Discuss the most important aspects of an issue first and continue through to the least important.

Your subject and thesis may determine which organizational approach will work best. If you have a choice of more than one, use the one with which you're most comfortable or that you feel will be easiest for you to write. (Nobody says you *have* to choose the hardest way!) Keep in mind that you can use a *blend* of two approaches—for example, you might mention events in chronological order and then discuss the cause/effect of each.

Rearrange your cards

If necessary, revise your general outline according to the organizational decision you just made. However, *don't* change the letters that you have assigned to the topics in your outline. If you decide to put topic "B" first in your new outline, for example, keep using the letter "B" in front of it. Otherwise, the topic letters on your note cards won't match those on your outline.

If you revised your outline, reorder your note cards so that they fall in the same order as your new outline.

Now, go through each group of cards that share the same topic letter. Rearrange them so that they, too, follow the organizational pattern you chose.

For example, let's presume you have been assigned a major paper (25 pages!): "Can The U.S. Trade Deficit Be Reversed?"

Your general outline might look like this:

A. Definition and explanation of causes.

B. History of trade deficits.

C. Political effects.

D. Special legislative/monetary programs.

E. Current economic opinions (leaders).

F. Implications (include potential countermeasures).

Go to your "A" stack of cards and go through the brief notes in the upper right-hand corner. Let's presume there are only three notes that appear on one or more of the cards—"Definition," "Cause—Overvalued Currency," and "Cause—Excess Demand." You now know what details you intend to include in the first part of your paper. Group the cards according to the topic they cover and, if you wish, start writing your detailed outline based on your notes.

Add any miscellaneous cards

After you sort all of the cards that have been assigned a specific topic heading, review the cards that are still marked with an asterisk or with your initials. Try to place them in your stack of cards.

Don't force a note card in where it does not belong. If there doesn't seem to be any logical place for the information on the card, it may be that the data just isn't relevant to your thesis. Set the card aside in a "leftover" pile. You can try again later.

Your detailed outline is done!

Flip through your note cards from front to back. See that? You've created a detailed outline without even knowing it. The topic letters on your note cards match the main topics of your outline. And those headlines on your note cards? They're the subtopics for your outline.

We simply transferred our note-card headlines to paper; they appear on our outline in the same order as they appear in our stack of cards.

Some instructors like to approve your outline before letting you proceed with your paper. If yours does, find out the specific outline format you are to follow. You may need to use a different numbering/lettering format from the one shown above—Roman numerals instead of capital letters for topic headings, for example.

Otherwise, you can get as detailed as you like with your outline. In most cases, a two-level outline—with topic headings plus subheadings—will suffice. Remember that you must have a minimum of two entries at every level of your outline.

Following is a sample detailed outline for your trade deficit paper.

Outline—U.S. Trade Deficit Paper

1. Introduction
    - A. Definition of deficit and trade deficit
    - B. What caused it?
        1. Overvalued currency
        2. Excess demand

2. History of Deficits
    - A. Resulting conflicts
    - B. Debtor/Creditor nations since World War I
    - C. Effects of tariffs
    - D. Effects on domestic employment
    - E. Effects on U.S. asset ownership

3. Political Effects
    - A. Germany—post-Versailles Treaty
    - B. Japan—quest for oil
    - C. OPEC oil embargo

4. Legislative/Monetary Programs
    - A. Role of central banks
    - B. Bretton-Woods Accords
    - C. Plaza Accords

5. Economic Opinions
    A. Nicholas Brady (U.S. Treasury Secretary)
    B. Alan Greenspan (Dir. Federal Reserve Board)
    C. Helmut Kohl (West German Chancellor)

6. Implications
    A. Effects on U.S. economy
    B. How to reduce problem (options)
        1. Trade barriers
        2. Import taxes
        3. Export restrictions
        4. Favored nation status
    C. Employment
    D. Creditor nation status
    E. Forecasts: Various scenarios

By George, I think you've got it!

If you haven't figured it out before, you should understand now why this note-card system is so valuable. If you had written all of your notes on several dozen sheets of paper, it would be quite a task to sort out information and put it in some logical order, let alone reorder it at will.

And this isn't the only stage at which having your notes on individual cards comes in handy. As you'll see in Chapter 7, the note-card system also is helpful when you tackle the next phase of your paper: writing your rough draft.

CHAPTER 7

WRITING YOUR ROUGH DRAFT

For some reason, this step is the hardest for most people. It's psychological, I guess—a fear that when your thoughts actually appear in black and white, there for all the world to read, you'll be judged a complete fool.

Well, you can't do a research paper without writing. And because the job has to be done, you might as well face it right now.

Using this book, you'll find this step a lot easier than your friends probably will, assuming, of course, that you have done everything as instructed so far—taken good notes, organized your note cards, and prepared a detailed outline.

You may not have realized it, but you've already *done* a lot of the hard work that goes into the writing stage. You have thought about how your paper will flow, you have organized your notes, and you have prepared a detailed outline. All that's left is to transfer your information and ideas from note cards to paper.

Still, as a writer, I know that this can be a scary prospect, no matter how well you've done up to now. So, in this chapter, I'll show you some tips and tricks that will make writing your rough draft a bit easier.

Because the things you will learn in this chapter and in Chapter 8 work together, read both chapters before you begin to write. Then come back and actually work through the steps outlined here.

Set the stage for good writing

Unfortunately for party-lovers, writing is a solitary activity. Good writing takes concentration and thought. And concentration and thought require quiet—and lots of it!

Find a quiet place to work, and do what you can to make sure you won't be interrupted. Nothing's more maddening than having the perfect phrase on the tip of your brain, only to have a friend pop in and wipe it out of your mind forever.

(As I continually point out, there are very few hard-and-fast study rules. And this is *not* one of them. Just as some of you may find it very easy to study with the radio blaring, a few of you may not need all this quiet to write, and write well. In fact, too much quiet may work against you. Do what works for *you.* As I've mentioned, I tend to write, study, and do a lot of other "concentration-required" tasks with the radio pounding away. I even took notes and organized my first book while watching daytime television—though *writing* anything of worth while watching TV can't, I'm convinced, be accomplished.)

You also need to have plenty of desk space, so you can spread out your note cards. Your work area should be well-lit, and you should have a dictionary and thesaurus close at hand.

If possible, work on a computer so that you can add, delete, and rearrange your words easily. Don't worry if your computer software doesn't have all the latest bells and whistles—a simple word-processing program is all you really need.

Don't psych yourself out

If you go into this thinking you're going to turn out a teacher-ready paper on your first try, you're doomed. That kind of performance pressure leads only to anxiety and frustration.

At this point, your goal is to produce a rough draft—with the emphasis on *rough*. Your first draft isn't *supposed* to be perfect. It's *supposed* to need revision.

Relax your expectations and you'll find that your ideas will flow much more freely. You'll be surprised at the intelligent, creative thoughts that come out of that brain of yours when you're not so worried about making a mistake.

Build the foundation first

The essence of good writing has little to do with grammar, spelling, punctuation, and the like. The essence of good writing is good thinking.

Sure, the mechanics of writing are important. You do need to make sure that you have everything spelled just right, that your participles aren't dangling, your periods and commas are placed just so.

But your thoughts, ideas, and logic are the foundation of your paper, and you need to build a foundation before you worry about hanging the front door. So, for now, just concentrate on getting your thoughts on paper. Don't worry about using exactly the "right" word. Don't worry about getting commas in all the right places. We'll take care of all that polishing later.

Do a note-card draft

Your note cards helped you come up with a detailed outline. Now, they're going to serve you again—helping you plot out the paragraphs and sentences of your paper.

We're going to do some more sorting and rearranging of cards. The end result will be what I call a "note-card draft." Here's what you do:

1. Your note cards should be arranged in the same order as your detailed outline. Take out all of the note cards labeled with the letter of the first topic on your outline.
2. Out of that stack, take out all the cards marked with the same "headline" as the first subheading in your outline.
3. Look at the information on those cards and think about how the various statistics, quotes, and facts might fit together in a paragraph.
4. Rearrange those cards so they fall in the order you have determined is best for the paragraph.

Building good paragraphs

I don't want to get into a lengthy discussion of English composition, but because we're dealing with how to build paragraphs, it makes sense to stop for a brief discussion of what's involved in good paragraph construction.

Each paragraph in your paper is like a mini-essay. It should have a topic sentence—a statement of the key point or fact you will discuss in the paragraph—and contain the evidence to support it. You shouldn't expect your reader to believe that your topic sentence is true just because you say so—you must back up your point with hard data. This evidence can come in different forms, such as:

- ☞ Quotes from experts.
- ☞ Research statistics.
- ☞ Examples from research or from your own experience.
- ☞ Detailed descriptions or other background information.

Paragraphs are like bricks of information—stack them up, one by one, until you have built a wall of evidence. Construct each paragraph carefully, and your readers will have no choice but to agree with your final conclusion.

If paragraphs are the bricks in your wall of evidence, transitions—sentences or phrases that move the reader from one thought to another—are the mortar that holds them together. Smooth transitions help readers move effortlessly from the summary of one paragraph to the introduction of another. (The first sentence in the paragraph you have just read is an example of a transition.)

Now put it all on paper

It's time to take the plunge and turn your note-card draft into a written rough draft. Using your cards as your guide, sit down and write.

Double- or triple-space your draft—that will make it easier to edit later. After you are finished with each note card, put a check mark at the bottom.

If you decide that you won't include information from a particular card, don't throw the card away—yet. Keep it in a separate stack. You may decide to fit in that piece of information in another part of your paper or change your mind after you read your rough draft and decide to include the information where you had originally planned.

If you get stuck...

Got writer's block already? Here are a few tricks to get you unstuck:

☞ **Pretend you're writing to a good friend.** Just tell him or her everything you've learned about your subject and why you believe your thesis is correct.

☞ **Use everyday language.** Too many people get so hung up on using fancy words and phrases that they forget that their goal is to *communicate.* Simpler is better.

☞ **Just do it.** What is it about a blank computer screen or piece of paper that scares would-be writers so badly? It happens to almost everyone, and there's only one cure I know: Just type *some*thing...*any*thing. Once you have written that first paragraph—even if it's a really *bad* first paragraph—your brain will start to generate spontaneous ideas.

☞ **Don't edit yourself!** As you write your rough draft, don't keep beating yourself up with negative thoughts such as, "This sounds really stupid," or "I'm a terrible writer. Why can't I express that better?" Remember: Your goal is a *rough* draft—it's supposed to stink a bit.

☞ **Keep moving.** If you get hung up in a particular section, don't sit there stewing over it for hours—or even for many minutes. Just write a quick note about what you plan to cover in that section, then go on to the next section.

Here's an example from one paper on 16th century Catholicism: "Give examples of changes that occurred in various monastic orders—Benedictines, Augustinians, Franciscans. Note growth of new orders and detail: Jesuits, Capuchins, Somaschis, Barnabites, etc."

If you can't get even that much out, skip the section altogether and come back to it later. The point is, do whatever you have to do to keep moving forward. Force yourself to make it all the way through your paper, with as few stops as possible.

The trouble with plagiarism

It's so tempting. You're having trouble with a sentence or section. The information you need was explained beautifully in that article you found in an old magazine. Why not just copy the section from the article? It so musty and obscure your teacher couldn't possibly know what you've done. Why not do it?

Because that would be plagiarism, that's why. And plagiarism—passing off another person's words or ideas as your own—is the biggest no-no of research-paper writing. It's a sure way to bring your grade down, down, down. It may even get you a failing mark. And, grades aside, it is simply *wrong*.

"But who'll ever know that I didn't write it myself?" you wonder. Sorry, but the odds are about 999 to 1 that you *will* be found out.

First, your teacher probably has been reading research papers—some of them undoubtedly on the same subject as yours—for a good many years. Those same "perfect passages" tend to pop up again and again. Do you really think your teacher will believe it's a coincidence that you wrote the exact same paragraph as that student in *last* year's class? Who flunked, by the way.

Second, your teacher is familiar with your work and your writing style. That "borrowed" paragraph, written in someone else's style, is going to be noticeably different from your own prose.

Then, of course, there is the moral issue involved—but I won't get into that. You learned that stealing was wrong in kindergarten. The principle applies to written words and ideas, too.

How to avoid it

To avoid plagiarism, you must give proper credit to the original author of material you use. You must also give credit for any facts, figures, or research data that you use. You do this through a *source note*—a footnote, endnote, or parenthetical note.

Sometimes, you might want to include a sentence or entire paragraph exactly as it was written by another author. If you do this, you must enclose the material in quotation marks and copy the material word for word, comma for comma. You must also offset the paragraph from the rest of the paper by indenting it from both margins, like this:

> "The author's paragraph you're quoting word for word is set off from the rest of the section by indenting it from both margins. It also is enclosed in quotation marks."

You should use this device sparingly, and only if the segment is so eloquently written or so meaningful that it makes a special impact on the reader. (Feel free, therefore, to quote any of the deathless prose from my books at any time.)

You should *not* do this to fill up your paper "the easy way"—if your teacher is anything like most of mine were, he won't buy seven pages of quotes in a 10-page paper.

We'll talk about how to write source notes in the next chapter. Because it's easiest to note which statements or sentences need documenting as you prepare your rough draft, go ahead and read Chapter 8 now.

But that's your only excuse for stopping or delaying your writing! As soon as you've learned the specifics about source notes, sit right down and finish your rough draft. If you keep in mind everything we've talked about in this chapter, writing your draft will be easier than you think.

I promise!

CHAPTER 8

DOCUMENTING YOUR SOURCES

You must give credit to the source of any fact, expression, or idea you use in your paper that is not your own.

For many years, the preferred way to credit (or *document)* sources was the *footnote.* Two other forms of documentation, *endnotes* and *parenthetical notes,* are popular now as well. For convenience, I'll refer to all of these different forms collectively as "source notes."

Whose rules are they, anyway?

In an earlier chapter, we discussed the fact that different authorities have set out different rules for bibliography listings. The same is true for source notes. Ask your instructor whose rules you are to follow.

If your teacher doesn't have a preference, you can use the method that seems easiest to you. Use the same method consistently throughout your paper—don't use a footnote on one page, an endnote on another.

Again, I'm going to give you the Modern Language Association of America (MLA) rules. And again, I'll give you the rules for three basic types of materials: a book, magazine article, and newspaper article. You can consult the *MLA Handbook* or other reference books if you want specific examples of how to prepare notes for more complicated types of material.

A reminder: What needs documentation

You need a source note when you put any of the following in your paper:

- ☞ Quotations taken from a published source.
- ☞ Someone else's theories or ideas.
- ☞ Someone else's sentences, phrases, or special expressions.
- ☞ Facts, figures, and research data compiled by someone else.
- ☞ Graphs, pictures, and charts designed by someone else.

There are some exceptions: You don't need to document the source of a fact, theory, or expression that is common knowledge. And you don't need a source note when you use a phrase or expression for which there is no known author.

For example, if you mention that Paris is the capital of France, you don't need to document the source of that information. Ditto for time-worn phrases such as, "When in Rome, do as the Romans do," or "A stitch in time, saves nine."

For a test of whether a statement needs a source note, ask yourself whether readers would otherwise think that you had come up with the information or idea all by yourself. If the answer is "yes," you need a source note. If you're in doubt, include a source note anyway.

Footnotes

A footnote is a source note that appears at the "foot" (bottom) of a page of text. The footnote system works like this: You put a raised (superscript) number at the end of the statement or fact you need to document. This serves as a "flag" to readers—it tells them to look at the bottom of the page for a note about the source of the data.

In front of that footnote, you put the same superscript number as you put next to the statement or fact in your text. This tells the reader which footnote applies to which statement or fact of text.

There is no limit to the number of footnotes you may have in your paper. Number each footnote consecutively, starting with the number 1. For every footnote "flag" in your paper, be sure there is a corresponding source note at the bottom of the page.

What goes into a footnote

You put the same information in your footnote as you do in your bibliography listing, with two differences: In a footnote, the author's name is shown in normal order, and the exact page number on which the information being documented appeared in the source is cited.

Most of the information for your footnotes will come from your bibliography cards, but you'll have to look at your note cards to get the actual page number from which various facts came. Arrange elements as follows:

1. Name(s) of the author(s), first name first.
2. Title of the book or article.
3. Publication information—place of publication, name of the publisher, date of publication, etc.
4. The number of the page(s) on which the information appeared in the work.

As with bibliography listings, the content of a footnote depends on the type of reference material. For a refresher on the specific information that you need to include and in what order, see the lists in Chapter 10.

Typing your footnotes

The following general rules apply to all footnotes:

☞ Put footnotes four lines below the last line of text on the page.

☞ Indent the first line of a footnote five spaces.

☞ Single-space lines within an individual footnote; double-space between footnotes.

☞ Always put the superscript (raised) number of the footnote after the punctuation in your text.

☞ Abbreviate all months except May, June, and July.

Punctuation guidelines for footnotes

There are specific rules of punctuation and style to follow when you write your footnotes.

For a book, type:

1. Number of the note (superscript).
2. Author's first name, middle name or initial (if any), last name (comma).
3. Title of the book (underlined); no period after the title.
4. In parentheses—place of publication (colon); name of the publisher (comma); year of publication.
5. Exact page(s) on which the information you're documenting appears (period). Do not write "page" or "pg." or "p."—just the number.

For a magazine article, type:

1. Number of the note (superscript).
2. Author's first name, middle name or initial (if any), last name (comma).
3. In quotation marks—title of the article (comma).
4. Name of the periodical in which the article appeared (underlined).
5. Day the periodical was published (for a weekly or biweekly periodical); month; year (colon).
6. Exact page number(s) from which the information was taken (period).

For a newspaper article, type:

1. Number of the note (superscript).
2. Author's first name, middle name or initial (if any), last name (comma).
3. In quotation marks—title of the article (comma).

4. Name of the newspaper in which the article appeared (underlined).
5. Name of the city and town in which the paper is published (if not part of the name of the paper and/or if the paper is not widely known)—enclose in brackets and do *not* underline.
6. Day the paper was published; month; year (comma).
7. Edition (abbreviate "edition" as "ed.") if more than one is published per day (colon).
8. Section and exact page from which the information was taken (period).

If there is other information on your card—for example, the name of an editor or series—you need to include it in your footnote. Arrange information in the same order you would for a bibliography listing. (See Chapter 10 for the order.)

Second references

The second time you cite a particular reference as a source of information, you use an abbreviated form of the footnote—just the author's last name and the page number on which the information appeared. (See sample footnote #4 following.)

If you have taken information from two different books written by the same author, you need to include the title of the book as well. If there is no author given for the work, show the title plus the page number.

Sample footnotes

Following is a sample excerpt from a research paper, followed by four sample footnotes—three that show the different styles necessary for various sources (book, magazine article, and newspaper article), the fourth to illustrate how to cite a source for the second time:

> Bob Smith was a leader in the history of Smiths in America. He earned $1 million by the time he was 18.[1] He was awarded honorary degrees in law from Harvard and Princeton.[2] At the age of 35, he invented the first successful widget-spinning gadget,[3] which gave manufacturers a new way to produce widgets.
>
> More than a savvy businessman and accomplished scholar, Smith was a devoted family man. A close friend and neighbor, Bill Jones, once said of Smith: "I never met a man who spent so much time attending to the needs of his wife and children."[4]

[1] Karen A. Jones, The Life and Times of Bob Smith (New York: Smith Press, 1989) 24.

[2] Stan Perkins, "The Life and Times of Bob Smith," Smith Magazine 24 Apr. 1989: 22.

[3] Bill Black, "Bob Smith: The New Widget Spinner," The New York Times 16 June 1976, late ed.: A12.

[4] Jones 38.

Endnotes

Endnotes are basically the same as footnotes. Within the body of your paper, you indicate the existence of an endnote in the same manner as you would for a footnote—with a superscript (raised) number. The only difference is that you put all of your source listings on a separate page at the end of the text, instead of at the bottom of each page.

Title the last page of your paper "Notes" and center that title at the top of the page. Leave a one-inch margin on all sides of the paper (top, bottom, left, and right).

List endnotes consecutively (put endnote 1 first, then note 2, etc.). As with your footnotes, indent the first line of each note. Double-space the entire page (both within individual notes and between notes). Follow the same punctuation rules as those given for footnotes.

Parenthetical notes

Parenthetical notes are probably the easiest way to document sources. In this system, you put a brief source note right in the body of your text, enclosed in parentheses (hence, the name—parenthetical notes).

Generally, your reference includes only the last name of the author and the page number from which the information was taken. For example:

> Bob Smith was a leader in the history of Smiths in America. He earned a million dollars by the time he was 18 (Jones 24).

To find complete details about the source, readers refer to your bibliography. In this case, they would look for a book or article by "(Somebody) Jones."

Make sure your note includes enough information so your readers will know exactly which source in your bibliography you are citing. For example, if your bibliography lists two different works, both written by authors with the last name of Jones, you should include the author's first name in your parenthetical note: (Karen Jones 24.).

If you have two books written by the same author, include the title of the book you are citing. You can use a one-, two- or three-word abbreviation of the title, if you want: (Jones, Life and Times 24.).

If your source is a one-page article, you don't have to give any page number in your note.

Now or later?

You can incorporate your source notes as you write your rough draft, or you can put them in during a later draft. I suggest you do the following:

1. As you write your rough draft, mark any statement of fact that needs to be documented. Note the number of the source (the number in the upper left-hand corner of your note card) and the page number from which the material was taken. For example: "Bob Smith was awarded honorary degrees from Harvard and Princeton. (#2-22)."
2. As you prepare your final draft, simply convert these "preliminary" notes into your formal ones.
3. Continue on through the rest of your text, consecutively numbering each note.
4. If you are using footnotes or endnotes: When you come to the first "preliminary" note in your text, replace the letter and number code with the superscript numeral "1." Find the bibliography card with the same source number as that in your preliminary note. Type your footnote or endnote, using the data from the bibliography card. Use the same page number that you show in your "preliminary" note.

5. If you are using parenthetical notes: Find the bibliography card that matches the source number in your preliminary note. Replace the number-letter code with your parenthetical note. Again, you already know which page number to cite, because you had that information in your preliminary note.

(Of course, if you're working on a computer, this will only work if you print out a hard copy of your rough draft. When you replace your "preliminary" note letter-number code, you'll lose the information about which source and page number you need to cite.)

CHAPTER 9

REVISING YOUR MASTERPIECE

You can breathe a big sigh of relief—your rough draft is done!

Now, you need to take that rough-cut diamond and polish it into a sparkling gem. In the remaining chapters of this book, we'll revise your rough cut—and revise it again—until we arrive at your final draft.

As we've done with other parts of your assignment, we'll break this process into several steps.

In this chapter, we'll work through two of those steps. First, you'll edit your paper for content and clarity. Then, you'll work on the finer points—grammar, spelling, sentence construction, etc.

Phase 1: Edit for meaning

As I said, we're not going to handle all your revisions in one pass. At this point, you still don't need to concentrate on grammar, spelling, and other technical aspects of your paper. Of course, when you notice flaws in these areas, fix them, but don't get hung up on them right now.

Rather, during *this* phase of the revision process, you should be trying to:

☞ **Improve** the flow of your paper—from paragraph to paragraph, sentence to sentence.

☞ **Organize** your thoughts and information better.

☞ **Clarify** any confusing points.

☞ **Strengthen** any weak arguments—by explaining your argument better or adding more data to support your point of view.

Revision checklist

As you review your rough draft, ask yourself the following questions:

☞ Do your thoughts move logically from one point to the next?

☞ Is the meaning of every sentence and paragraph crystal clear?

☞ Does every sentence make a point—or support one?

☞ Do you move smoothly from one paragraph to the next? Or do you jump randomly from one topic to another?

☞ Do you support your conclusions with solid evidence: research data, examples, statistics?

☞ Do you include a good *mix* of evidence—quotes from experts, scientific data, personal experiences, historical examples?

☞ Do you have a solid introduction and conclusion?

☞ Did you write in your own words and style? Or have you merely strung together phrases and quotes "borrowed" from other authors?

☞ Have you explained your subject thoroughly? Or assumed that readers have more knowledge about it than they actually might? (Remember: *You're* familiar with the topic now, but you've spent *weeks* on it. Just because something is now "obvious" to you doesn't mean your readers will know what you're talking about.)

☞ Have you convinced your readers that your thesis is valid?

Mark any trouble spots with a colored pencil or pen. If you have an idea of how to fix a section, jot it down on your rough draft.

Then, ask a friend or parent to read your paper. Ask them which sections were confusing, which didn't seem to fit in as written. Make notes on your draft about these trouble points.

Now, sit down and begin to rewrite. Focus on all of those problem areas you found. If necessary, add new information. Play with sentences, paragraphs, even entire sections.

If you're working with a computer, this is fairly easy to do. You can flip words, cut and add sentences, rearrange whole pages with a few keystrokes.

If you're still hunched over a typewriter or scratching along with pen and paper, you can do the same thing, using scissors and tape. Just cut up the pages of your rough draft and tape them together in their new order.

If you can't figure out how to fix a bothersome sentence or paragraph, take some time out from writing. Think about what it is you're trying to tell the reader—what point are you trying to get across?

Once you get your thoughts straight, the words will usually take care of themselves.

Phase 2: Do the detail work

When you finish editing for content and meaning, print or type out a clean copy of your paper.

It's time to double-check all of your facts for accuracy and deal with those things I've been telling you to delay: sentence structure, grammar, punctuation, spelling, etc.

Comb through your paper and check every piece of factual information against your note cards:

- ☞ Did you spell names, terms, and places correctly?
- ☞ When you quoted dates and statistics, did you get your numbers straight?
- ☞ Do you have a source note (or preliminary source note) for every fact, expression, or idea that is not your own?
- ☞ If you quoted material from a source, did you quote that source exactly, word for word, comma for comma? Did you put the material in quotation marks?

Mark any corrections on your new draft. Again, use a colored pen or pencil so you'll easily spot corrections later.

Smooth out the edges

You've already fixed major problem areas in your paper. Now take an even closer look at your sentences and paragraphs. Try to make them smoother, tighter, easier to understand.

- ☞ Is there too much fat? Seize every opportunity to make the same point in fewer words.
- ☞ Are there places where phrasing or construction is awkward? Try to rearrange the sentence or section so that it has a better flow.
- ☞ Did you use descriptive, colorful words? Did you tell your reader, "The planes were damaged" or paint a more colorful and creative picture: "The planes were broken-down hulks of rusted metal—bullet-ridden, neglected warbirds that could barely limp down the runway."
- ☞ Consult a thesaurus for synonyms that work better than the words you originally chose. But don't get carried away and use words so obscure that the average reader wouldn't know their meaning. When in doubt, opt for the familiar word rather than the obscure, the shorter vs. the longer, the tangible vs. the hypothetical, the direct word vs. the roundabout phrase.
- ☞ Have you overused particular words? Constantly using the same words makes your writing boring. Check a thesaurus for some other possibilities.
- ☞ How do the words *sound?* When you read your paper aloud, does it bounce along like a Sousa march? Or plod drearily like a dirge? Vary the length of your sentences and paragraphs to make your writing more exciting.

☞ Always remember the point of the paper: to communicate your ideas as clearly and concisely as possible. So don't get lost in the details. Yes, we've all heard of one famous writer or another (Flaubert comes immediately to mind) who filled a wastebasket with discarded pages before he got one page of usable prose. Whose every word seemed to be drawn screaming and kicking from her belly. Hey, this isn't *War and Peace* you're writing here. Relax. If you have to choose between that "perfect" word and the most organized paper imaginable, opt for the latter.

Again, mark corrections on your draft with a colored pen or pencil. No need to retype your paper yet—unless it's gotten so marked up that it's hard to read!

Check your grammar and spelling

Here's the part that almost nobody enjoys. It's time to rid your paper of mistakes in grammar and spelling.

I know that I've told you all along that your thoughts are the most important element of your paper. It's true. But it's also true that glaring mistakes in grammar and spelling will lead your teacher to believe that you are either careless or downright ignorant. Neither of which will bode well for your final grade.

So, get out your dictionary and a reference book on English usage and grammar. If you don't happen to own the latter, check one out from the library, or better yet, buy your own copy. Ask your instructor to recommend a few good choices.

Scour through your paper, sentence by sentence, marking corrections with your colored pen or pencil. Ferret out:

- ☞ **Misspelled words.** Check every word. Ask yourself: "If I had to bet $100 that I spelled that word correctly, would I pull out my wallet?" No? Then you'd better look it up in the dictionary! Watch out especially for words your spell-check program may not catch, like "too" instead of "to."
- ☞ **Incorrect punctuation.** Review the rules regarding placement of commas, quotation marks, periods, etc. Make sure you follow those rules throughout your paper.
- ☞ **Incorrect sentence structure.** Look for dangling participles, split infinitives, sentences that end in prepositions, and other "no-no's."

Again, review the rules about such matters in your reference book.

Phase 3: Prepare the almost-final draft

Retype your paper, making all those corrections you marked as you completed Phase 2. As you prepare this draft of your paper, incorporate the following three steps:

1. Format the paper according to your teacher's instructions—use the specified page length, margins, and line spacing. If you haven't been given any instructions in this area, follow these guidelines:
   - ☞ Type or print on one side of the paper only.
   - ☞ Use 8½ x 11 paper.
   - ☞ Leave a one-inch margin all around—top, bottom, right, and left.
   - ☞ Indent the first word of each paragraph five spaces from the left margin.

- ☞ Double-space all text. (Single-space footnotes, but double space between each.)
- ☞ Number your pages in the upper right-hand corner of the paper, one half-inch from the top.

Think this is an inconsequential step? Don't kid yourself. After all, if you can't follow the simplest directions about things like margins, why should your instructor believe that you've gotten anything else correct?

2. Incorporate your final footnotes, endnotes, or parenthetical notes. For specifics on how to do this, refer back to Chapter 8.
3. Give your paper a title, if you haven't already done so. Your title should be as short and sweet as possible, but it should tell readers what they can expect to learn from your paper. Don't get cute or coy—that's for magazine covers (and it's pretty annoying even then).

You may want to have a headline and a subhead—for example, "Women Air Force Service Pilots: The Almost-forgotten Veterans of World War II." If so, separate your subhead from your main head with a colon and two spaces.

Some teachers prefer that you put your title, name, date, and class number on a separate title page. Others want this information to appear at the top of the first page of your text. As always, ask your instructor which page format to follow.

Now, give yourself a big pat on the back! The toughest parts of your assignment are all behind you now.

CHAPTER 10

COMPILING YOUR FINAL BIBLIOGRAPHY

By the time you've completed the revision process outlined in Chapter 9, your paper should be in very good shape. Give yourself a round of applause!

You need to prepare your final bibliography, which I'll show you how to do in this chapter. Lastly, you'll need to proofread your paper and type or print out your final draft. Those steps are covered in Chapter 11.

"Works consulted" vs. "works cited"

Your teacher may ask for a *"works consulted"* bibliography, a list of all reference materials you reviewed during your research, *even if nothing from them was incorporated in your paper*. Or you may be asked to do a *"works cited"* bibliography, listing only the materials you mentioned in the footnotes, endnotes, or parenthetical notes.

If your teacher does not specify which type of bibliography to include, choose the first. It will be a better indication of the range of research you've done.

There are some very specific technical rules you must follow when preparing your bibliography. These rules are the same whether you are doing a "works consulted" or "works cited" bibliography.

Your bibliography listings contain virtually the same information as footnotes or endnotes. But as we've already learned, there are two big variations: 1) The format and punctuation are different and 2) the page number references are different.

Somewhere along the line, people made up these rules. I'm sure there were good reasons for the things they decided, but the reasons aren't important. What *is* important is that you follow the rules—like them or not.

Remember, different authorities prefer different rules, so check with your teacher to find out which rules he or she prefers you follow. Because we've been following MLA rules so far, we'll stick with them.

Laying out your bibliography page

Your bibliography should be at the end of your paper, on a separate page or pages:

- ☞ One inch from the top of the page: Center the title "Works Cited" or "Works Consulted," depending upon which type of bibliography you're doing.
- ☞ Use the same margins as you did for the rest of your paper—one inch all the way around.

- ☞ Treat your bibliography pages as if they are a continuation of the text of your paper and number them accordingly—don't start repaginating.
- ☞ List sources alphabetically, by the author's last name. If no author is given, list by the first word in the title of the work (unless the first word is "A," "An" or "The," in which case list by the second word of the title).
- ☞ The first line of each listing should be flush with the left margin. Indent all other lines five spaces from the left margin.
- ☞ Double-space all listings and double-space between entries.
- ☞ Abbreviate all months except May, June, and July.

Sort your bibliography cards

You will take all of the information for your bibliography directly from your bibliography cards. Before typing, put your bibliography cards in the correct alphabetical order. Then, just transfer all the information, card by card, following the style guidelines that I have listed below.

For a bibliography listing for a book, type:

1. Author's last name (comma), first name, and middle name or initial (period and skip two spaces).
2. Title of book, underlined (period, skip two spaces).
3. Place of publication (colon and skip a space); the name of publisher (comma and skip a space); year of publication (period).

For a magazine article, type:

1. Author's last name (comma), first name, and middle name or initial (period and skip two spaces).
2. Title of article (in quotation marks, with a period before the ending quotation marks, then skip two spaces). Note: If the name of the article ends with its own punctuation, such as a question mark, don't put in the period.
3. Title of periodical in which the article appeared, underlined.
4. Day of publication (if one is given); month; year; (colon and space).
5. Page numbers on which article appeared (period). If article didn't appear on consecutive pages, just type the number of the first page followed by a plus (+) sign—for example, 23+.

You do not need to include the volume numbers of a magazine, unless it is a scholarly journal. But if in doubt, include it—better too much information than too little.

For a newspaper article, type:

1. Author's last name (comma), first name, and middle name or initial (period and skip two spaces).
2. Title of article (in quotation marks, with a period before the ending quotation marks, then skip two spaces). Note: If name of article ends with its own punctuation, such as a question mark, don't put in the period.
3. Title of newspaper in which article appeared, underlined.

4. Day of publication; month; year.
5. *If paper publishes more than one daily edition:* Put a comma after the year, then type edition information (colon and space), then page numbers on which the article appeared. Include section letter or number if applicable—for example, A8.
6. *If paper publishes only one daily edition:* Type a *colon* after the year (space), then section and page numbers on which article appeared.

If the newspaper isn't a nationally published or well-known paper, add the name of the city and state where it is published after the title. Enclose this information in brackets, but don't underline it. Example: Lawrence Times [Lawrence, NJ].

You do not need to include the volume or issue numbers of the newspaper.

Sample bibliography listings

This excerpt from a sample bibliography page includes listings for a book, a magazine article, and a newspaper article (in that order):

Jones, Karen A. The Life and Times of Bob Smith. New York: Smith Press, 1989.

Perkins, Stan. "The Life and Times of Bob Smith." Smith Magazine 24 Apr. 1989: 22-28.

Black, Bill. "Bob Smith: The New Widget Spinner." The New York Times 16 June 1976, late ed.: A12.

Did you get them all?

Check your bibliography against the text of your paper. Be sure that you have included all the works cited in your source notes.

CHAPTER 11

APPLYING THE FINISHING TOUCHES

Can you see it? That light at the end of the tunnel? You should—you're 99 percent of the way *through* the research-paper tunnel.

Don't shut down your mental engine just yet, though—there are a couple of tricky turns left to negotiate.

First, you need to proofread your paper. Then, you need to type or print out a perfect copy of your manuscript—and proofread it again.

To be a good proofreader, you need a sharp eye. Unfortunately, your poor eyes are probably pretty tired by now. And you've become so familiar with your paper that it may be difficult for you to see it clearly. You're likely to read phrase by phrase, rather than word by word. And that means that you'll likely skip right over some typos and other errors.

Not to worry, though. In this chapter, I'll show you some tricks that will help you overcome these problems and catch all those little bugaboos in your manuscript.

Trick #1: Read your paper aloud

Go to a quiet room, and read your paper aloud. Not in your head—actually speak the words you have written. Sound them out, syllable by syllable. You'll quickly pick up on typos and misspelled words.

Mark any errors that you find with a brightly colored pen or pencil, and circle them. You want to be able to spot them easily and quickly when you type up or print out your final draft.

Trick #2: Work backward

This is another great trick. Read your paper from back to front, starting with the last word on the last page, working backward toward your introduction. This will help you to focus on each individual word, rather than on the meaning of your phrases and sentences.

Trick #3: Use your computer "spell check"

If you're working on a computer that has a "spell-check" program, be sure to use it. But don't rely on it alone! Yes, the computer will pick up misspelled words. But what if you've used the *wrong* word altogether—used "their" when you meant "there"? If you've *spelled* it right, the computer might not detect your error. (some grammar/usage programs will).

Trick #4: Have someone else read it

Ask a parent, sibling, or other relative to read your paper. Or trade papers with a classmate—you read his if he reads yours. Someone who has never seen your paper before is much more likely to catch a mistake than someone who has read it again and again. (Just be careful about the person you pick and the instructions you give. If you're two days away from turning in your paper, you don't want to hear from your anal-retentive friend how *he* would have organized the paper.)

Prepare your perfect copy

After you've proofread your paper several times *(at least* three times), type or print out a clean draft. Then proofread it *again,* to make sure you caught every single error. Miss one or two? Fix those pages *and proofread again.* Continue until you're sure your paper is error-free.

Get it all together

Be sure to put your final draft on good quality, white typing or computer printer paper. Don't use that erasable typing paper! It smudges easily.

If you've written your paper on a computer, avoid printing your final draft on a low-quality dot matrix or bubble-jet printer. Manuscripts printed on such printers are sometimes hard to read—and the last thing you want to do is make it difficult for your teacher to read your paper. (Some instructors do not even accept such printer copy.)

You can also save your paper on a disk and take it to a quick-print shop. Providing you're working on a compatible computer system, the shop can print out your paper on a laser printer, which produces typeset-quality printing.

If you don't have access to a good printer, or if you're just a lousy typist, you may want to have your final draft prepared by a professional typist or computer service bureau. Just make sure the one you select can have your paper done in plenty of time to meet your final deadline!

As soon as you complete your final draft, head right for the copy shop. Pay the buck or two it costs to make a copy of your paper. In the event that you lose or damage your original manuscript, you will have a backup copy (even if it's already "backed up" on your hard drive. Never crashed your hard drive? You will, probably right after you *don't* make a copy of that paper!)

Turn in your assignment

Put your paper in a new manuscript binder or folder, unless your instructor asks you to do otherwise. Then, turn in your paper—on time, of course!

And congratulate yourself!

You have just completed one of the most challenging assignments you will face as a student. You should feel a real sense of accomplishment. Remember, you can use many of the same strategies you learned as we put together your research paper when you prepare essays, oral reports, and other school assignments (which, as it turns out, I discuss in the next chapter). And the skills you developed during the past few weeks or months will be useful to you long after you've left the classroom behind for good.

So accept my congratulations, and treat yourself to a little celebration.

CHAPTER 12

ESSAY TESTS AND ORAL REPORTS

Approach essay questions the same way you would a paper. Although you can't check your textbook or go to the library to do research, the facts, ideas, comparisons, etc., you need are in your own cerebral library—your mind.

Don't ever, *ever* begin writing the answer to an essay question without a little "homework" first. I don't care if you're the school's prize-winning journalist.

First, really look at the question. Are you sure you know what it's asking? What are the verbs? Don't "describe" when it calls for you to "compare and contrast." Don't "explain" when it tells you to "argue." Underline the verbs. (See pages 403 and 405 for a list of the most-used verbs in essay tests and what each instructs you to do.)

Then sit back a minute and think about what you're going to say. Or less than a minute, depending on how much time you have, but *don't* just start writing.

Here's the step-by-step way to answer every essay question:

Step one: On a blank sheet of paper, write down all the facts, ideas, concepts, etc., you feel should be included in your answer.

Step two: Organize them in the order in which they should appear. You don't have to rewrite your notes into a detailed outline—why not just number each note according to where you want to place it?

Step three: Compose your first paragraph, working on it just as long and as hard as I suggested you do on your papers. It should summarize and introduce the key points you will make in your essay. *This is where superior essay answers are made or unmade.*

Step four: Write your essay.

Step five: Reread your essay and, if necessary, add points left out, correct spelling, grammar, etc. Also watch for a careless omission that could cause serious damage—leaving out a "not," making the point opposite of the one you wanted to.

If there is a particular fact you know is important and should be included but you just don't remember it, guess if you can. Otherwise, just leave it out and do the best you can. If the rest of your essay is well-thought-out and organized and clearly communicates all the other points that should be included, I doubt most teachers will mark you down too severely for such an omission.

Remember this: Few teachers will be impressed by length. A well-organized, well-constructed, specific answer will always get you a better grade than "shotgunning"—writing down everything you know in the faint hope that you will actually hit something. Worry less about the specific words and more about the information. Organize your answer to a fault and write to be understood, not to impress. Better to use shorter sentences, paragraphs, and words—and be clear and concise—than to let the teacher fall into a clausal nightmare from which he may never emerge (and neither will your A!).

If you don't have the faintest clue what the question means, ask. If you still don't have any idea of the answer—and I mean *zilch*—leave it blank. Writing down everything you think you know about the supposed subject in the hopes that one or two things will actually have something to do with the question is, in my mind, a waste of everyone's time. Better to allocate the time you would waste to other parts of the test and do a better job on those.

The best-organized beats the best-written

I think numbering your notes is as good an organizational tool as jotting down a complete outline, but there is certainly nothing wrong with fashioning a quick outline. Not one with Roman numerals—it will be a simple list of abbreviated words, scribbled on a piece of scrap paper or in the margin of your test booklet. The purpose of this outline is the same as those fancy ones: to make sure you include everything you need and want to say—in order.

No one is going to grade this outline. In fact, no one else is even going to *see* it. I might as well make my "quality, not quantity" speech here, too. I hope you write well. It's important. But excellent writing, even pages and pages of it, will not get you an excellent grade unless you have the quality—hard-hitting, incisive, direct answers.

Again, most teachers won't fall for the beautifully crafted, empty answer. Don't depend on your good looks or your command of the subjunctive to get you by. Study.

Think of the introduction and the conclusion as the bread in a sandwich, with the information in between as the hamburger, lettuce, tomato, and pickle. Everything is necessary for it all to hang together, but the main attraction is going to be what's between the slices.

Proof it!

Budget your time so that you can go back over your essay, slowly, and correct any mistakes or make any additions. Check your spelling, punctuation, grammar, and syntax. (And if you don't know what that is, find out. You'll need to know for the SAT.) It would be a shame for you to write a beautiful essay and lose points because you had those kinds of errors.

When you're done, you're done...almost

Resist the temptation to leave the room or turn in your paper before you absolutely must. Imagine the pain of sitting in the cafeteria, while everyone else is back in the room, continuing to work on the test, and you suddenly remember what else you could have said to make your essay really sparkle. But it's too late!

Make sure you can't, simply *can't*, add anything more to any of the essay answers before you walk out of the test.

If you're out of time are you out of luck?

Although you should have carefully allocated sufficient time to complete all the essays on a given test before you started working on the first, things happen. You may find yourself with two minutes left and one essay to go. What do you do? As quickly as possible, write down everything you think should be included in your answer and number each point in the order in which you would have written it. If you then have time to reorganize your notes into a better-organized outline, do so. Many teachers will give you at least partial credit (some very near *full* credit) if your outline contains all the information the answer was supposed to. It will at least show you knew a lot about the subject and were capable of outlining a reasonable response.

One of the reasons you may have left yourself with insufficient time to answer one or more questions is because you knew too darned much about the previous question(s). And you wanted to make sure the teacher *knew* you knew, so you wrote...and wrote...and wrote...until you ran out of time.

Be careful—some teachers throw in a relatively general question that, if you wanted to, you could write about until next Wednesday. In that case, they aren't testing your knowledge of the whole subject as much as your ability to *edit* yourself, to organize and summarize the *important* points.

Just remember that no matter how fantastic your answer to any one essay, it is going to get one-fifth the overall score (presuming five questions)—that is, 20 points, never more, even if you turn in a publishable book manuscript. Meanwhile, 80 points are waiting for you.

Oral reports

There are some key differences between writing a report and presenting it orally, especially if you don't want to make the mistake of just reading your report in front of the class.

Good notes are your lifeline when you stand up to say what's on your mind. They should act as cues to remind you where your talk should go next, and they should make you feel secure that you can get through the ordeal.

However, notes can also be a crutch that guarantees not success, but audience boredom. You've probably seen any number of people get up in front of an audience and just read some papers they have in front of them. I guarantee you that, as a relative novice at public speaking, you will make one (and maybe all) of these "Big Three" mistakes if you bring your entire text with you:

1. You will read from it, failing to make eye contact with your audience. This will help to ensure that you lose *their* interest and *your* credibility. How familiar can you be with a subject if you have to *read* your entire speech?
2. If you stop reading for a second to ad lib or look at your listeners, you will lose your place. It's much harder to find that key word that will jog your memory on a full page of text than on an index card.
3. You won't be familiar enough with your speech, because, after all, you'll have it there with you, so why bother rehearsing or memorizing anything?

Getting ready to get ready

Exactly what sort of talk is this going to be? Odds are, if you've been assigned to give a talk for a class, it will fall into one of the following categories:

☞ **Exposition:** a straightforward statement of facts.

☞ **Argument:** tries to change the opinions of at least a portion of the audience.

☞ **Description:** provides a visual picture to your listeners.

☞ **Narration:** storytelling.

The most common forms of oral reports assigned in school will be the exposition and argument. You'll find that you will research and organize your information for these types of speeches pretty much the way you would a term paper.

A note of caution: If you're preparing an *argument*, don't convince yourself you don't have to research *both* sides of the topic just because you're only presenting *one* of them. You should be doubly prepared with all the facts, as you might be challenged with questions or the arguments of other speakers.

As you gather information for your report, making notes on index cards as you did for your term paper, keep this in mind: In order for you to be effective, you must use some different techniques when you *tell* your story rather than *write* it. Here are a few:

☞ **Don't make your topic too broad.** This advice, offered for preparing written reports as well, is even more important when preparing a talk. Try giving an effective speech on George Washington, Hemingway's novels, or French politics in 15 minutes, frequently the amount of time assigned for oral reports. These topics are more suited to a series of books!

George Washington's effect on the two-term limit or the imagery of "The Old Man and The Sea" or the rise of the Socialists in post-war France are more manageable. Narrowing the scope of your talk will help you research and organize it more effectively.

- ☞ **Don't overuse statistics.** Although they're very important for lending credibility to your position, too many will only weigh down your speech and bore your audience.
- ☞ **Anecdotes add color and life to your talk.** But use them sparingly, because they can slow down your speech. Get to the punch line before the yawns start.
- ☞ **Be careful with quotes.** Unlike a term paper, a speech allows you to establish yourself as an authority with less fear of being accused of plagiarism. So you can present a lot more facts without attribution. (But you'd better have the sources in case you're asked about your facts.) You can use quotes, though, when they contain distinctive language or elicit an emotion. Be sure to attribute the source.

I've found that trying to shuffle a bunch of papers in front of a class is difficult and that note cards that fit in the palm of my hand are a lot easier to use. But only if the notes on them are very short and to the point, to act as "triggers" rather than verbatim cue cards—hanging on to 300 note cards is as difficult as a sheaf of papers.

Remember: You'll actually be holding these cards in your sweaty palms and speaking from them, so write *notes,* not whole sentences. The shorter the notes—and the more often you practice your report so each note triggers the right information—the more effective your report will be. (And the less you will have to look at them, making eye contact with your class and teacher easier.)

Here are some other ways to make your oral reports more effective:

- ☞ Pick out one person to talk to—preferably a friend, but any animated and/or interested person will do—and direct your talk to him or her.
- ☞ *Practice, practice, practice* your presentation. Jangled nerves are often the result of a lack of confidence. The more confident you are that you know your material, the less nervous you will be and the better and more spontaneous your presentation will be.
- ☞ If you are like me and suffer from involuntary "shakes" at the mere thought of standing in front of a roomful of people, make sure you can use a lectern, desk, or something to cling to.
- ☞ Take a deep breath before you go to the front of the class. And don't worry about pausing, even taking another deep breath or two, if you lose your place or find your confidence slipping away.
- ☞ If every trick in the world still doesn't calm you down, consider taking a public speaking course (Dale Carnegie, *et al)*, joining the Toastmasters Club, or seeking out similar extracurricular help.

Instructional verbs on essay tests

Compare Examine two or more objects, ideas, people, etc., and note similarities and differences.

Contrast Compare to highlight differences. Similar to *differentiate, distinguish.*

Criticize Judge and discuss merits and faults. Similar to *critique.*

Define Explain the nature or essential qualities.

Describe	Convey the appearance, nature, attributes, etc.
Discuss	Consider or examine by argument, comment, etc.; debate; explore solutions.
Enumerate	List various events, things, descriptions, ideas, etc.
Evaluate	Appraise the worth of an idea, comment, etc., and justify your conclusion.
Explain	Make the meaning of something clear, plain, intelligible and/or understandable.
Illustrate	Use specific examples or analogies to explain.
Interpret	Give the meaning of something by paraphrase, by translation, or by an explanation based on personal opinion.
Justify	Defend a statement or conclusion. Similar to *support*.
Narrate	Recount the occurrence of something, usually by giving details of events in the order in which they occurred. Similar to *describe*, but only applicable to something that happens in time.
Outline	Do a general sketch, account, or report, indicating only the main features of a book, subject, or project.
Prove	Establish the truth or genuineness by evidence or argument. Similar to *show, explain why, demonstrate*. (In math, verify validity by mathematical demonstration.)
Relate	Give an account of events and/or circumstances, usually to establish association, connections, or relationships.

Review	Survey a topic, occurrence, or idea, generally but critically. Similar to *describe, discuss, illustrate, outline, summarize, trace.* Some test makers may use these words virtually interchangeably, although one can find subtle differences in each.
State	Present the facts concisely and clearly. May be used interchangeably with *name, list, indicate, identify, enumerate, cite.*
Summarize	State in concise form, omitting examples and details.
Trace	Follow the course or history of an occurrence, idea, etc.

INDEX

9